Praise for
Can We All Be Feminists?

"As timely as it is well-written, this clear-eyed collection is just what I need right now."
　　　—Jacqueline Woodson, *New York Times* bestselling author of
　　　　　　　　　　　　　　　　　　　　Brown Girl Dreaming

"In an eloquent and searing introduction . . . Eric-Udorie calls to mind a young Audre Lorde."　　　　　　　　　　—*Kirkus Reviews*

PENGUIN BOOKS

CAN WE ALL BE FEMINISTS?

June Eric-Udorie is a twenty-year-old British writer and feminist activist. Named *Elle* UK's Female Activist of the Year for 2017, she has been included on lists of influential and inspiring women by the BBC, the *Guardian*, and more. A cofounder of Youth for Change, an initiative that works to combat female genital mutilation and forced marriage around the world, she recently spearheaded a successful campaign to overturn the British government's decision to remove feminism from the nationally mandated A-level (high school) politics syllabus. June has spoken at the Southbank Centre's Women of the World Festival, the United Nations, and elsewhere, and her writing has appeared in the *Guardian*, the *Independent*, *New States-man*, the *Telegraph*, *ESPN The Magazine*, and *Fusion*, among others. June is currently an undergraduate at Duke University, where she is a recipient of the University Scholars merit scholarship and a Global Human Rights Scholar at the Kenan Institute for Ethics.

CAN WE ALL BE

FEMINISTS?

New Writing from Brit Bennett, Nicole
Dennis-Benn, and 15 Others on
Intersectionality, Identity, and the Way
Forward for Feminism

EDITED BY

June Eric-Udorie

PENGUIN BOOKS

PENGUIN BOOKS

An imprint of Penguin Random House LLC
375 Hudson Street
New York, New York 10014
penguinrandomhouse.com

Library of Congress Cataloging-in-Publication
Control Number: 2018018203 (print)

ISBN 9780143132370 (paperback)
ISBN 9780525504351 (ebook)

Printed in the United States of America
1   3   5   7   9   10   8   6   4   2

Set in Adobe Caslon Pro
Designed by Katy Riegel

CONTENTS

INTRODUCTION

June Eric-Udorie

THERE WAS ONCE a time when I didn't have the language for the discrimination and gender inequality I witnessed inside and outside my childhood home. As a young girl growing up in Lagos, Nigeria, I'd see stories on the news about men beating up their wives, and the people around me would say things like, "That's what she deserves." I listened as older women gossiped about grown men leering (or worse) at teenage girls, and watched as they shrugged their shoulders, calling it "unfortunate." When I asked my mother about these things, she ignored me and changed the subject, or asked if this was the sort of behavior—asking about things that were not my business—I planned to take to my husband's house. "Why can't it be *my* house? Why is it always *his* house?" I would retort, angry that I couldn't legally own property because I was born a girl. "*Mechi onu*, shut up!" she would shout back. "What is wrong with you, *ehn*? You think this is how you will find a husband? *Ngwa*, get out of here."

In my Nigerian home, there was a clear set of norms that governed how a girl should behave. "Good" girls, my mother taught us, were seen and not heard. Good girls knew they would grow up to be wives and mothers. Good girls would be submissive to their husbands; they would never use their voices. Good girls crossed their legs, wore long skirts, prayed and were active in church, were never loud or boisterous, kept their opinions to themselves, didn't look at boys, and always focused on school. Good girls didn't rebel.

For a long time, I tried to be a "good" girl. I was an exemplary student and active in Sunday school. Even after I moved from Nigeria to a UK boarding school when I was ten, I held on to traditional expectations of girls and women. When I was fourteen and my family was visiting our old church in Lagos over the Christmas holiday, the youth pastor asked me to stand up, and pointed me out as a role model for all the young women in this church. I knew why he'd picked me. I didn't talk to boys; I had many Bible verses memorized; I advocated against abortion; I wore a purity ring and was saving myself for my husband.

By the middle of the following year, I'd thrown my purity ring in the trash, stopped praying, and come to believe that abortion is a woman's choice. I let go of the homophobic teachings I'd internalized from the Pentecostal church, and argued with my father that gay people *do* deserve the right to marry. Where did this change come from? Feminism. Namely, Mary Wollstonecraft's *A Vindication of the Rights of Woman*, which a teacher had given me that year. And after that, Naomi Wolf's *The Beauty Myth*, which I'd bought myself. So much went over my head as I read these books at age fifteen. But the feminism I encountered in them seemed so simple and appealing.

It was a struggle to end the oppression women faced.

I was not aware then of the myriad ways in which mainstream feminism has historically excluded marginalized women. And it would be even longer before I understood that twenty-first-century feminists were still battling those issues. All I knew was that feminism seemed to be the most useful tool available to me and to other women to fight against the oppression stacked against us. And so, I called myself a feminist, at home, in public, with friends, and at church.

When we returned to visit family in Lagos the next Christmas, one of the youth leaders cornered me and said, "That feminism thing you're doing, we don't do that here." I smirked at her, before answering back, "I'm sorry, but I'm doing this everywhere."

AT SIXTEEN, I was full of passion for feminism and desperately wanted to contribute to the discussions online and in the media. In 2014, I created a Twitter account and started interacting with feminists there. At the same time, I began sending editors pitches for stories I wanted to write on feminism, politics, and pop culture. After seven months of failed pitches, I cowrote a column in the *Guardian* with Carlene Firmin, founder of the MsUnderstood partnership, on protecting children and young people from sexual abuse. This marked the beginning of my writing about feminist activism, campaigning, and organizing for major UK news outlets.

The editors to whom I pitched my stories were almost exclusively white women, and the vast majority of them identified as feminists. Good, I thought, excited at the idea that I would be edited by other feminist women. As these editors worked on my pieces, I, in turn, started reading their journalism and following them on Twitter. At first, I internalized their discriminatory views. But Twitter exposed me to Black feminist scholarship, and as I started reading tweets and articles by Flavia Dzodan, Reni Eddo-Lodge, Mikki Kendall, and Jude Wanga, my perspective shifted. It quickly dawned on me that their feminism didn't care about a Black, queer, disabled young woman like me. Their feminism was entirely focused on the experiences of women who were white, wealthy or middle-class, heterosexual, and able-bodied. Feeling powerless, I made the choice to ignore their blind spots and carried on accepting writing assignments. But it was horrifying to watch these editors, and so many others who prided themselves on being feminists, dismiss women of color and laugh at the concerns raised by LGBTQIA+ women. In one case, an editor criticized the idea that people should be able to define their own gender, arguing that men can't just decide that they're women. Many editors complained when marginalized women asked for more inclusion in feminist discourse, saying that they were asking their white female counterparts to be perfect. One editor went so far as to argue that being "trans" is a cover-up that male rapists employ to gain access to the spaces frequented by women and nonbinary folks.

Eventually, my silence made me uncomfortable, and it shifted to rage. Instead of continuing to pitch to these editors, whose views I was scared I was internalizing like I'd done with my family's and church's views while growing up, I picked up books by Black women: Angela Davis, Audre Lorde, bell hooks, and Patricia Hill Collins. Reading bell hooks's *Feminist Theory*, I came across a definition of feminism that I felt included me, that made me feel understood and seen:

> Feminism is the struggle to end sexist oppression. Its aim is not to benefit solely any specific group of women, any particular race or class of women. It does not privilege women over men. It has the power to transform in a meaningful way all our lives. . . . Feminism as a movement to end sexist oppression directs our attention to systems of domination and the inter-relatedness of sex, race, and class oppression. Therefore, it compels us to centralize the experiences and the social predicaments of women who bear the brunt of sexist oppression

as a way to understand the collective social status of women
in the United States.

hooks makes it clear that the purpose of feminism is not to
benefit any one group of women while leaving the others
behind. She also argues that women's intersecting identities
should be central to feminist analyses.

After reading this chapter, I found it hard to reconcile
ascribing the word *feminist* to Black feminist thinkers such
as the ones I've mentioned, as well as to those white feminists who held classist, racist, cissexist, Islamophobic, ableist,
and transphobic views. Could the latter group even be
considered feminists? I found it difficult to see how they
could, given that, for example, when campaigning for equal
pay, they would only talk about the gender pay gap, which by
default focuses on the gender pay gap between men and
white women, which adheres to a narrative that the gender
pay gap is not racialized, for instance, and thus ignoring the
fact that Black women, Latina women, and disabled women
were earning even less than their white female counterparts.
I did not understand how they could be called feminists
while they spoke for Muslim women in the debate on
whether the hijab is oppressive, denying Muslim women
their agency. As a Black woman, I was offended when I attended a feminist rally in London and saw a white woman
holding a sign that read, WOMAN IS THE NIGGER OF THE
WORLD. In the 2017 Women's March, millions of women and
men marched worldwide to protest the election of Donald J.
Trump as the US president and rising levels of fascism and
xenophobia. Many of the women wore pink "pussy hats" as a
response to Trump's comments about gabbing women "by the
pussy." It was an empowering sight of unity and resistance to
see tens of millions come together, all of them marching for
a common cause. But it also stung when I thought about the

gender-nonconforming people and trans women for whom the pink pussy hats suggested that womanhood is contingent upon having a vagina, thereby excluding them. I found it painful to stomach how many women marched carrying signs with slogans like PUSSIES AGAINST FASCISM and VIVA LA VULVA. With such signs, did they not see how they were furthering the cissexist idea that trans women are not "real" women because they do not have vaginas?

When I looked at all of these examples of blind spots and willful exclusion in mainstream feminism, I had to ask: Why is it so hard for privileged feminists to see our humanity—to see my humanity? Don't white feminists know that they have so much more privilege and power than the average trans woman, queer woman, or woman of color? Why are they always asking that I think only of my gender—putting aside the fact I am Black, queer, and disabled—in service of the "wider cause"? What kind of feminism is that? Unsurprisingly, this is a question that women like me have been asking for centuries.

In 1851, African-American abolitionist and women's rights activist Sojourner Truth attended the Women's Rights Convention in Akron, Ohio. After a number of activists had already spoken in favor of women's suffrage, Truth rose to speak. According to some reports, the white women around her tried to silence her, fearing that she would change the subject to emancipation. In what is now a famous speech, Truth declared:

> I think that 'twixt de niggers of de South and the women of de North, all talking about rights, the white men will be in a fix pretty soon. But what's all this here talking about? That man over there say that women needs to be helped into carriages, and lifted over ditches, and to have de best place everywhere. Nobody ever helps me into carriages, over mud-

puddles, or gives me any best place! And ain't I a woman? Look at me! Look at my arm! I have ploughed, and planted, and gathered into barns, and no man could head me! And ain't I a woman? I could work as much and eat as much as a man—when I could get it—and bear the lash as well! And ain't I a woman? I have borne thirteen children, and seen most all sold off to slavery, and when I cried out with my mother's grief, none but Jesus heard me! And ain't I a woman? Then they talks 'bout this ting in de head; what this they call it?" ["Intellect," whispered someone near.] "That's it, honey. What's that got to do with women's rights or nigger's rights? If my cup won't hold but a pint, and yours holds a quart, wouldn't you be mean not to let me have my little half-measure full?

Reading these words, I felt an instant jerk of recognition. The issue that Sojourner Truth faced in 1851 is one that Black women and many other women who feel excluded by feminism are still grappling with today. Like me, Truth was fighting for women's issues, but also for Black women's issues. "I feel I have the right to have just as much as a man," she said in 1867. "There is a great stir about colored men getting their rights, but not a word about the colored women; and if colored men get their rights, and colored women not theirs, the colored men will be masters over the women, and it will be just as bad as it was before."

Despite Truth's speech and her sustained activism in the decades following the convention, the suffrage movement in the United States continued to exclude Black women and women of color. In 1869, white women suffrage leaders including Elizabeth Cady Stanton and Susan B. Anthony rallied against the Fifteenth Amendment, which enfranchised freed Black men, accusing the Republicans of ignoring fifteen million women's rights in favor of empowering two million Black men. Anthony declared, "I will cut off this right arm of mine before I will ever work or demand the ballot for the Negro and not the woman," ignoring the fact that there are people who exist at the intersection of Negro and woman. Fast-forward to the 2016 presidential election, when thousands of white women flocked to Susan B. Anthony's grave to cover it with their "I Voted" stickers, many of them ignorant of or privileged enough to disregard her racist legacy, thus sweeping it under the rug. Meanwhile, in the UK, white British suffragettes often compared the plight of women to slavery without weighing how entitled and ludicrous that false equivalence was. For example, in 1913, Emmeline Pankhurst said, "I would rather be a rebel than a slave." On both sides of the Atlantic, renowned white feminist activists did not come close to understanding that Black women experience both racism and sexism.

It wasn't until much more recently that a word describing the experience of existing under multiple oppressive systems entered the lexicon. In 1989, Black feminist legal scholar Kimberlé Crenshaw coined the term *intersectionality* to encourage us to think about the ways in which racial and gender discrimination overlap. In her words: "Intersectionality . . . was my attempt to make feminism, anti-racist activism, and anti-discrimination law do what I thought they should— highlight the multiple avenues through which racial and gender oppression were experienced so that the problems would be easier to discuss and understand." Though Crenshaw originally intended the term to apply to Black women, the theory has been widely adopted and expanded. Intersectionality offers us a way to understand how multiple structures— capitalism, heterosexism, patriarchy, white supremacy, and so on—work together to harm women: women who are poor, disabled, queer, Muslim, undocumented, not white, or a combination of those things. Intersectionality is a way for marginalized women to talk about how their lives are affected by multiple oppressive structures—ableism, racism, and sexism, for example—that thus hit them harder and cause them to exist in double or even triple jeopardy.

Failing to take these intersections into account means leaving a huge swath of women out of feminist politics. But mainstream feminism—often referred to as "white feminism"—is still catching up to this idea. Many feminists are still ignoring the women who don't fit into the white, cisgender, heterosexual, upper- or upper-middle-class, able-bodied mold, and focusing only on the concerns of women like them. And while some white feminists have blind spots around disability, race, sexuality, and other marginalized identities, others are outright discriminatory and exclusionary. This is not a new phenomenon.

From Sojourner Truth's day on, feminists of all ages and types have ignored or actively excluded marginalized groups. At a National Organization for Women meeting in 1969, Betty Friedan argued that lesbian women were a threat to feminism because they were a distraction from the group's goals of economic and social equality. In response, queer women involved in the National Organization for Women and the Gay Liberation Front created the group known as Lavender Menace, protesting the exclusion of lesbian women at the Second Congress to Unite Women in 1970. Following this, at the next national conference of the National Organization for Women, the delegates adopted a resolution that recognized lesbian rights as "a legitimate concern for feminism."

For the past five decades, many feminists have refused to acknowledge that trans women are women. In her 1999 book, *The Whole Woman*, notable and well-respected third-wave radical feminist Germaine Greer shared her trans-exclusionary views, writing:

> Governments that consist of very few women have hurried to recognise as women, men who believe that they are women and have had to castrate themselves to prove it, because they see women not as another sex, but as a non-sex. No so-called sex-change has ever begged for a uterus-and-ovaries transplant, if uterus-and-ovaries transplants were made mandatory for wannabe women they would disappear overnight. The insistence that man-made women be accepted as women is the institutional expression of the mistaken conviction that women are defective males.

Greer was espousing the same trans-exclusionary feminism that prominent second-wave feminist Janice Raymond had embraced two decades earlier, when she argued that "all transsexuals rape women's bodies by reducing the real female form to an artifact, appropriating this body for themselves. . . . Transsexuals merely cut off the most obvious means of invading women, so that they seem non-invasive." Today, many feminists still hold transmisogynist views, and can be found arguing that trans women are a violent threat to cisgender women in restrooms. The arguments of these trans-exclusionary radical feminists, or TERFs, are not only false, but represent a reprehensible failing on the part of feminism to include and advocate for a community of women that is already under attack. The rates of assault and murder on trans women are shocking. According to the National Center for Transgender Equality, more than one in four trans people have suffered a bias-driven assault, with higher rates for trans women and trans people of color. A 2011 study from the Anti-Violence Project found that 40 percent of anti-LGBT murder victims were transgender women. Mainstream feminism's refusal to take intersectionality into account and to advocate for a group of women who are among the most threatened has devastating consequences.

As a result of the marginalization and exclusion that persists to this day, being active in the feminist movement can be an anger-inducing, isolating, and exhausting experience. Sometimes I avoid attending feminist group meetings unless they are led by a Black woman, because I'm tired of being asked to leave my Blackness at the door. Other times, I worry about going to Black feminist group meetings because of the homophobia that is endemic in many Black communities. I spoke to a friend, another Black queer woman, about this, and we both wondered: What would happen if we were openly queer in these spaces? What if I walked into that room as openly bisexual? It seemed too difficult, too dangerous. When I do attend feminist gatherings, I come expecting to struggle to read the material. I'm visually impaired, and I've never been in a feminist space that has catered to a woman like me.

Sometimes I wonder: What would my life be like if I had more power and privilege? Imagine not having to worry about whether a professor will accommodate you in their classroom; not needing to brace yourself for the cost of prescriptions you need to manage your mental health. Imagine not having to pass on attending a queer feminist meeting for fear of racism. Imagine how luxurious it would be to not have to navigate the daily microaggressions that come with living and studying, or working, in a predominantly white environment.

In my work as an activist, I regularly speak on panels and at workshops. More than once, a white woman has cornered me afterward to thank me for not being like other Black women.

"They're *so angry!*" they say. "I don't get it, June. Why do they hate us?" In most cases, I smile and nod, before leaving the area as quickly as possible. I try to keep my emotions under control. *O Zugo*, that's enough, I whisper, soothing myself in Igbo. Don't show them you're angry—don't let them win.

In my early activism—whether I was campaigning against female genital mutilation or successfully petitioning the UK government to keep feminism on the A-level politics syllabus—the fear of being stereotyped as an Angry Black Woman haunted me. I did everything I could to prevent myself from being seen that way. I strived to be measured as I spoke; I made myself smaller; I tried to make my points about exclusionary feminism without raising my voice. But I'm not invested in that anymore. Why? Because I *am* angry. I'm *pissed*. I'm so angry and I'm so tired of mainstream white feminism. And why shouldn't I be? I've spent the past five years watching white women ignore women like me who exist on the margins. It's infuriating to watch prominent, often career feminists debate whether women can "have it all" when I can't stop thinking about my Black and trans siblings dying at the hands of the police. And then there's the recent election of Donald Trump. Throughout his presidential campaign, Trump attacked women and immigrants, using racist, homophobic, and xenophobic rhetoric. But come election day, 53 percent of white women voted for him, compared to the 94 percent of Black women and 68 percent of Latina women who voted for Hillary Clinton—pointing again to the privilege that allows white women to remain ignorant of and insulated from the issues facing women of color, Muslim women, immigrants, and other marginalized groups, a problem that also plagues mainstream feminism.

The problem with mainstream feminism, again and again, is the frivolity of the issues it is concerned with: manspreading, "girl power" and female "empowerment," articles with headlines like CAN YOU BE A FEMINIST AND WEAR MAKEUP? As they fight these lesser battles, white women ignore the ways that their Black and brown, disabled, and trans sisters are still shackled by multiple forms of oppression. In the United States, Black women and girls make up only 13 percent of the population, but according to a 2015 #SayHerName report by the African American Policy Forum, they account for 33 percent of all women killed by the police. The #Say HerName movement was put together by the African-American Policy Forum to make visible the names of Black women killed by the police, who were often sidelined in the conversation in favor of Black men. Where was mainstream feminism when Rekia Boyd was killed, when Sandra Bland was killed? What about Alteria Woods or Charleena Lyles? Where were white women when Black women marched, asking that they #SayHerName? In the UK, an organization called Women's Aid found that one in two disabled women will be abused in their lifetime. Half! What has mainstream feminism done to bring attention to that? In 2015, Amnesty International published research and policy recommendations in support of the "decriminalization of all aspects of consensual adult sex," sometimes referred to as "the New Zealand Model." Prominent British feminists attacked Amnesty International for not following the Nordic Model, which does not criminalize the selling of sex, but does aim to punish clients by criminalizing the purchase of sex. Despite the fact that in the report Amnesty made it very clear that they were responding to the wishes of sex workers, white feminists from Hollywood, including Lena Dunham, Kate Winslet, Meryl Streep, and Emma Thompson, joined with their British counterparts in criticizing the human rights organization, signing an open letter asking Amnesty to reverse its position. Do these so-called feminists just not care about the voices of sex workers? What makes it so hard for them to respect their needs? Then there's rural America, where in 2015, pregnant women were 64 percent more likely to die of complications than women in urban areas. The time and distance from hospitals with resources and specialists for obstetric emergencies renders so many women vulnerable. Did we see mainstream feminists rallying around this issue? Or the fact that, according to the National Latina Network, one in three Hispanic or Latina women have experienced physical violence from an intimate partner in their lifetime? Where is the mainstream feminist outrage about that?

When white feminists focus their attention on issues that mostly affect affluent, cisgender, heterosexual, white women like themselves, they fail to address life-or-death issues facing millions of women of color, disabled women, queer women, trans women, poor women, and other marginalized groups. I wonder: Do these so-called feminists ever stop to consider the fact that there are women who can't even get through the door—whether because of racism, fatphobia, homophobia, or transphobia—let alone into the boardroom? And when we fail to think of these women—to advocate for them, to rally for them, and to listen to them—it's the equivalent of saying that their lives, their experiences, and their struggles aren't important. This kind of feminism is not only wrong but also dangerous. Mainstream feminism's lack of an intersectional focus could be a mortal threat to its very existence if a plurality of women and nonbinary folks don't see it as a tool that has the power to change their lives.

INTERSECTIONALITY MATTERS. It has always mattered. Long before the word existed, it was a lived experience for millions. And yet, current mainstream feminist politics still takes a one-size-fits-all approach. Returning to bell hooks's definition, feminism aims to end sexist oppression for all.

So how can a feminism that excludes tens of millions of women succeed?

If feminism is to cease to be a movement for the few, privileged women must start listening to women who are poor, women who are undocumented, women who are queer, women who are on the margins of society, elevating *those* voices instead of their own. White women must also acknowledge their privilege, despite the fact that they face sexist oppression. Often, when marginalized women ask white women to do so, they complain that it goes against "unity" and finding "common ground." White women often call for a "sisterhood" that requires marginalized women to subsume part of our identities in service of the battle for gender equality, to separate our identities in the politics we practice. For me, this is impossible—how can I separate my Blackness from my womanhood? And is it really a "sisterhood" if I cannot bring all of myself to the room? I want no part of a feminism that asks me to ignore parts of my identity. And neither should you. Instead, I seek a feminism that, as Audre Lorde wrote in 1984 in her seminal speech, "The Master's Tools Will Never Dismantle the Master's House," acknowledges privilege and is open to difference:

> As women, we have been taught either to ignore our differences, or to view them as causes for separation and suspicion rather than as forces for change. Without community there is no liberation, only the most vulnerable and temporary armistice between an individual and her oppression. But community must not mean a shedding of our differences, nor the pathetic pretense that these differences do not exist.

Of course, no political movement is going to be perfect. There's bound to be disagreement. And challenging each other is healthy. But if the aim of feminism is to end multiple forms of oppression and transform our lives—*all of them*—then we must heal fractures, build bridges, and come together as we work toward achieving that goal. I agree wholeheartedly that building an (albeit imperfect) united sisterhood that focuses on the liberation of all women is a necessary step. But we won't get there by abandoning our own concerns and shutting off parts of ourselves.

We will only get there when privileged feminists start listening—really listening, no matter how uncomfortable it might be—to women like me, who exist on the margins, and amplifying our voices.

To those women with privilege, this is what we need from you: Organize with us, but let us be the authority on our own experiences and in our activism. Don't speak for us—we can speak for ourselves. And if we can't, because it's too dangerous or the consequences might be too much to bear, then use your privilege to raise our voices and our struggles. Show up and show out for us. Put yourselves and your bodies on the line. Yes, that means attending that rally about police brutality and showing up for that vigil when yet another trans woman of color is murdered. When you organize, look at who's in the room, and who's not, and do what you can to get them in the room. If that fails, go to where those women are. Move beyond the digital sphere to accommodate women who can't access it because of poverty, geography, a lack of internet literacy, age, and other factors. Consider each issue through as many different lenses as you can: race, class, disability, sexuality, poverty, neuroatypicality, and gender identity. Broaden your view of what is considered a feminist issue. Pay us for our work and organizing. Help us when we run for office. Bail our families out of jail. Volunteer with immigrants' rights groups. Campaign for better access to family planning services, for better childcare, for better health care. Make your organizing rooms and marches accessible for disabled women. Use our preferred pronouns. Fight against mental health stigma. Work to do this in every aspect of your life. But crucially, don't come to us for the solutions to problems that were not caused by us. Take initiative. Learn. Make mistakes. Do better.

To my marginalized sisters: I see you. I know how hard it is to move through the world while living at the intersection of oppression. I know what it's like to have no money, to be poor and homeless and roaming the streets, to perm your hair for a job interview, to walk into a room and wonder if the people present will see you as human. I also realize that I might not know your struggles, or fully understand all that you're experiencing right now. But I take heart from the fact that, despite the odds stacked against us, so many of us are thriving. Yes, some of us are struggling to survive and some of us are dying, but those of us who can are fighting for you, and we will remember your names and your stories. We have to keep going. It seems simple to say, and harder to do, but in a world where we experience extortionate levels of violence and so much is stacked against us that you may wonder if this world even wants us alive, our mere existence is a radical act. Take care of yourselves. Put yourselves first. Find moments of joy. Celebrate yourselves. Hold on to all the good we've done—and are yet to do. Listen to and learn from your sisters: undocumented women, trans women, Black women, disabled women. Hold their hands. Work across lines of marginalization. Support each other. Keep fighting, the best that you can. Keep trying, the best that you can. Learn. Make mistakes. Do better.

For those not already versed in the challenges facing, and debates within, feminism today, reading this anthology is a great place to start. For those of you who, like me, live and breathe these issues, I hope you'll find some common truth, or see experiences like yours represented in this collection, which includes only marginalized voices and so puts them front and center.

For privileged women, I hope it will help you begin to grasp the struggles of women who are different from you, as well as why some marginalized women who believe in equality nevertheless struggle to identify with feminism. I am one of those women.

I chose to call this anthology *Can We All Be Feminists?* because as a marginalized woman, I've sometimes wondered if feminism has space for me. In my late teens, I discovered *womanism*, a term coined by Alice Walker that explicitly focuses on the experiences of Black women. For some time, that label felt more apt because of Walker's spotlight on Black women's needs and her inclusion of queer women, writing that a womanist is "a woman who loves another woman, sexually and/or non sexually." I felt like womanism wouldn't leave me out in the way that feminism often did. Ultimately, I'm comfortable with calling my beliefs by either term—feminism or womanism—because I still believe that feminism can improve, can be so much better, and has been and will continue to be a powerful framework for women to achieve so much. But I know that many other women feel excluded by feminism, or see it as useless because it is not concerned with the issues that affect them.

In this anthology, you'll hear from seventeen women as they grapple with their relationship to feminism, especially as it relates to their marginalized identities. Novelists Brit Bennett and Nicole Dennis-Benn examine religion and lesbianism respectively, with the additional lens of Black womanhood. Performance artist Selina Thompson discusses the issue of fat and feminism. Gabrielle Bellot and Juliet Jacques remind us of the precarious position in which trans women find themselves. Frances Ryan chronicles the issues facing disabled women. And Wei Ming Kam demonstrates how immigration is a feminist issue. These are just some of the voices in these pages. Of course, there's no way this anthology can raise every issue and represent all women. It's impossible to do that. But we've done our best to bring together as diverse a group of women as possible. I hope their insights and arguments will challenge you, galvanize you, and start conversations.

Despite its shortcomings, I'm really grateful for feminism. Thanks to feminism, I found my voice and my purpose: campaigning, fighting, and standing up for the rights of *all* women. Feminism also gave me the permission to reject the notions of being a "good" girl. I like being a rebel girl. I hope this anthology helps spark your own rebellion. I have no idea where it might take us. But let's begin.

CAN WE ALL
BE FEMINISTS?

NO WAVE FEMINISM

Charlotte Shane

IF YOU FEEL like feminism is failing you, you are not alone. I sometimes have the impression that I'm as thoroughly feminist as I am thoroughly human, that feminism is as intrinsic to my constitution as my skeleton is to my body. But in my thirty-five years, I've struggled with or outright rejected feminism on several occasions: first, as an ignorant adolescent ("What do women need feminism for if we've already got the vote?"); then, as a sex worker who saw how regularly and even gleefully feminists stoked the public's long-standing antipathy toward professionally sexual women; and now, again, as someone moving ever further into the far left, who cannot abide the forms of feminism that embrace and are complicit with the worst aspects of liberalism.

The more I learn about the intersecting, oppressive forces that continue to shape the Western world—colonialism, patriarchy, capitalism, xenophobia, and racism—and the network of cruel social machinery to which these systems give rise—incarceration, crippling debt, disenfranchisement, deportation, and so on—the less sense it makes to use gender as the primary lens through which to regard human-engineered suffering. Feminism doesn't feel like the sharpest weapon to wield against white supremacy or border policing, for instance, or even the best tool with which to approach basic civic concerns like vibrant schools. That's not because those issues don't impact women; obviously, they directly and indirectly impact many. But they don't necessarily impact women more or in dramatically different ways than they do men. In other words, the most significant challenges those issues present aren't tethered to one's sex. And so prioritizing gender above other aspects of identity limits one's realm of ethical response.

Here's an example. American prisons often keep female prisoners shackled while they give birth. There are variations on the theme: Some women are shackled during labor, some are unshackled during but then shackled again almost immediately afterward, and almost all are shackled while heavily pregnant. There's some variation of what shackling entails, too. It can mean being cuffed at the wrists, or at the ankles, or both—or cuffed to a hospital bed, or chained at the waist. Articulating these details makes the sadism even starker.

A class action federal lawsuit in 2017 alleged more than forty women at the Milwaukee County Jail suffered this horror. It was preceded by lawsuits in 2014 and 2016 against the same jail for similar practices. But the appalling practice is hardly confined to one city or even one state. In 2015, New York prisons were found to be shackling prisoners in labor in spite of a state law that made it illegal to do so. And according to a 2016 report by the Prison Birth Project and Prisoners' Legal Services of Massachusetts, jails and prisons in Massachusetts were guilty of similar violations.

Most feminists probably agree that this is a feminist issue; the topic accordingly receives coverage on feminist websites and sometimes in women's magazines. But does a feminist obligation to attend to the rights of the imprisoned extend only as far as pregnancy and labor? Is it a feminist issue when a nonpregnant woman is shackled? Or when she is caged for years and exploited for her labor, denied face-to-face visits from loved ones, held captive in a compound in the name of "justice"? If the answer to these questions is yes, then is it also a feminist issue when men are shackled during various health emergencies—seizures, say? (In 2014, a male inmate in Colorado died after undergoing several seizures while in restraints and receiving no medical treatment.) Is it a feminist issue when incarcerated men are denied the right to visit with family, or exploited for their labor? Is it a feminist issue that so many men are raped while in prison? Or does feminism's responsibility begin and end with gender-based mistreatment?

The feminists hired by prominent media outlets often advocate for measures that would result in higher levels of incarceration. They write op-eds in favor of further criminalization around sex work, and call for longer prison sentences for men convicted of assault—which we've known for decades is not necessarily synonymous with "men who've committed the crime." They also, disturbingly, relish the theater of sentencing like that enacted by Judge Rosemarie Aquilina, who told serial sexual abuser Larry Nassar that if she could, she would "allow some or many people to do to him what he did to others." (So, sexual violation is an atrocity . . . unless it happens to the right person?) They capitalize on women's justified fear and anger around mistreatment by men to shore up the status quo, to suggest that our current problems are not the result of fundamentally unjust institutions, but rather institutions that are only incidentally sexist. That means those same institutions could become less so with the right adjustments, like more draconian sentencing for crimes against women, or more female judges.

But the prison system is racist and brutal *by design*, not by accident or mismanagement, just as the court system regularly fails the most vulnerable because it was built to protect the powerful. "The challenge of the twenty-first century is not to demand equal opportunity to participate in the machinery of oppression," revolutionary thinker Angela Davis has written. "Rather, it is to identify and dismantle those structures." Yet leveraging our existing legal system for criminalization remains the go-to strategy for most feminists when it comes to dealing with objectionable behavior. Criminalization entails fines and incarceration; it does not meaningfully concern itself with rehabilitation, education, victim care, or prevention. Its ability to deter other potential offenders is unproven—or, arguably, proven to be nonexistent, as is especially demonstrable with laws against drug use and possession—and the recidivism rate is astronomical. Moreover, the legal system is not accessible to everyone. Undocumented people cannot use it. People leading already criminalized lives, like sex workers, often cannot use it, and marginalized people are also discouraged from or outright prevented from using it by a slew of means. (The most obvious of which is usually time and money.)

This instinct to turn to the state is not unfamiliar to me. I, too, learned from a young age that laws and courts and police are the way to deal with almost everything: You notice something is wrong, you get a law passed or use an existing law to stop it, and the problem is solved. This is not how our current laws work in practice, and it is incumbent upon us to face that fact with honesty and creativity. When activists speak out against police and prisons, people immediately demand that they offer a replacement apparatus, but it is an impossible demand. The transformation needs to be more profound than a simple swap. Prison abolitionist Mariame Kaba speaks on this point with great eloquence: "We have to transform the relationships we have with each other so we can really create new forms of safety and justice in our communities. [The work of abolition] insists that it is necessary that you *change everything*." [emphasis added.]

Many feminists, though, have lost their foremother's radical vision of changing everything. Instead, they are ready to work within the tight confines of an ineffective system, and they endorse and invest in a de facto police state. The "feminist" modifier itself is useless for indicating a stance on this issue, as it is for many others: protecting the rights of trans women, for instance, or even the legality of abortion.

This tension is long-standing and perhaps inevitable given that feminism is assumed to galvanize people under a banner of gender rather than shared ideological and moral commitments, as a formal organization, like a political party or a local activist group, would. There's no explicit platform for feminism because it's an idea, ownerless and atomized, based on the observation of one specific, persistent source of imbalance in a stunningly unfair world. It can be invoked (cynically or sincerely) by anyone, which is part of why it's been so easily co-opted by corporations who use superficial gestures of pro-women sentiment for brand management, and by a mainstream media that anoints clueless celebrities like Lena Dunham, Taylor Swift, and Amy Schumer as the vanguard of righteous, pro-lady politics.

Aside from for-profit institutions muddying the waters, there's also the matter of individual dissent. Even groups with clear and detailed mission statements run into internal disagreement. That's healthy and good. But today's concept of feminism provides such a wide net that some women (and men) assume gender alone makes one eligible for membership, regardless of actual convictions. "Feminist" has become synonymous with hollow phrases like "female empowerment" and "strong women" and "girl power." If a woman's ambition were automatically feminist by virtue of her gender alone, that would hold true whether she's directing her energies into exploiting workers in other countries, trying to overturn affirmative action, or working to keep her neighborhood free from immigrants.

Sheryl Sandberg's Lean In campaign notoriously exemplifies this sort of self-serving attitude. In her 2010 TED Talk and 2013 book by the same name, Sandberg exhorted working women to throw themselves into the corporate world, implying that women's general lack of representation in the boardroom was a function of their own timidity and emotionality rather than workplace discrimination or intractable secondary obstacles (like being unable to afford childcare, or simply not wanting to sacrifice quality of life for a title). Why is it important that women assume more prominent roles in corporations? Because their absence indicates sexism, and sexism is bad. Or because they'd bring "diversity," and diversity makes a company stronger. A number of similar platitudes could be offered in response to this question, but none would be sufficient. By assuming that having more women is better, period, we relinquish the opportunity to question what it is the corporation does (read: who it harms and how it harms them), what's inherently good about climbing to the top of any hierarchy, or how it socially benefits all women for one particular woman to earn an obscene amount of money.

The feminism espoused by Sandberg goes by many names—neoliberal feminism, white feminism, corporate feminism—but whatever it's called, its priority is to help a small number of people further consolidate power and money without rocking the proverbial boat. Few systems are threatened by slotting women into roles traditionally held by men, because absolute wealth and absolute power tend to corrupt absolutely. Few want to dismantle the means by which they achieve tremendous success; rather, they want to further consolidate that success in all its forms: influence, wealth, and so on. If patriarchy's worst offense were keeping women out of the workplace, then sure, women like Sheryl Sandberg would be triumphs of the cause. But the notion that women shouldn't work outside the home was always unique to the white upper and middle classes. Poorer women never had the option to stay at home, and Black women in the United States have virtually always been expected to work, if not in the fields then in white homes as "domestic" servants. The far more noxious effects of patriarchy, like rendering women incapable of exercising autonomy over their reproduction or paying them lower wages for their work, can and do endure even with more women "on top." You never have to look very far to find female politicians voting to make abortion less accessible, or female activists trying to take down Planned Parenthood, just as you don't have to search very hard to find powerful women who explicitly blame other women for their own sexual assault or who, à la Ann Coulter, go so far as to suggest women shouldn't have the right to vote.

So not only is Lean In feminism useless for achieving a truly pro-women future wherein *all* women see their lives improved, but it actively undermines that vision. It's a feminism that purports to push for progress while wedding itself to the perpetuation and justification of patriarchy's equally insidious attendants: capitalism, imperialism, racism, ableism, and so on. Every other hierarchy may remain intact as long as (some) women are allowed a shot at approaching the top. By participating in unjust power structures, and giving those same structures a fresh patina of legitimacy, this feminism places a radically reimagined future further out of reach for the people—women and men alike—who so desperately need it.

Ignoring the problems of less advantaged women to secure the rights, and later, the high-profile achievement, of the privileged has been part of feminism's legacy since the beginning. Suffragettes (who were primarily white and middle or upper class) were often outspoken racists who fomented anti-Black sentiment, participating in segregation and endorsing colonialism. Various white figureheads of feminism in the 1960s and 1970s were willfully ignorant about and explicitly unconcerned by the social concerns shared by women of color; they also disavowed lesbians and tried to keep them apart from the larger movement. Today, many prominent British feminists stoke anti-trans fears among their followers and rally for further criminalization and stigmatization of sex work—in spite of the fact that doing so demonstrably keeps female (and male, and non-gender-conforming) sex workers extraordinarily vulnerable. American feminists are quieter on these issues, but then, they're quiet on a lot of issues—namely, almost anything that doesn't revolve around (white, cis) women's reproductive options and (white, cis) women's experience of sexual assault or harassment, or cultural representation as measured by women directing big-budget films and winning awards.

Mainstream feminism fails us because, by definition, it adheres to the status quo and nudges it only slightly to the left, if at all. It wouldn't be mainstream if it didn't play by these rules. But the status quo is actively harmful to almost everyone, regardless of gender. It concentrates wealth in the hands of the .01 percent (US' 3 RICHEST MEN HAVE MORE WEALTH THAN HALF OF THE POPULATION was a repeated headline in late 2017 following the release of a report by the Institute for Policy Studies in Washington, D.C.) It keeps many of us underemployed and terrified of getting sick, lest we need medical care that far outstrips our resources. It allows police officers to murder with impunity. It renders voting inaccessible to huge swaths of the adult population. It ravages communities with gun violence. It breaks our hearts, and it makes it harder to start every day with enough hope to work for something better.

Perhaps the most apt name for this kind of feminism, then, is *sabotage feminism*. It exists to stymie the efforts of the most radical feminist values—those that put the most disadvantaged among us *first*, not last—by turning the very idea of feminism on itself, by feeding feminism its own tail. Second-wave feminists—those active in the late 1960s through the '80s—envisioned a profound remaking of society on sexual, familial, and economic levels. These years birthed the dreams of wages for housework, the Equal Rights Amendment, and unapologetic abortion on demand, and it offered women a fantasy of solidarity as they rallied behind those efforts. But whatever wave of feminism we're experiencing now might be best described as *no wave*, for it leaves us bereft of unity, momentum, and power as we compete against each other to sit with men on the boards of companies with track records of unremitting mendacity.

I know a lot of feminists are more progressive and intelligent than what the largest news outlets suggest. When I use "us" and "we," it's with this reality in mind; it is an attempt to encompass people of any gender who desire less suffering for all, and who believe their own freedom, comfort, and pleasure should not come at the expense of someone else's. But because Lean In feminism—the feminism that says any conventionally successful woman is likely to be an example of feminist success—still has a near-monopoly when it comes to the dominant public discourse, excoriating and disavowing it is an important step in pushing against the ways it's leveraged to silence more substantive concerns.

I'M NOT READY to abandon feminism, because misogyny and sexism are real. But I'm disheartened by the derelict quality of what my generation inherited and helped build, or at least permitted to be built on our watch. I believe feminism is both necessary and (in its current state) regularly superfluous—both urgent and too often a distraction. Nothing illustrated this dynamic more horribly than the campaign and election of Donald Trump, a man who bragged about sexual assault, spent decades publicly insulting women in the most reductive ways possible, and has a history of dramatic and crude sexist behavior when it comes to his marriages and his involvement in beauty pageants. He is a vile and enthusiastic chauvinist—there's no lack of confirmation there—but for all the public hand-wringing over his well-documented misogyny, his worst acts as president have hardly been confined to the "pussy grabbing" that became the central rallying cry against him as the election approached in late 2016. As far as we know, he's not leveraged his office to sexually harass or assault anyone; with a few notable exceptions, he's not even spent much time verbally attacking specific female enemies on Twitter. It doesn't seem he's opposed to women in high places earning lots of money and making big decisions, and he has a number of women in top positions within his White House staff and cabinet—which, as I've mentioned, is entirely consistent with the Lean In era's definition of feminist progress.

What he's done instead is incite his followers—and I say "followers" not only to reflect the parlance of social media but because it seems the most accurate word to describe his fervent fans—and the authority figures among them to enact a wide range of brutal aggression against Muslims, Mexicans, transgender people, the lower classes (meaning anyone outside his own tax bracket), and anyone from protesters to journalists who oppose or irritate the ruling class. Listing some of his recent offenses feels both futile and necessary as his atrocities continue to amass, only to be wiped away by each new headline. At the time of this writing, he's held rallies to further agitate for white supremacy, defended the neo-Nazis who terrorized Charlottesville, Virginia, in mid-August 2017, and laid blame for "violence" at the feet of left-ists who protected peaceful clergy members. He is, at least superficially, trying to follow through on his promises to build a wall between the United States and Mexico. The Supreme Court has allowed his infamous Muslim travel ban to take full effect. Despite the vast unpopularity of such a decision, his administration has managed to overturn net neutrality and pass a heinous (and again, hugely unpopular) tax bill.

All of which is to say that rather than attacking women as a discrete group, Trump has followed in the footsteps of the presidents before him (yes, even the Democrats) and instead focused on waging war both at home and abroad against people of color, the poor, our natural environment, and tools of active political participation (like the right to vote and to protest). Again, women are impacted by all of this, because many women are poor, most women are not white, and all women, like all humans and indeed all mammals, need a hospitable environment in which to live. But feminism without intersectionality—in other words, without sensitivity and equal attention to other nexuses of discrimination and oppression, such as race and sexuality—is worthless. And the feminism on tap in this moment is emphatically not intersectional.

Misogyny is alive and thriving, and we cannot tolerate a world in which this is so. Yet we also know misogyny is rarely the dominant motivation behind the most destructive work of politicians, corporate leaders, and other multimillionaires or billionaires not already among those two groups. They operate under other more immediate and selfish concerns, like how to crush challenges to their outsize power, further inflate their bloated wealth, and deflect responsibility for all the misery they inflict. With its gender-based wage asymmetries and its outsourcing of reproductive labor (the unpaid work of bearing and raising children) to primarily women, sexism is useful, but rarely the end goal in and of itself. Sabotage feminism, the feminism that's visible to most Americans and to most women, that's espoused by both celebrities and op-ed columnists, has trouble grappling with this. It can say plenty about how Trump habitually demeans women, but it hasn't developed the sort of trenchant, comprehensive critique that would allow it to speak meaningfully on the racist and fascist legacy he has adopted so completely, one in which the state is entitled to any and all of our personal data; to carry out massive attacks overseas with heavy civilian casualties in countries with which we're not even officially at war; to cage its own citizens before they're found guilty of any crime and then indefinitely thereafter; to violently aggress against peaceful protesters and to murder citizens with impunity through an unrestrained and anti-Black police force.

As many have pointed out since November 2016, none of what Trump advocates is new. He is unusually offensive to middle- and upper-class propriety, but it is only the bluntness of his rhetoric that's unique to him, not its content. His continued support from the Republican Party, and the limpness of elected Democrats' response, speaks to just how entrenched his beliefs are. How can we concern ourselves with unreasonable beauty standards when families are being ripped apart by deportation? How can we harp about a wage gap when even men aren't earning enough to live?

But of course, those are false dilemmas. There should be nothing incompatible about feminism and any other movement for social justice; on the contrary, true feminism should be essential to the success of all other progressive movements. Conflict materializes when we buy into the notion that feminism is a narrow aperture through which to consider our world, one that can only inform our analysis on issues that break down neatly around gender. When feminism is treated as if it can respond solely to oppressions that move neatly from men to women—with no complicating factors or contextual ambiguity—it becomes the agent of our enemies, lending itself to the adoption of a victim mind-set in which all women are threatened by all men and where other vectors of power, like race or able-bodiedness or wealth, are immaterial. It conveniently obfuscates just how easily women can participate in oppression of other women, and of men, too—and always have.

If feminism were a vehicle of rescue or even just improvement for individual women, as opposed to being a radical vision with the power to remake society on a grand scale, it would still have to intervene in health care, in childcare, in gun control. It would have to grapple with exploitative workplaces, and with incarceration, and environmental degradation, because women's lives are deeply degraded by and even lost to these conditions. Feminism should expand our commitment to each other as human beings, not contract it by replicating the same power structures we should be decisively overthrowing. And the good news is: It can. Just as we expect men to speak out around other men who evince sexist or misogynist attitudes, so should we commit ourselves to confronting and educating women (or anyone) who depict feminism as a strategy of personal betterment by any means necessary instead of a political cause organized around the goal of a more just world. We have to hold ourselves to high standards and invite those around us to join.

I'M NOT SURE if I'm a "feminist" or not. Some hateful people have identified as feminists over the years, and while I'm loath to ally myself with them, I'm equally loath to cede the word without a fight. But it's not a name I need to call myself anymore, perhaps, because its tenets feel sufficiently absorbed into the gestalt of who I am. Plus, the neurotic insistence on labeling things "feminist"—not just ourselves and each other, but personal products and companies and movies and ad campaigns—feels like part and parcel of a diminishing of what the word could mean. Feminism itself is a practice, a tool, a weapon, an insight. It is the truth that in our current world, women are often intentionally, systematically disadvantaged and exploited because of their gender. Therefore, "feminist" should be regarded as a promise, a mode of being, a commitment carried into all our efforts to recognize and reject sexism, and to let that inform our rejection of *all* types of injustice. Never again should it be treated as a static label that anyone can put on or take off like a piece of statement jewelry.

The current condition of feminism is not the permanent condition of feminism. Though there are some (sadly, many) people who work to make it an ideology that doesn't recognize or incorporate the specific rights and needs of trans women, sex workers, Black women, disabled women, and poor women—among others—feminism itself has no gatekeepers. It is not a club from which others can exclude you. No one can keep you from living in concert with its core realizations, and what you call yourself while you act from that foundation ultimately means very little. Coherent, ethical feminism is available to anyone who recognizes that gender is relevant only inasmuch as a society makes it so; that gender alone determines nothing about a person's worth, aptitude, intelligence, or character; and that policies and laws and rhetoric to the contrary are not only unjust and harmful, they are incorrect and born from self-serving biases.

To make feminism work for where we are now, I propose we break it open. Let our vision be confined not to one wave but to an entire sea. I want a flexible feminism that floods into every other cause we adopt, that girds every framework we erect, as so many abolitionist and socialist and anarchist women before us proved it can. Because we need feminism still, no matter how badly it disappoints us in its most visible form. We will probably need it forever; its work will never be complete. It's because it is so indispensable to any and every convincing vision of a better world that we must continue to demand feminism itself be better, no matter what word we rally around.

UNAPOLOGETIC

Nicole Dennis-Benn

I WAS GUILTY. Every time an R. Kelly song came on the radio, I danced and sang along to the lyrics, closing my eyes to the glaring headlines in the media about his sexual abuse allegations. I even debated with friends about whether an artist's work should be regarded as separate from the artist's personal life, pleading with them to pardon him for his indiscretions. "The man is a genius," I'd say, joining the chorus of Black women and men whose sympathy for the young Black girls and the damage done to them wasn't as powerful as their allegiance to the artist and his work. In this case, it was classic R&B by a man who has written music for the likes of Michael Jackson, Madonna, Aaliyah, Toni Braxton, Lady Gaga, Britney Spears, and many more chart toppers. It was the same for Bill Cosby. When it came out that he had been raping women for decades, many Black folks felt we had to choose between the women who came forward—mostly white, with the exception of supermodel Beverly Johnson—and the man who gave us the distinguished Huxtables on *The Cosby Show*, which was crucial at a time when we craved to see good images of ourselves on television.

Little did I know at the time that what I was silently agreeing to by lamenting the fall of these men was a rape culture that continued to fuel their power. Little did I know, too, that in my lame argument that we should "protect the artist," I was participating in silencing the women who had the courage to come forward despite the power of these men—women who, like Anita Hill, valiantly stood their ground in the face of denials from their harassers and assaulters (in her case Clarence Thomas, a federal circuit judge who had been nominated to the US Supreme Court) and were told their truth could not be so. *For how could he do such a thing? He's beloved! You sure you weren't mistaken? He's a Black man. Do you know how hard it is for Black men?* Answering those questions, many Black women like me gag ourselves with explanations and rebuttals. We believe for the sake of believing in something other than our own demise. For we were socialized to protect Black men, to coddle them, to be the rocks on which they stand tall.

I must admit that I sat uncomfortably with my silence. Somehow, it became fury that fed my rage—not against the culprits, but against the women who came forward, doing something I never thought I'd have the guts to do. For in my mind, I internalized the fears and silences of my elders— women who have warned against these things. *Nevah wash yuh dirty draws in public river, gyal.* Or *Suck salt an' you'll succeed.* These voices remained in me, merging with mine when I dared to utter things like, "But he's legendary!" Or "How do we know these women aren't lying? How do we know they're not doing this for their own fame?" And the deadliest statement of them all, which often looms above the room full of Black women, holding our corners as the cornerstones we were raised to be: "Every other Black man is in prison. Why are we going to be responsible for putting more of them there?" (Now I wonder: Has anyone ever thought the same about Black women?)

Forgive me. I knew not what I had bought into the day I was born a Black woman. I did not know that day as I stared up into my mother's smiling face that I had joined an allegiance to shame and silence, bearing the indiscretions of others and justifying these hurts with phrases like "Turn the other cheek," "Be humble," and "Be strong."

In college, I had no idea what feminism was and quite honestly did not care. I was grappling with a lot more adjustments—my other identities as immigrant, lesbian, female, and black, all closing in on me like four walls. Certainly there were women who had inspired me to be independent and powerful. But as I came of age as a Black woman, I knew I had to privilege the most obvious of my identities—my skin color. For it's the cover on which people's eyes fall, their own minds adjusting like Rubik's Cubes to see how I should be treated, addressed. Or not. Truth be told, my Black skin also made it easier for me to fit into my new country, America, becoming friends and roommates with other Black students on a mostly white college campus, given that white students weren't the first ones to welcome me. I felt closer to other students of color, yet still alienated because of my Jamaican accent and my sexuality, which I kept hidden for the first two years of college for the sake of fitting in.

In my junior year, I lived with a group of Black women who eventually learned of my sexuality. It was a painful experience when I was told by one of my housemates that she didn't feel comfortable living with me. This was not my only experience of distrust and homophobia among heterosexual Black women. Perhaps they couldn't—and still cannot—understand how anyone could deny the Black man, and more specifically, the Black penis. Many of them gave me strange looks, and a few even went as far as to draw their towels tighter after stepping out of the shower and seeing me. Therefore, I made myself even more scarce. I retreated to the other side of campus and tried to forge relationships with other lesbians, who were almost always white and had their own prejudices.

The pang of rejection remained with me for years, much like the realization that my Black male professors, like Black heterosexual women, preferred the Black male students to the Black female students. And how could they not? They were so scarce on Cornell University's campus compared to the Black women, though we were also a small population. Like the Black women, Black professors found it refreshing that these young Black men were in their classrooms and not in prison or selling drugs on the street. Therefore, they were highly favored. People leaned in to hear their analysis of questions I could've answered better, dismissing me and the other women in the classroom. They could do no wrong. Therefore, it is no surprise that in Black culture, men like R. Kelly, Clarence Thomas, O. J. Simpson, Bill Cosby, Russell Simmons, Thomas Sayers Ellis, Bishop Eddie Long, and all the other so-called upstanding Black men could get away with committing the crimes they were accused of for so long. For in the eyes of Black women, they are victims of a racist society ready to emasculate the Black man.

I am sad to admit that I found myself lowering my raised hand in those classrooms in college and graduate school, telling myself, "Maybe he said it better," or "Maybe my accent would've gotten in the way," or "He deserves to be here as much as I do. It's good to see a Black man thrive. It's good to see him here, warming these seats, rather than behind bars. His voice deserves to be heard. To be louder than mine."

Forgive me. I knew not what I pledged my allegiance to then. I faded into the background, refusing to look around me, stand up, and speak. But this was before I sat in a feminist theory course in the spring of my junior year.

I needed an elective to balance all the heavy science courses I had been taking as a premed major. I needed this elective to graduate. My naïveté led me to believe that feminist theory would be easy, at least compared to biochemistry. I was wrong. I often burned the midnight oil studying for this class. It was in my feminist theory course that I discovered the word *womanist* after reading an essay written by Alice Walker, who felt that feminism at the time did not incorporate the needs of women of color and other marginalized groups. I never removed that word from my vocabulary. Though I went on to graduate the following year and continued to try miserably to compartmentalize all my identities, I couldn't help but think about the word: womanist.

IN 2015, I participated in my first march. By then, I had a new identity as a writer and was about to publish my first book, about three working-class Jamaican Black women trying to survive their fates. I donned a hoodie that summer and marched against police brutality with a group of Black women who organized against the injustices done to Black men. These women coined the phrase "Black Lives Matter." I, like many Black women across America, joined in holding up the "Black Lives Matter" banner as we marched. Even my wife wore the sticker on her book bag to work each day. We—Black lesbian women—marched for the justice of our fallen Black soldiers, possessively holding on to the legacies of Black men and Black boys as though we ourselves had birthed them from our wombs. Meanwhile, no one marched for us. Black girls and Black women were being raped and killed every day, and no one dared to take the time to make a banner for them, for us. No one cried for us. The only time we were seen crying was on television, next to Al Sharpton or another civil rights leader, presumably a man, mourning the death of sons, fathers, brothers, nephews, uncles, husbands. We utter, "I forgive. I forgive. I forgive," because it is what Black women are taught. We are taught to be selfless. We are taught to get along. We are taught to be meek. For God forbid we raise our voices and express the rage stirring inside our souls, inside our hearts. God forbid we're perceived as angry, feeding into the "angry Black woman" stereotype. Look how quickly Michelle Obama was ridiculed when she spoke on behalf of her husband during the early days of his campaign. And God forbid we dare turn against our brothers and admit that they hurt us. We risk bringing down the whole race with an allegation like that. So we remain silent, bow our heads, and numb our rage with anything we can find—food, sex, retail, drugs, alcohol, or Granny's personal favorite, religion.

Alice Walker's words ring truer than ever as I contemplate how the world never sees Black women. Somehow, we are pegged as nurturers but simultaneously stripped of our gender. Are we supposed to be gods? Is that why we are told that our bodies are temples? But then again, if our bodies are temples, we are nothing but edifices, lacking heart and desire and rights to our own bodies. It was Alice Walker, who describes in her essay "In Search of Our Mothers' Gardens" the depiction of Black women in the eyes of a very observant poet of the Harlem Renaissance, Jean Toomer. According to Walker, Toomer's description was written in the post-Reconstruction South. He had visited the South in the early 1920s and observed the intense religiosity of Black women there. In the excerpt, Toomer comments on this intense religiosity's numbing effect on Black women against the backdrop of social injustices being done to them. He describes

Black women as "crazy" saints, women whose eyes wander from themselves toward heaven, stuck in hopelessness. Alice Walker writes that according to Toomer, "[Black women] stumbled blindly through their lives: creatures so abused and mutilated in body, so dimmed and confused by pain, that they considered themselves unworthy even of hope. In the selfless abstractions their bodies became to the men who used them, they became more than 'sexual objects,' more even than mere women: they became Saints."

Though it's beautifully written and precise, I could not help but reflect on the fact that Jean Toomer was a Black man. I also couldn't help but wonder if this was intentional on Walker's part, to write this Black man's observation of defeated Black women as an example to bolster her argument. However, though Toomer's observation may seem contradictory in a feminist/womanist argument—especially one about self-expression—there's something powerful about Walker's choice to use a mere observer, an outsider, recounting these images of beautiful, stoic women frozen in place before their time. Stones.

Growing up, I was always aware of this act of sainthood, but never had these words to describe what I was seeing. In fact, I never knew that I, too, was subtly beginning to adapt to this unspoken rule, growing up as a Black girl inside a body already deemed public property, available to the lusts of older men. I was thirteen years old when Lady Saw, a notorious female emcee, suddenly appeared in the Jamaican dancehall sphere, brash and opinionated, with gyrating hips and songs that oozed sexuality. As a high school girl, I had heard her taboo phrases within our Jamaican cultural context. I sang along to songs such as "Hice It Up" and "No Long Talking" every day of the week except Sundays—when I simply hummed lyrics in Sunday school or while doing chores. I even did the neck rolls as I told imaginary haters,

"Chat to me back!" There was an appeal to the lyrics that I had not fully understood then, a sudden sense of freedom I felt as my narrow hips moved like I was trying to balance a hula hoop.

Growing up in Jamaica, up until that point it had been hard for me to picture grown women as anything other than pious and godly. I used to wonder if the women I knew had ever dared to put their skirts between their legs to play hopscotch or double Dutch; or if they had ever flung their bony arms around each other's shoulders, carefree, and whispered secrets about crushes that wiggled in their abdomens like earthworms after a generous October shower. I yearned to know who they were before they clutched their Bibles, folded themselves up, adjusted masks of sternness or displeasure with the secular world, and covered their bare brown legs with long skirts. Before they became good at silencing us with one look and murmuring statements like "God help us." I often imagined a giant pendulum swinging from the sky with many women of a certain age gazing up at it while they repeated that phrase—"God help us." Hunched down on their knees, they prayed and waited, waited and prayed for a salvation they thought didn't exist on earth. Jamaican working-class girls begin to perform womanhood around eleven or twelve years old, their childlike wit suspended in the frozen glance of female elders, their youthfulness covered in starched uniforms and slips underneath, their animated curiosities discouraged by the tension of responsibilities like dodging the invasive lusts of older men. By twenty-five, any hint of animation is drained out of them, the muscles of their faces tightening, downturned mouths fixed in a meanness that mocks any form of gaiety and weary eyes holding contempt for anyone who fails to conform. For what's there to smile about when there's no silver lining? No laws protecting the Black female body? No access in a country where upward mobility is hard? We were told to look to heaven—a place where redemption, joy, and validation are promised, a place away from the so-called paradise where we lived. For while Jamaica is paradise to many tourists and privileged expats, it's also where poor Black bodies are regarded (or disregarded) as the mere foundation on which the ruling class build their wealth, their fantasies. I never knew any other way of being a woman; never dared consider the types that existed outside the norm of piety, grace, and respectability.

Until Lady Saw.

Her music made me feel bold and daring. I had never before heard a woman make such demands in the bedroom, making statements about what she wanted and how she wanted it. I can remember everything she said as if it were yesterday, telling men that anything they do, she can do, too; for her, pleasure is just as sweet when she's in control. The fact that she beat Jamaican men at their own game—men whose masculinity is defined by how many women they can get—was phenomenal. Gender equality at its best, in my view. To turn on Fame FM and hear horns blasting and deejays screaming, "Big chune! Big chune!" over Lady Saw's lyrics calling out men on their egos excited me. Her aggressive rhymes, sung with a gravelly voice, charged the airwaves, turning femininity as a role on its head.

Lady Saw, queen of the dancehall, was my Jamaican working-class feminist scholar. Her voice was not amplified via microphones connected to lecterns planted in ivory tower lecture halls. Instead, her melodic realism literally "sawed" down sound systems and cultural norms, revamping womanhood in our music industry and beyond. A survivor of sexual violence, Lady Saw was determined to reclaim her sexual freedom. There was an underlying female anthem in every song that spoke against the respectability factor that so many Black women in our culture grappled with. For example, in 1997, she released her hit single "Sycamore Tree." This song is about a woman being pressured into giving oral sex and daring to exercise her agency, her right to say no regardless of the man's expectations of her. When I heard these words as a young girl who constantly dealt with the advances of older men, I felt protected by Lady Saw's courage and voice. She emboldened me, empowered me to utilize my own agency.

Nevertheless, in my very Christian surroundings, there was nothing as ungodly as Lady Saw. For a great majority, she was deemed too raunchy. Too dangerous. Many a prayer meeting was held inside the small Christian fellowship that I was a part of, damning Satan's influence over our youth, and dousing every thought, every action, and every mention of anything secular with the blood of Jesus. Lady Saw's arrogance infuriated the elders; her reign as a prominent Grammy Award–winning Jamaican artist who was vocal about her demands of pleasure incited men and women in our church to speak in tongues.

Furthermore, Lady Saw sang in Jamaican patois, a language we were discouraged from speaking in public. For no one wanted to risk sounding like a *buttu*, a word that supposedly cultured Jamaicans use to describe the working-class—working-class women in particular—whom they perceive to be uncivilized. While I spoke patois at home, I was forbidden to speak it at the elite high school I attended in Kingston, where the Queen's English was standard. I had already felt alienated in my new environment, being of a different social class and hue from the girls who attended the school—girls from homes with hired help and satellite dishes; who traveled on a weekly basis to Miami to shop, given that their parents were wealthy; and who had privileges from being mixed with white and Lebanese family, most of whom owned businesses on the island. Therefore, I became self-conscious of my language and was careful not to speak it. Such shame and silence felt like a form of punishment—an iron prison. When I heard Lady Saw speak patois as though it never entered her mind to be ashamed of it—owning it as a part of her identity as much as she owned her body and her sexuality—my insecurities dissolved. For while Lady Saw might not have used the Queen's English, she was royalty to me.

In the midst of all the condemnation of Saw and her music, I was coming into my sexuality. I moved around cautiously, aware of my newly formed breasts, hips, and thighs. I was glad for the British-style pleated knee-length school uniforms that hid my new body. But that did not prevent the leering and lewd gestures of men. Even men in my church gave me the kind of looks that made me want to cover every part of my flesh. I was disturbed by the sexual overtones, the seemingly dark mystery of the thing they saw—my body— embellished by their fantasies. Except this body was young and inexperienced. Those were the days when I felt the most bewildering panic of my life, a need to touch myself and make certain that my body existed and that I was inside it. At thirteen I knew I was powerless against the way men in our society see young girls, especially since I was surrounded by saints who simply hummed their secrets and offered only ominous warnings against unladylike behavior. For them, men were to be coddled for their flaws and women were to be blamed for those men's indiscretions. I knew deep down that these women were not malicious or heartless, but resigned to patriarchy, and in some cases afraid of it. I had not counted on the booming voice and beautiful face that stared at me in every flier advertising popular dancehall sessions like Passa Passa and Weddy Weddy in Kingston. It was a face that reminded me of Grace Jones, with high cheekbones, angular features reminiscent of a smooth stone carved by a thoughtful sculptor, and a piercing gaze that dared anyone to challenge her autonomy. Lady Saw.

A woman has the right to her own body. This message was inherent in every Lady Saw song—that and the fact that a woman has the right to express herself sexually and still be in control of what happens to her body. I was inspired by Lady Saw, who entered a male-dominated industry and became the greatest musical influence of all time in our country before retiring. She showed me that a woman is no less competent in male-dominated fields, and that a woman's role is not to magnify the hierarchal dominance of masculinity by keeping egos erect, but to forcibly establish herself as an equal. In other words, Lady Saw taught me what feminism is: unapologetic.

I REALIZED THAT I needed Lady Saw's attitude to get through a world so willing to strip me of my dignity and humanity based on who I am. It is in writing that I finally was able to make sense of the various silences I kept—like the identities I struggled to reconcile in college. Now I strongly identify as a Black lesbian immigrant woman from a working-class background in Jamaica. Therefore, like Alice Walker's, my feminism looks a lot different. My feminism has to account for the fact that Black women are invisible; Black women, especially the immigrants among us, are still very much overworked and underpaid compared with our white counterparts. My feminism has to also account for the fact that Black women—like Anita Hill, Beverly Johnson, the fifteen-year-old girl in Jamaica who was raped by her pastor—much like those young girls who came forward about R. Kelly, suffered in silence for years out of fear of being called traitors or accomplices to the demise of "upstanding Black men."

Most important, my feminism has to account for Black lesbians who are mere shadows of any movement, falling through cracks. We are as invisible as we are taboo—a deadly strike. Audre Lorde accurately describes the dilemma of Black lesbians as "being caught between white women's racism and the homophobia of [other Black women]." There's nothing more painful than being dismissed by your own group—be it the sisters you look to for community, the brothers who deem your sexuality a threat to their manhood, or the culture you claim that doesn't claim you back because you're gay.

So what does the sister outsider do? What does she call herself when she struggles to fight against layered oppression? I left that box blank for a long time. Instead, I wrote around it. In writing I find my voice and use it to give voice to those women like me who are unable to tick that box—women who are overlooked because of their Blackness, queerness, immigration status, or otherness. I write for all the women who still feel powerless against three-dimensional, sometimes four-dimensional, oppression—sister outsiders who, like me, never knew they, too, could wear a pink knitted hat and march together with the white women who had always been the cover girls for feminism. That event was met with a lot of apprehension from women of color, particularly Black women, who feared that history might repeat itself with upper-middle-class white women not owning their privilege and thus putting their needs over other women's. The march ended up being very successful when three women of color—Tamika D. Mallory, Carmen Perez, and Linda Sarsour—were brought on board to organize, and with that came the unifying logo of the multicolored fists that sent an instant message of inclusion to marginalized groups of women. With our voices represented and our unique narratives and needs as women acknowledged, it became easier for me to wear that pink knitted hat.

Lastly, I began to write to prove to myself that I can break down the walls built by the internalized oppression that I've been carrying as a Black lesbian woman. To be honest, January 2017 was the first time I ever called myself a feminist. Because for Black women, regardless of country and culture, feminism is a layered concept. One has to take into consideration the allegiance we were born into by virtue of being Black. Somehow, this very skin—this beautiful velvet skin of various shades of brown—has lovingly wrapped itself around our eyes, ears, and mouths, too, when it comes to seeking justice for ourselves, especially against Black men. For the whole world sees our skin color first. The whole world responds to it first. Even Sojourner Truth had to beg the question, "Ain't I a woman, too?" Sometimes, we forget that ourselves. So, when it comes to speaking our truths and our sufferings, the whole world, including white women, hears murmurs sounding somewhat different from theirs. Similarly, Black heterosexual women might think Black lesbian women's sexual preferences make us alien, our cries on a different frequency. Therefore, we clamp our ears shut to each other based on these perceived differences.

It is my belief that before we can successfully dismantle patriarchy, we have to learn to pledge allegiance to ourselves, and empathize with each other as women. And like Lady Saw, be unapologetic, be loud, be defiant in our will to love and save ourselves as Black women.

FAT DEMANDS

Selina Thompson

I REMEMBER DISTINCTLY the moment when the need for intersectional feminism occurred to me. I was twenty-one, in my room at university reading Susie Orbach's seminal feminist text, *Fat Is a Feminist Issue*. In it, she instructs women who are trying to give up dieting to "load up your house with bad foods," so that anything they could possibly crave is there, and as such they will not need to binge eat. I was perplexed. What kind of world was this woman living in, where I could afford to have a kitchen full of any kind of food I might desire? And how, as a single woman, could I justify the kind of guaranteed food waste that would accompany such an act? I didn't have the language for it then, but it was the first time I realized that a feminist writer had been so busy thinking of all women as simply women that she had not seen all of my womanhood. She had not seen that my womanhood was broke and single. And she had definitely not seen that my womanhood might not want to lose weight.

I believe that in its purest form feminism, along with the other emancipatory projects that it is bound up in, seeks to liberate all of us from the shackles of the default body and living a life that is tailored to it. Feminism must demand full and rich lives for those of us who are not white, who are not financially comfortable, who are not thin, who are not able-bodied or neurotypical. Feminism must demand rich and full lives for those of us who are not heterosexual, cisgender, monogamous, or sexually active. Feminism must demand rich and full lives for those of us who do not fall within a specific age range, those of us who do sex work, those of us who are subject to the violence of various immigration systems. You cannot fix misogyny without fixing all the -isms and phobias that it is part of. Unless we build a feminism that starts from the needs of the most vulnerable and most maligned—those furthest from what has historically been the default body—our feminism will always be a shadow of what it could be.

There are times when I feel a deep resistance to wearing the feminist label, largely as a result of how many parts of myself I am still required to leave at the door before I can enter, and how rapidly anything radical loses its potency and meaning. We can see this in the ongoing appropriation of the body-positivity movement, and its shift from prioritizing bodies typically marginalized by the mainstream to encompassing and uplifting the same bodies that are celebrated by the status quo. A quick look on the #bodypositivity Instagram hashtag can find a smorgasbord of diet advice, weigh-ins, and before-and-afters, and elements such as these have fatphobia ingrained in them. However, it is also worth noting that body positivity and its presence within feminist circles can be what Charlotte Cooper describes as a proxy in her landmark text, *Fat Activism: A Radical Social Movement*: something that encourages us to see fat activism as being all about loving your body, when actually it is richer and far more complex than this.

Asking that feminism be intersectional is not asking it to do anything other than make sense. We know that gender politics, race, and class are not just a discussion of the personal. We know they are a discussion of economic factors, of how we live together as a society, of how we live with the earth and its resources, and of the dominant narratives that shape our understanding of "health." If what we are fighting is present across multiple levels, our resistance must be also.

I have chosen to speak about fat here because it is so frequently overlooked and misunderstood. Historically, fat feminism has had a huge race and class problem, despite the fact that the construction of fat as an identity has been intimately linked to racial formation, gender, disability, and class. In *Fat Shame*, Amy Erdman Farrell locates fat's inception as a discrediting factor in the pseudoscience of the late nineteenth century: "A physical state that marked its bearers as people lower on the evolutionary and racial scale— Africans, 'native' peoples, immigrants, criminals and prostitutes. All women were also considered to be more at risk of fatness." Since the late nineteenth century, fat has held a very specific resonance of laziness and gluttony; of being uncivilized, primitive, and out of control; of being somehow less than human; and all of these attributes are also placed on the bodies of other marginalized identities. Feminism must be able to hold all of who we are, or it will exclude those who need it most.

Fat activism began to emerge in the late 1960s, and its short, chaotic history has been consistently marginalized and erased. Feminism that isn't taking fat liberation on board enthusiastically is failing, because it will never be all that it can be if it is not standing staunchly against *all* forms of bodily control. It is this factor in particular that makes me think that fat feminism may hold the radical seeds that could take our collective liberation further and develop how we all might live rich, fulfilling lives within our bodies, regardless of size.

1. Disentanglement

Fat is messy. I wanted to find an isolated way of writing about it, a clean way, but I quickly became entangled.

First and foremost, as a Black woman, I got tangled up in race. I got tangled up in images of the mammy, and of the sassy fat Black friend. I got tangled up in endless articles about just how fat Black women are, and why, how we fail to recognize that our children are fat, and how this fat is just another example of failure for a group in society that is perceived as "fat, sick, and crazy."

I got tangled up in assumptions about what people of color (POC) eat and how we eat it. I was enmeshed in the colonial fantasy that in other cultures fat is allowed to exist unfettered and free, but this myth silences those whose experiences are vastly different. I drowned in the endless images that reinforce our expectations that a fat Black body will be giving and nurturing above all else, like Jennifer Hudson's character Louise in the *Sex and the City* movie, who arrives, sorts out Carrie Bradshaw's life, and then promptly disappears back to St. Louis. I was reminded that we will be punished if we fail to do this, like Hudson's character Effie in *Dreamgirls*, who, despite having the stronger voice than her thinner rival, Deena Jones, is cheated on, demoted from lead vocalist, and then kicked out of the group into alcoholism and near-poverty with her child, to the words of the song "Heavy" ("Come on baby baby, lose some weight"). I was silenced by the way in which Blackness, fat, and poverty come together in the American Welfare Queen and her counterparts all over the world.

The figure of the mammy and all that she represents— among other things, the absence of Black female sexual desire—led me to try to disentangle fat and sex. I'm trying to disentangle the fetishized body, the desired body, and the desiring body. I'm trying to disentangle the mechanics of fat sex, the awkwardness, but also the sense of achievement of broken beds, giggling at positions that maybe won't work, rolls and folds that may need moving but still warrant a loving touch or a sexualized touch or a rough touch, if this is what is desired. I'm trying to disentangle what kind of touch the fat body is told that it deserves, and what happens to the soul of a person with a fat body if these messages sink too deep. What space is left for them to love and be loved? I try to disentangle this from the lover who tells you that you are lucky that they deign to love your fat body and from the one-night stand who announces, damp with anticipation, that fat girls just try harder. I'm trying to disentangle the hand-wringing that surrounds the chubby chaser, and the respectability politics—policing within community so as to appear amenable to the mainstream—bound up in this. I'm trying to disentangle the fat body from the ever-present background hum of pornography, from the politics of sex work, where both hand-wringing and the fetishizing gaze might be at their most potent—but where one also might feel power, and first and foremost be able to pay the bills.

This only compounded the problem because I found that I had stumbled into the mess that is the fat worker, or rather the fat person who would work but is defeated at every turn. The person who negotiates uniforms that don't fit, and has to hope that they will not go up against a fatphobic interviewer. I'm thinking about how this works when somebody is fat and unemployed for long periods of time. I am thinking about the assumption that a fat body is a sick body, that a fat body will cost an employer money, and how this becomes a reason not to hire—and how tenuous the legal protections for fat people are. I am thinking about how demanding this kind of change requires a visibility that many fat people would find violating and potentially dangerous. I am thinking of those who are fat to an extent that work may become completely inaccessible, those for whom fat makes leaving the house insurmountable, for a variety of reasons.

How do I disentangle the fat body, the fat person, from discourse around health? How do I disentangle discourse around health from the impact that government policy has on health provision? How do I disentangle fat from the fact that our ideas of health always serve the political agendas and societal mores of the day, and as such hold all their violence? How do I draw out that being fat under a left-wing, liberal government and being fat under a more right-wing government are two very different things—but both are the sum total of being fat under neoliberalism? How do I disentangle this from endless reels of the torsos of fat people on the news with statistics plastered over them? How do I disentangle my fat body from the knowledge that it can be refused medical care on the basis that it is a drain to society? How do I disentangle my body from death, when I can literally be told that I am obese to a morbid extent? What happens to the people whose bodies are consistently misdiagnosed or to those made so unwelcome in spaces of medical care that they simply stop attending? How do I disentangle my body from the clutches of a doctor who has nothing to tell me other than that I need to lose weight?

The longer I sat untangling, the worse it got. I ran into the tangle of fat liberation and the social model of disability. This model argues that no single body is abnormal, that there are limitless variations of what our bodies can be, and that we are disabled not by these variations, but instead by societal attitudes that do not accommodate them. When we apply this to fat, it becomes just another variation and it is society that needs to adapt to the needs of fat people, as opposed to fat people needing to find a way to fit better. Are there ways in which this crossover is appropriative? Do we risk erasing those who are physically disabled in other ways and also fat?

I stumbled on fat liberation and the toxicity of the diet industry, the deception that hides in plain sight: that diets often change our relationships with our bodies in harmful ways without delivering the desired and promised results, and still we go back. I tripped over the links between fat and food justice—endless articles about how the foods we eat might be filled with chemicals that make them addictive—but then found myself staring down fat and class, and the fact that food is often a way in which value judgments are made about the tastes and lifestyles of the poor. In the words of writer and activist Amy Lamé, we're not putting an obesity tax on foie gras, but we are on the 80p sausage rolls at Greggs, and there's a reason for that. Even this got me tied up in thinking about fat and mental health, about the long-term psychological impact of street harassment, about agoraphobia rates among fat people, about how difficult it is to find mental health care provision for eating disorders that doesn't also hold fatphobic attitudes buried within it.

It's a mess. It is a historic mess. I can find the concerns I've outlined threaded throughout 1983's *Shadow on a Tightrope: Writings by Women on Fat Oppression*, and see them reiterated ten years later in 1994's more optimistic anthology, *Journeys to Self-Acceptance: Fat Women Speak*.

Almost twenty-five years on, it is still a mess.

2. Killing the Myth of Control

Every single element of this mess comes back to control: control of the body that is not the default, control of the body that is other. This is one of the founding stones of patriarchy, of fat stigma, of class, and of race.

It is one of the greatest thefts that patriarchy enacts on bodies—on all our bodies—to tell them that they don't belong to us. That desire to control is there when we give birth. It is there when we experience puberty. It is there when we experience sexual pleasure as well as when we don't, and it is there when we experience menopause. It is there when our periods cause us excruciating pain and there is no provision for that; it is there when we wish to express our gender differently and are harassed in public as a result. It is there when our bodies respond to the demands of capitalism with anything other than productivity. It is there when we choose not to bear children, it is there when we age, and it is there when our bodies are fat. In our society a fat body is one perceived as deeply out of control, as primitive, uncivilized, and animal. These are all things we are encouraged to despise and fear.

We enforce this othering with interrogation. Fat bodies are endlessly asked to explain themselves. Why? Why are you so fat? Why?

Is it trauma? Did you eat too much? Not exercise enough? Is it depression? Your genes? The way you were raised? The labels on your food? Why?

Each question stands in for the real question: How do you fix it? And even that question stands in the place of the primary concern: How do I, the corporation, make money off of fixing it? Or perhaps more accurately: How do I fail to fix it while making it look like I am succeeding and the failure is your fault?

I am referring to the fix-all solution that is the diet industrial complex.

In *Fat and Proud*, Charlotte Cooper describes dieting as the perfect product, for it always fails and when it does, the blame lies with the consumer. Not only that, dieting doesn't just fail, it exacerbates the supposed problem. With every failure, more weight is gained, and this is a widely known, statistically proven fact; 97 percent of people who lose weight on a diet will regain that weight and more within three years. Despite this, the pressure is ramped up, the diet is returned to with renewed vigor, and usually this translates to additional expenditure. I would go even further and say that the fat dieting body is not only the perfect consumer body, it also becomes the perfect advertisement—a success story when weight is lost and a cautionary tale when it is not. At every stage of the cycle of dieting that many, many people know so well is a push and pull with control—lose weight, gain weight, fight the body's reaction systems to restriction, fight any fatigue or hunger we might feel, navigate the voices of others while the body that loses weight becomes public property, and do all of this while self-deprecating and pretending it all feels good. It's exhausting. It's maddening. It leaves one enraged. There are few things more flawed than the idea that one body type can represent health for the billions of human bodies that live on this earth, with all their lifestyles and needs. And yet this is the myth that dieting feeds us.

This myth is also apparent when we look at how modern approaches to health manifest themselves. It is easier for doctors to tell us that our bodies' problems are the result of fat and that we need to lose weight than it is for them to re-educate themselves on the potential needs of fat bodies. It is easier for physiotherapists to lay the demand of weight loss at your feet than it is for them to think about what exercise regimes tailored to bigger bodies might look like. It is simpler, not to mention more cost-effective, to say that fat people are the problem than it is to acknowledge that bodies are chaos, that control of them is almost always an illusion. It is easier to ignore the fact that the body's default is to keep us alive, and that some of the changes we may seek to make to our bodies do not fit with that.

3. Beyond Consumption

There is a growing, rich oeuvre of body-positive work.

At present, it is focused on consumption, by which I mean two interlinked ideas. The first is wanting more images and representations of yourself to consume in art, advertising, and entertainment. The second is building your activism around the individual, with the assumption that this will lead to systemic change: "If individuals change, the world changes."

It is consumer oriented, most at home in advertising or on blogs and social media. It is one of many feminisms that prioritize young fashionable women with active social lives and disposable income. I fit this description to an extent, and must admit that it has been transformative to me and many others. Better clothes can improve the quality of one's life, seeing more fat bodies on your Instagram feed can make you feel better about your own, and all of this can help us live more embodied, richer lives, which is something that all fat people deserve. Memoirs about fat, such as Roxane Gay's *Hunger*, can help to decalcify hard pockets of trauma, and online fat-activism communities offer advice on everything from how to negotiate flying while fat, to dating, to giving you the confidence to go into your doctor or into a massage session like an avenging angel heading into war, knowing a virtual community surrounds you. These things make up the day-to-day of life, and they matter. Activism is a rich and varied thing, happening as much in intimate conversations and Twitter threads as it is in marches, writing, and campaigning for legislative change, but this work is not without its flaws.

Fat feminism that starts and stops with the concerns outlined here, many of them dependent on disposable income, is brittle. It should not, for example, be enough to ask for a wider range of clothes if we are not also considering how they are produced. There is nothing radical about a plus-size dress produced in a sweatshop. If stylish, comfortable clothes for fat people are only available online, then there is a limit to who has access to them. Fat feminism needs to be an anti-capitalist project. At all times we need to remember that when we speak of fat, when we speak of bodies and their relationship to capital, we are speaking of power.

When it comes to representation, fat liberation needs to ask hard questions about who becomes an acceptable fat spokesperson and why. Is it because they are white, cisgender, and hourglass figured? Or is it because they have enough disposable income for an ever-changing wardrobe? Are they deemed acceptable by a fatphobic world because they are heterosexual and in a relationship? Do you only get to take up space if you are a size 26 at an absolute push and no older than forty? Did they get that book deal because they are simply telling a variation on the transformation story, one in which they are not transformed by losing weight but are instead transformed by romantic love, avid consumption of plus-size products, or an internal acceptance of a body positivity that is well suited to advertising campaigns? Perhaps they have received bonus points because they are also exercising in ways seen as exclusive to thin people and eating in a manner deemed healthy by current trends. In short, in spite of being fat they have enough of a relationship to the default body to be accepted, to become a point of aspiration.

I demand a fat liberation that destroys the concepts of beauty and success: It is not enough to simply bring fat into the fold. Fat aspiration has as much capacity to harm as thin aspiration if not examined.

4. True Radicalism and Its Ally, Constant Vigilance

I do not wish to lay the work of changing the world at the feet of the fat, but I know that as people at the fringes, we have the capacity to build something truly radical, because we are working from a vantage point that allows us to see a little bit more of the big picture.

As with other feminisms and emancipatory movements, a great deal of this fat liberation work now takes place online, and has done so since the early days of the internet. In many ways this is brilliant, allowing for a multiplicity of voices and combating much of the isolation that can be a part of life for many fat people. My concern is that often online activism prioritizes and only really reaches a limited audience, namely those who are already actively seeking out what it has to say. I want to figure out who is not in the room and why. I believe feminism must always be asking this: Who is dominating the conversation, and what doesn't get spoken about as a consequence of this?

I also worry about where fat feminism cannot be found. Often a fat body reveals the limits of people's feminism, reveals what still feels a freedom too far. It has been interesting to note the absence of fat bodies in a movie like *Lemonade* and the abjection of fat bodies in a movie such as *Mad Max: Fury Road*. These are celebrated feminist pop culture moments, and rightly so, but what they lack when it comes to fat is both illuminating and disheartening.

Even the most radical of feminisms and political movements can struggle to countenance fat. Fatphobia is rampant in veganism, with organizations such as PETA claiming that fat is a result of meat and dairy consumption to fat-shame people into veganism. Within the radical left and socialist circles, the idea of the fat cat—bloated, gluttonous, and greedy—endures, continuing to use fat as a discrediting factor. It can be a struggle to find discussions of fat within transfeminism, but there have been documented cases of young transfeminine and transmasculine people being refused treatment or overlooked because of fat. Like all blind spots, this limited vision holds these movements back, and as a committed feminist, I want to push them forward.

I do this by asking more of feminism. I ask for a feminism that moves beyond consumption by being staunchly anti-capitalist, for body chaos that prioritizes true care of our bodies, and for a severance from causality, from the presentation of fat as a problem in need of a solution.

What might an anti-capitalist fat theory, an alliance of fat people taking a stand against profit, a group of fat people who saw adequate care of fat bodies and all their needs as a stand against violence look like? Where would it be located? How might fat activism liberate itself from a system that feeds off fatphobia, and how might nuanced discussion of the political standing of fat bodies radically transform other movements?

I want to know what happens if we lean into the fear of the primitive body, if we swan-dive into it. I want body chaos, body anarchy—a cacophony of bodies that are respected, loved, desired, and cared for without caveat, in all shapes and sizes. For our bodies to belong to us when we go to great lengths to change them and for our bodies to belong to us when we wish to change them as little as possible. For our bodies to be free from judgment. For a health at every size that acknowledges that the doing of health might look different from the end result. I want a chaos of body that actively accepts and acknowledges that thin privilege exists and is built on the oppression of fat bodies, that this oppression is enforced when we surround ourselves and each other with ceaseless diet talk. That this oppression is embodied by those who comment on my body in public spaces. That the facade of concern trolling—the act of criticizing somebody's lifestyle choices under the guise of it being for their own good—does not mitigate its violence. For an end to the ceaseless demand that you control your body, that you do everything you can to make it behave like anything other than a body.

I believe that body anarchy is the antithesis of the diet and that it demands true care. This goes against everything that the societies we live in value. Such care would be tailored, time consuming, expensive, and thoughtful. It would be in active dialogue with the cared for, a care that puts profit second.

To achieve this, we have to genuinely ask ourselves how comfortable we are with people making health decisions for themselves that we dislike. Any and all prescriptions risk being filled with unchecked prejudices and assumptions.

My worry about asking for anything less than fat liberation—and the reason that I find myself writing a polemic, as opposed to something funnier or warmer or more gentle—is that I don't want the fate of fat people to forever be ambivalence. For there to always be a gap between how we would like to live in our bodies, how we feel we should live in our bodies as feminists, and the reality of how we live in them as defined by the material realities of the world that we live in. I want to be able to write about fat with nuance rather than ambivalence. I don't want to write with a desperate desire to lose weight sitting on my shoulder, because weight loss is not freedom. I know that my thin siblings often do not feel free in their bodies either, and that how we feel is beside the point when so much of how we live in the world is controlled by systems that go on, undeterred by how we feel.

For true fat liberation to take place, feminism and other emancipatory movements must ask themselves how the changes they are fighting for impact every body of every size and capability. Just as important, we must all sit honestly with where our prejudices lie, where we set our unconscious limits. When does my body stop being human for you? When does the body become significant enough for you to include it in your analysis? At two hundred pounds? Three hundred and fifty? Five hundred? Honest answers and positive change might transform our feminist communities beyond recognition.

5. Liberation

These demands are big, and like all demands for societal change, they may take generations to put into practice. So what do I offer my fat siblings for now?

In the first instance, I offer you this, which I remind myself of often:

I am not a Russian doll.

There is not a thin woman inside me waiting to come out.

There is not a gap between my soul and my body; they are one.

My life and body changed when I truly began to take that message into my heart.

Began. It is a lifelong absorption, and as such needs reiterating regularly:

She/we/ I
Is/are/am
One body.
Fat just is
Fat just demands to be
Neutral.
But
When one dares to live with a fat body
In this society, as it is right now

Happy and grumpy and free and sexy and talented, dancing and loving and eating and exercising, drinking and sleeping and reading and working, swimming and hiking and lifting and twisting, stretching and yearning and arching, sometimes loving it, sometimes hating it, touching and being touched, sacred, profane, humdrum, every day, sometimes lethargic and sometimes energetic in short, human

We make something glitch in our society, just a little bit. Yes, it is too simple to say that mere existence is radical. I am at the beginning of my own journey within fat activism, and I know that there is a rooting in community that needs to take place, that there is much learning to be done that cannot take place alone. But when a fat body lives and exists as human, our systems struggle to use it as an abject object, a specter to keep those around it in line with capitalism, consumerism, and patriarchy. This is deeply revealing. This is radical.

At the core of so much feminism is a demand for agency, for freedom. And so I say to my fat siblings, exercise that agency. You do you. Your body is your own—let it be chaos, let it be anarchy, let it be animal, let it be you. Know that this is a radical act, an act of pure feminism. Know that agency and power are always in dialogue with each other. If this is possible for you, think critically about what makes it possible. Ask what work we need to do to make this possible for others.

And get to it, if you can.

BORDERLANDS

||||||||||||||||||||||||||||||||||||||||||||||||||||||||||||||||||||||||||||||||||||||||||||||||||||||||||||||||||||||||||||||||||||||||||||

Gabrielle Bellot

UP UNTIL MARCH of 2017, I venerated Chimamanda Ngozi
Adichie, the Nigerian novelist and avowed proponent of
feminism whose TED Talks on gender equality and the
dangers of single stories—that is, of overly simple narratives
about people or places—had become so popular around the
world that they seemed to eclipse her fiction. I taught her
first TED Talk, "The Danger of a Single Story," in nearly all
of my global literature and creative writing classes; I felt
moved by her grace, eloquence, and—I thought—open-
mindedness to the vastness of the world. As a trans woman
of color from the Caribbean who was then living in Florida,
I was accustomed to the failures of authority figures, including prominent cisgender feminists, when they decided to
speak about transgender people—trans women and nonbinary individuals in particular, as trans men tended to be
erased from their discourse altogether. But Adichie represented empathy to me, as well as humility. She had confessed
in her lecture, multiple times, to having naively held a single
story about either a person (an impoverished family servant)
or a place (Mexico), until she learned, by spending more
time with each, that she had been wrong. She was one of the
last people I expected to fail me. I almost felt as if I knew

her, in the way our favorite authors and all the people who star our skies seem so close to us, despite their distance.

But then she began to speak about trans women as if we were the Other. On Britain's *Channel 4 News* in March 2017, she declared, after being asked unceremoniously what she thought of trans women, that we are not "women," but rather, a separate category, segregated forever from women because cis and trans women have, supposedly, been raised differently. If men possess male privilege, then trans women, she argued, do as well. A brouhaha ensued in the media. Even then, although I was hurt and incensed, I was willing to give her a second chance; surely she, of all people, would be able to climb out of the cavernous hole of her mistaken, reductive views. If she apologized and vowed to learn more, I would forgive her, even if I would still struggle a bit more than usual to place her in my private constellation of stars.

I had come out as trans in my late twenties. Because I was already androgynous, when I began to present as female in public, I almost instantly "passed" visually as a woman. Male strangers saw me as a woman, and they catcalled me, spoke down to me, asked me to have sex with them, objectified and minimized me in the way we so often come to expect as women, cis or trans. Surely, I thought, Adichie would realize that if one walks through the world being perceived as a woman, one learns, gradually, the language of experience shared by many women.

What male privilege did I have when a lecherous male taxi driver tried to keep me from leaving his cab because he wanted me to fuck him, or when security guards propositioned me, or when I felt terror walking alone because I did not know if the man trailing behind me was a benign pedestrian or a rapist stalking his prey? When a man I went on a date with would not stop doing something that hurt me during sex when I told him *no, no, stop* until I almost had to yell, because he assumed his sexual desires superseded mine?

Instead, however, Adichie doubled down on her views. She expressed shock that she, whom LGBTQ people had seemed to adore, was under attack. Later, I would realize that her shock came specifically from the fact that her pride in her own assumed infallibility, her own presumed public belovedness, had been wounded. She parroted the talking points of trans-exclusionary radical feminists, presenting them as if they were simply obvious foundational truths of life. Men were socialized as men, Adichie argued, and women as women, and socialization determined who one was, so a transgender woman socialized as a man could never, ever be a woman. We were cursed and consigned to a perpetual definition of the self. (Never mind the question of how trans girls raised from a young age as girls, or the cis girls *not* socialized in the way Adichie described, might factor into this, or the bigger question of why socialization—a simplistic, essentialist idea—is used to discredit the science of gender identity, which, like sexual orientation, is simply an internal sense of self that all people possess.)

It hurt, too, because I had not transitioned on a whim. On the contrary, I chose to begin to transition only after being brought to the point of suicide over my depression from gender dysphoria, and I gave up my home and being able to see most of my family in return.

In the Commonwealth of Dominica, where I grew up, being openly queer seemed unthinkable: At best, you would become the target of jokes or social ostracism; at worst, you could be beaten up or killed. Earnest expressions of queerness were topics of susurrus, of quiet acts in rooms when everyone had hopefully left, surreptitious trysts in bamboo patches under the moonless night in the botanical garden whose gates were closed and had to be scaled. Homosexuality was casually described as a biblical abomination, as something squalid and disgusting, as something that deserved corrective punishment. I didn't even know the word *transgender* existed until I went to college in the United States; I knew what I was, but had no language to express it for many years, so I simply thought something was broadly queer about me—which, of course, was true. "Bun out di chi chi," a then-popular song by Jamaican dancehall artist Capleton advised his audiences, and I would bounce my head, even dance, to a song about people like me being immolated because I was so afraid of my queerness being uncovered that I tried to mask it behind a bulwark of bland, brutish homophobia.

Even as I was always trying to smile and seem happy, I lived in a tropical winter. I loved my beautiful island, yet a part of me felt like I didn't belong. If I were to come out, I knew, I would likely sacrifice my chances to be happy. Even if I escaped getting beat up, I would be relegated to the isolated sadness of a sunken ship. I could never have a normal romantic life, could never marry, could never even go out with my friends without fearing some confrontation. Better, it seemed, to swim into a sea of quiet lies, even if the water pressure down there thumped in my ears and swirled up the silt until all the world I swam in was a murky mess. Better that, I thought, than the pelagic danger of clarity, of revealing myself too much.

By the time I got to college in Florida, I was less religious, but I still vaguely believed I might be tortured for eternity in the sadistic fires of hell if I so much as entertained anything I had been taught was sinful: homosexuality, gender nonconformity. Even thinking of it could damn me, I sometimes feared. I had already tried, for years, to banish that ghostly-ghastly internal girl, ghastly because I had been indoctrinated to think that my gender dysphoria—a term I wouldn't even know until years later—was symptomatic of sin, a chain linking and pulling me to hell. Yet she was anchored to me. I wouldn't come out until I was twenty-seven and in graduate school in Florida; after nearly killing myself from the torment of living a lie for so long, corpse-living, I decided I had to take the risk of revealing that I was trans. After this, I lost my ability to return to Dominica, as I knew I could not live a normal, happy life there as an openly trans woman.

Adichie's comments seemed detached from my experience, as if my pain and struggles had been little more than a silly joke. Yet they had been proffered with authority. While mainstream feminism debated whether trans women were women, people like me were trying to deal with finding homes, losing family, trying not to seem too scared when a cop with a visible gun pulled us over and asked to see an ID we knew still said *M*, trying to find love, trying to find jobs that wouldn't fire us at a whim if a customer complained about our "disturbing" presence, trying to use a public bathroom without being afraid of causing a panic or being escorted out by security guards. Trans women, particularly trans women of color, are already among the most at-risk groups in America and, sadly, in much of the world. When highly visible figures like Adichie call our womanhood into question, thus encouraging the general public to focus on that rather than on expanding and improving the few legal rights we possess, it only makes all the other challenges and oppression we face more difficult.

None of this was new. Adichie's rhetoric echoed, if somewhat tamely, a long history of feminists excluding trans women. In 1952, Christine Jorgensen became the most famous trans woman in America, if not the world, when her then-radical reassignment surgery made headlines—EX-GI BECOMES BLONDE BEAUTY, the New York *Daily News* announced. At first, the media described her, progressively, with female pronouns, but when Jorgensen revealed that she couldn't menstruate or become pregnant, many publications reacted indignantly by misgendering her, as if to imply that she couldn't be a woman unless her body matched the exact specifications of most cis women's. Radical feminism, which evolved from second-wave feminism in the 1970s and '80s and frequently focused on domestic violence, particularly rape, by men against women, earned a reputation for virulent transphobia, as many prominent radical feminists simply lumped trans women in with those dangerous men. In 1973, the West Coast Lesbian Conference in Los Angeles erupted into controversy over whether to allow a trans folk singer, Beth Elliott, to perform. The keynote speaker, Robin Morgan, furiously declared that her "thirty-two years of suffering in this androcentric society" made her a woman and asked how a "transvestite . . . *dares* understand our pain? No, in our mothers' name and our own, we must not call him sister." The Michigan Womyn's Music Festival, founded in 1976 by Lisa Vogel and catering to thousands of women each August, only allows cis women—"womyn-born womyn"—to enter. To let trans women in, Vogel has argued, would make cis women uncomfortable, rather than "allow[ing] women to let down their guard." The annual RadFem Collective conference routinely excludes trans women from participating, despite being billed as a space for women to discuss women's issues. In 1997, feminist Sheila Jeffreys argued in a paper that "transsexualism should be seen as a violation of human rights." The renowned feminist Germaine Greer has repeatedly courted controversy for saying that trans women are "not women" because we do not "look like, sound like, or behave like women," as she told the BBC in 2015. Such comments will appear every few months in the news, when yet another celebrity or politician announces that we are "really" men.

Paradoxically, given mainstream feminism's failure to include me, I came to understand feminism best—internally, experientially, in bones and brain—by transitioning into someone who is almost always perceived by strangers to be a woman. Not only was there the aforementioned catcalling, but men also spoke down to me and spoke over me, assuming my inferior abilities and expertise before I had revealed anything about either. I learned, too, simple sacrosanct things about being a woman: what a sisterhood can feel like when women love and support each other. Living as a trans woman of color forced me to redraw my maps of the world, to redesign the topography of dreams and reality alike. It's one thing to say you support women's equality and liberation; it's another to feel, experientially, where those desires for equality and liberation come from. I learned, in other words, what it was like to be perceived as a woman in the world by being one, yet I knew I would still be barred, inexorably, from many "women's" spaces simply by virtue of being the wrong kind of woman.

Months later, when journalist David Remnick asked Adichie onstage at *The New Yorker* festival about the backlash she had received from the left over her comments, she laughed condescendingly at the trans women who had critiqued her. They just didn't get it, Adichie smirked. It was, she continued, just another example of the left "creating its own decline"; to disagree with her views, she suggested, by affirming the right of trans women to be *recognized* as women, was to send liberalism into self-destruction by asking too much of people. (Her views echoed an idea frequently raised by comedian Bill Maher and others after Donald Trump's election: that transgender rights were "boutique issues," as Maher put it, rather than central ones, and so the left had sealed its loss to Trump by visibly supporting the rights of such divisive, freakish people as me.)

So hermetically sealed was Adiche from criticism that she had decided everyone else must be wrong; she had chosen to retain a single story about trans women, contradicting the very core of what I had once believed she valued. The same woman I had dreamed of sitting next to and speaking with on a stage suddenly shifted; I now wondered what she would think of someone like me being seated next to her, what she might say—what *I*, in my confused indignation, might say. The dream deliquesced. It no longer made sense. I felt as if I had lost a friend. Laughter, Elias Canetti argues in *Crowds and Power*, expanding on comments by Thomas Hobbes, is a way of expressing superiority over one who has fallen, an acknowledgment that the person we are laughing at *could* have been our prey; rather than dominate or devour them, we laugh. When I heard Adichie's supercilious laughter, I felt hurt anew.

I'm accustomed to feeling like I live in the borderlands of a world, not fully belonging anywhere culturally, racially, or in terms of my gender. (One of my favorite video game series, fittingly, is named Borderlands.) But I didn't want someone I respected to tell me, condescendingly, that I *had* to live in the borderlands, that I could never really be what I had almost killed myself in order to be: a woman.

Despite the firestorm ignited by Adichie's comments, a variety of powerful outlets soon returned, as if nothing had happened, to lauding her as a model feminist. *The New Yorker* festival had advertised her as a feminist authority, and the kicker to a starry-eyed profile of Adichie for the *New York Times Style Magazine* by Dave Eggers labeled her "a defining voice on race and gender for the digital age," while the article itself neglected to even mention her transphobic remarks. The implication was clear: One can be a "defining voice on gender" for the twenty-first century by suggesting that trans women will never be women because all "real" women grow up the same way—a way, according to this line of reasoning, entirely distinct from trans women's experiences. It is difficult not to feel excluded from feminism when one of its most visible faces decides, with a derisive chuckle, that you don't really belong.

ULTIMATELY, HOWEVER, events like these create important teachable moments. One important takeaway from this one is that we should not assume we are authorities on all aspects of feminism simply because we are authorities on some of them. When a feminist icon, like Adichie, decides that her high standing in the feminist community allows her to speak glibly on anything proffered to her, she runs the risk of assuming a false sense of universalism, of all-encompassing authority. Success can become its own form of privilege: When we succeed, we begin to think that we can do no wrong. In reality, we need to listen humbly to each other's stories, lest we fall victim to perpetuating single stories ourselves. We can certainly ask questions and be critical, but we need to be willing to listen and learn before putting ourselves on an authoritative pedestal. The mere fact that a trans woman who transitioned later in life may have been perceived, prior to her coming out, as male and, ergo, potentially had the privileges of such a gender designation does not render her the recipient of such privileges after coming out, or for that matter, unable to interrogate the privilege she may have had previously by weighing it against her experiences now, and the stories of her cis-female sisters.

Yet the danger when a voice as influential as Adichie's presents such parochial views is that many people will simply take what she says at face value as a politically incorrect truth. Overly clean, essentialist narratives like Adichie's are rarely able to encompass the messy largeness of reality. To deny this is to give ammunition, as she unwittingly did, to anti-trans political groups (almost uniformly on the right) who wish to restrict access to hormone replacement therapy and gender-confirming surgeries, oppose legal concessions that would change our genders or sexes on our IDs after meeting certain criteria, and limit our abilities to move through public spaces such as restrooms—each of which relies on some tenet of the argument that we are "really" men illegitimately and iniquitously attempting to invade cis women's spaces.

This is the recurring pain of being trans and a feminist: knowing that every few months, if not every few days, some new, popular op-ed that excoriates our existence will appear, some of them written by people you formerly admired, even avowed feminists. You will see, over and over, comments under these articles from people expressing relief that finally—*finally*—someone has had the courage to speak out against such dangerous freaks as us. You will be asked, as I often am, why I do not wish to debate my gender. The ones who ask will be well-meaning, even excessively polite. They will not understand when I say that it is akin to asking a lesbian to debate her sexual orientation or a Black American if the old racialist rumors peddled by Charles Murray and others about IQ and ethnicity are true. When you cannot take it anymore and get upset, you will be asked why you are so angry. Why, indeed, are trans women of color so upset, when we face these condescending, demeaning inquiries day in and out?

After the anger, it hurts. And then, at some point, we are expected to smile and let it all go.

We wear the mask, as Paul Laurence Dunbar says in his famous poem, the mask that grins and lies.

This is the sadness, subtle and salient as petrichor, of being a trans woman of color: never knowing if we will fit in, and always knowing there is somewhere we will not.

"IMAGINE A WORLD," I said, in front of the White House at a vigil with other poets and writers a few months after Donald Trump's tumultuous election, "in which a trans woman of color could be president. Imagine a world like that." Some people chuckle-smiled. It was a telling reaction. In a country where banning us from the military would, months later, be met with enthusiasm from many everyday Americans, the notion of electing someone as unutterably, unspeakably bizarre as a trans woman—and one of color, no less—seemed too far-fetched to be entertained as a real possibility. It seemed perhaps as improbable, or even more so, as Americans electing a Muslim or avowedly atheistic woman or a woman who was physically disabled, regardless of whether this particular woman's experience and policies would demonstrably better the nation. A saccharine, supposititious, substance-conjured, just plain silly dream. Electing a woman is still too difficult for the United States; what of a figure who would have to contend not only with misogyny, but also with transphobia, homophobia (when people refuse to accept our gender and thus view us with contempt as effete gay men), and racism?

What would a world where such an election was plausible look like?

It seems fantastical, strange, absurd. Even I struggle to believe such a world could exist, where a trans woman could be America's president, where bigotry against both women broadly and trans people specifically has become so scarce that we could be considered viable candidates at all. If we were more likely to be taken as people than as political precepts, it might cease to seem so utterly unlikely. Yet we are the very embodiment of the Other, the strange thing lurking liminally on the dangerous borderlands of society. Rather than as ordinary and extraordinary people, we exist in this public imagination as flittering funhouse reflections, at once gargantuan and tiny. We are sexual kinks in the weird part of porn sites, death-deserving men deceivers seeking to corrupt the fertile grounds of some poor lad's heterosexual manhood, men trying to invade women's spaces and women seeking men's approval by appearing as whichever gender is appropriate for whichever social conquest, freaks in a lurid carnival, biblical abominations, destroyers of bodies. We are nearly universally negative *things*, rather than humans.

And this is in America, the land where you can supposedly be anything, do anything, achieve anything. In Dominica, where LGBTQ individuals have zero legal protections, it would indeed be impossible, at least for now, to imagine an openly trans woman holding any important office—if she could work in any office at all. In both countries, as in many others, the reasons are endemic and eclectic, from zealous and bigoted religious dogma to anti-LGBTQ political propaganda—the latter of which is often propped up in developing countries by American anti-queer activists, like Scott Lively, who travel abroad with the specific goal of preventing nondiscrimination laws from passing by disseminating dangerous stereotypes about LGBTQ populations to would-be voters. But the fact that it is so difficult to imagine a trans woman viably leading either nation is also symptomatic of feminism's failures: that even as our public profile in America and elsewhere has unquestionably improved, we are still, so often, stuck at the ground floor of debating whether trans women should be included in women's conferences or restrooms. It is fine to be bad feminists, à la Roxane Gay; it is terrible for feminism to be bad.

There's a special isolation that shadows so many trans women in certain feminist circles. When I spoke in 2017 at a women's caucus at AWP (Association of Writers and Writing Programs, a yearly conference oriented around writing and publishing) on behalf of VIDA (an American feminist organization well known for its annual VIDA Count, which surveys how many women and nonbinary people are published in major outlets each year), I was nervous. It wasn't just that I had signed on at the last minute and was talking extempore; I was nervous because I did not know if my voice and appearance would "pass" and, if they didn't, if I would cause other women to walk out, to tell *me* to walk out, or to ask me why something like me was taking up the space a *real* woman could occupy. Whether I could feel comfortable and accepted as someone who might have something to add to the table became a benchmark for assessing other so-called feminists.

However, in addition to being trans-exclusionary, so much contemporary feminist discourse that purports to be universal in its claims is still suffused with a stubborn, simplistic Americentrism that can work to exclude feminists who grew up outside America. Far too many contemporary activists—who usually mean well—casually use terms like *Black* and *white* in ways that reflect America's history and present of casual white supremacy and traditionalistic misogyny, yet what it means to be Black—or any racial designation—is always informed by where and when we are in the world. There are overlapping discriminations, but there is no universal racialized experience that will forever define everyone. This overly simple, non–culturally nuanced language erodes the potential power of feminism to change things. And at times it isolates me. The experience of being multiracial—like me—in one country does not necessarily reflect that of being multiracial in another.

To be trans in the world is to almost always fear exclusion or violence, even for those of us who pass. It is to always have a shadow of doubt, if not outright terror, trail us into the restroom, the locker room, airport security lines, the grocery store, the hospital, the dressing room, the lamplit—or even brightly lit—sidewalk where eyes watch too intently as we pass, the panels where women speak about women's issues, the beds where we fuck, the places where we must present our legal names and genders to have services rendered, and even the places where no one else in the world is but us. I usually pass, but the fear of being aggressively, angrily, violently outed and rejected as trans is always with me. This is not a crying cult of victimhood, as right-wingers often put it; it is merely an uncomfortable reality. As a woman of color, this is even more the case; I am more likely to face discrimination, from various groups, simply because my skin is brown. Neither of these things should ever be true in feminist spaces.

The tension between being trans and being recognized as my gender or race molded my perceptions of feminism—and led me to the murky place I find myself now, where as a result of these failures, I do not always feel welcome in the very world I want so much to help build.

But despite all this, I have hope. I am as integral to feminism as any other kind of woman in the wide, stelliferous constellation of womanhood.

One can dream. And when we wake up, we need to find a way to turn the dream I described at the White House vigil into a non-dream, so that that incredible world in which we have progressed so far that a trans woman of color could, credibly, preside no longer leaves an audience, as well as the dreamer-speaker, incredulous. We need to learn to translate our dreams, so our constellations on our waking nights and days will look fuller and more beautiful. But we will never get there unless we keep weaving and wielding our dreams, so that someday, some young brown trans girl will think, without being told it is absurd, that she, too, could one day guide some drifting piece of the world.

INTERSECTIONALITY AND THE BLACK LIVES MATTER MOVEMENT

Evette Dionne

THERE CAME A TIME when police violence seemed as routine and ordinary as brushing my teeth. I can't remember when it happened, but I'm sure it was after George Zimmerman stalked Trayvon Martin in a Florida suburb, confronted him, got beaten up, and decided that a teenager's life mattered less than his pride. That was in 2012. I was twenty-two. Or maybe it was after Mike Brown Jr.'s body was left to rot on the concrete, baking in Ferguson, Missouri's unrelenting August heat, his mother's piercing screams of "That's my son!" echoing through the air for a long time after his spirit had left his bullet-riddled body. Four hours earlier, police officer Darren Wilson had shot him for allegedly stealing cigarillos from a corner store. That was in 2014. I was twenty-four. Or maybe it was after Tamir Rice, an innocent twelve-year-old Black boy with a face sweet enough to make my teeth ache, met his end in less than two minutes from the start of his encounter with police. Since Black children are perceived as adults long before their voices crack or their breasts sprout, Cleveland police officers presumed Rice to be a threat. When they approached him, jumped out of the car, and shot him for brandishing a pellet gun on a recreation center playground, they didn't consider his age or the value of his life. I imagine how startled he must've been. I imagine how scared he was right before he inhaled his last breath. That was in 2014. I was twenty-five, and teaching a social justice class to low-income eighth-graders of color at a junior high school in Denver. I was struggling to keep them safe, and to reassure them that a bullet from a police officer's gun wouldn't end their young lives.

Tamir Rice was killed midway through our six-week section on race and, more specifically, the relationship between police violence and sustained activism. The timing of the lessons was both perfect and haunting. As we discussed how they could use their newfound knowledge to enact change in their communities, new names and verdicts became classroom discussions. In the time that I taught those curious and brilliant eighth-graders, Brown's killer wasn't indicted; Keith Childress was killed in Las Vegas; Jamar Clark took his last breath in Minneapolis; and Jessie Hernandez, a queer sixteen-year-old Latina, was killed by Denver police officers. Hernandez's death rocked them most of all because she, like them, was a teenager who inhabited Denver. She felt deeply familiar to them because she had walked the same streets they walked, and was killed on those streets by officers tasked with protecting and serving them. Her death resonated deeply for children who were still understanding police violence as a foreign problem that couldn't possibly come to their doorsteps. Near the end of the semester, I hosted a Jeopardy review game to jog their memories of the various victims we'd studied—and that's when I had a startling realization that's continued to haunt me long after I've left the classroom: Hernandez was the only female victim of police violence that we'd focused on. Sandra Bland hadn't died yet.

Charleena Lyles was still alive. Korryn Gaines hadn't been killed yet. But there were other girls and women of color who'd been killed by police or died while in police custody whose names never graced our classroom's SMART Board.

While I'd taught them about racism, white supremacy, and police violence, I'd also inadvertently framed police violence as a cisgender man's issue. Through my teaching and my rhetoric, I'd extended the patriarchal lens that police violence is often seen and theorized through. I also understood, in that moment, how internalized sexism can get the best of us: I was able to recite the names of Black cisgender and heterosexual male victims of police violence, but I couldn't even name three Black women or women of color who'd been killed by an officer. I could even recall what happened to Black men in their final moments. Philando Castile was shot dead in his car in Saint Paul, Minnesota, in 2016 while his girlfriend, Diamond Reynolds, and her daughter bore witness to the carnage. Eric Garner was choked to death by an officer in Staten Island, New York, after being approached for selling loose cigarettes to customers in front of a convenience store. Walter Scott was fatally shot in Charleston, South Carolina, after police officer Michael Slager pulled him over for a broken brake light. Their last moments, many of which were captured on video and played on a loop on social media, are memories that I can recall without prompting, but for a long time, the same couldn't be said of the Black women who found themselves on the wrong end of a police officer's gun.

Black feminism calls for us to examine erasure and re-center those who've been sidelined. In theory, Black feminism is a lens through which to see and understand the world, but it also requires both a reckoning with and an ongoing unlearning of oppression, including sexism, racism, and the critical juncture of misogynoir—a term coined by queer Black feminist scholar Moya Bailey and strengthened by Trudy, creator of the now-defunct blog *Gradient Lair*, to describe the marginalization of Black women at the intersections of race and gender. I know the language. I've read the canon. I've taken Black feminism courses. Yet, when it came to the issue of police violence, I had on blinders that prevented me from seeing how female victims of police violence were marginalized in the cultural narrative about brutality. On the surface, that makes perfect sense because more Black men are killed by police than Black women. Plus, no government entity tracks the number of people killed by police, and it wasn't until 2015 that the *Guardian* and the *Washington Post*, respectively, created databases that quantify the killings. Media organizations, which are often led by men, shone a spotlight on select male victims, leaving the sixteen Black women killed by police officers in 2016 without national attention. Yet, as a Black feminist writer and scholar whose life's work centers on Black women, how could I overlook this erasure?

Unfortunately, I'm not the only one to have done so. Because police violence isn't considered a core feminist issue, it's often viewed through the lens of Black male activists, many of whom are well versed in issues of race but lack a fundamental understanding of how race and gender intersect to oppress Black women. It's not accidental that we know the names and stories of male victims, including Freddie Gray, Alton Sterling, and Terence Crutcher, but are less familiar with Pearlie Golden, a ninety-three-year-old Black woman killed in her Texas home in 2014 by Stephen Stem, an officer who fatally wounded another person in 2012. Many of us are unfamiliar with Yvette Smith, a forty-seven-year-old Texas woman who called the police to break up a fight between two men but was shot dead when Officer Daniel Willis arrived on the scene. What about Tarika Wilson? Tyisha Miller? Gabriella Nevarez? Charleena Lyles, who was pregnant when she was killed by a Seattle police officer? Rekia

Boyd? Aiyana Stanley-Jones? Tanisha Anderson, a thirty-seven-year-old with a mental illness, was killed by officers a little more than a week before Rice met his demise. Both shootings happened in Cleveland. Only one dominated news headlines, brought resources and organizers to the Midwestern city, and became, for many, the tipping point of police violence. The lack of national attention paid to Anderson's death haunts me because I could've used that intimate classroom space to have conversations about both Rice and her. It also raises a question I've worked toward answering since I left the classroom and pivoted toward writing: How do we make police violence a core feminist political commitment, so better attention can be paid to the issue?

The Arc of History

Civil rights advocate Sandra Bland often used social media to call attention to state-sanctioned police violence. She used the hashtag #SandySpeaks to call out white people's usage of "all lives matter," to push back against the idea that discussing race is divisive, and to speak honestly about the impact of depression and post-traumatic stress disorder. Like so many others who use social media to raise awareness, Bland created a platform to have public conversations about ideas that are often discussed privately. When the twenty-eight-year-old was found dead in a Waller County, Texas, jail cell on July 13, 2015, a national spotlight was shone on her work and her death—a rare feat for people, particularly Black women, who are killed by police or die in police custody.

When authorities ruled Bland's death a suicide, protests erupted in twelve cities, and more than two hundred thousand people tweeted her name over the span of three days. Activists began demanding the state of Texas release the video of her arrest and that state trooper Brian Encinia be charged for unlawfully detaining Bland. The sustained attention paid to a Black woman found dead in a jail cell is an anomaly in the national conversation about police violence. Yet Black women and girls are also brutalized and killed by those tasked with serving and protecting them. Although Black women and girls make up only 13 percent of the US population, the African American Policy Forum (AAPF) found that they comprise 33 percent of all women killed by police.

Yet the trauma of police violence isn't an issue that mainstream feminist organizations are devoting resources to ending. While Equal Pay Day, the day when white women will earn the same amount that white men earned the year before, is recognized as an unofficial feminist holiday because of the impact of the wage gap on white women, rallies that recognize Black female victims of police violence are sparsely attended, don't dominate social media timelines, and aren't considered worthy of day-to-day media coverage.

Take, for instance, the death of Rekia Boyd in 2012. Though off-duty Chicago police detective Dante Servin fatally shot the twenty-two-year-old in a park, he was still acquitted of involuntary manslaughter charges in April 2015. When Black women activists organized a vigil in New York City's Union Square to protest Servin's acquittal, only one hundred people showed up. Although thousands of people flooded New York's streets mere months before to protest Eric Garner's death, again, a Black woman victim was left to be mourned in isolation, without an effort to shine a national spotlight on her death.

As columnist Jarvis DeBerry explained in the *Times-Picayune* newspaper a week after the deflated protest, "sexism can leave us blind to the taste of brutality that Black women are getting from the police." In order to make female victims of color integral to the police violence narrative, police violence itself can't be treated as a parallel, never-intersecting issue with feminism. We've heard this record before, and it always ends poorly for Black women. While the exclusion of women of color and Black women from the narrative around police violence seems like a recent phenomenon, there's a storied history of Black men and white feminists being centered in liberation movements. During the suffrage movement, for instance, journalist and activist Ida B. Wells worked alongside white suffragists to force the federal government to grant women the right to vote. Simultaneously, she fought with white suffragists, including Frances Willard and Susan B. Anthony, to recognize the systematic lynching of Black men as an integral part of their push for voting equity, and to fight to end the inhumane practice. Many of those white women rebuffed her because they, like so many white women historically and contemporarily, understood feminism as a tool for accruing equal power, prestige, and access to that of white men. Wells implied as much in a speech delivered in Chicago in 1900. "Under this reign of the 'unwritten law,' no colored man, no matter what his reputation, is safe from lynching if a white woman, no matter what her standing or motive, cares to charge him with insult or assault," she said. "It is considered a sufficient excuse and reasonable justification to put a prisoner to death under this 'unwritten law' for the frequently repeated charge that these lynching horrors are necessary to prevent crimes against women."

Men, particularly white men, have gone to dangerously violent extremes to hoard and protect the perceived virtue of white women, and suffragists used that foundational toehold of white supremacy to argue their case. "I do not want to see a negro man walk to the polls and vote on who should handle my tax money, while I myself cannot vote at all," Rebecca Ann Latimer Felton, the first female senator, said after passage of the Fifteenth Amendment, which guaranteed African-American men the right to vote. "When there is not enough religion in the pulpit to organize a crusade against sin; nor justice in the court house to promptly punish crime; nor manhood enough in the nation to put a sheltering arm about innocence and virtue—if it needs lynching to protect woman's dearest possession from the ravening human beasts—then I say lynch, a thousand times a week if necessary." Wells and other Black suffragists understood that the right to vote couldn't be an island of its own, separate from the trauma inflicted on Black families over and over again, the fear that sits in the back of our minds that our relative may leave for work and come home in a casket. Yet, Wells's inherent wisdom was sidelined, the needs of white women were centered, and Black women didn't earn the unfettered right to vote until the Voting Rights Act of 1965 was passed. When feminism is solely about the issues pertinent to middle-class, cisgender, heterosexual white women, the issues that impact women of color, such as police violence, are sidelined, and it becomes a parallel problem rather than an integrated one that feminists with access to power and privilege and resources can work toward dismantling.

During the civil rights movement, for instance, cisgender heterosexual men, including Martin Luther King Jr. and the Greensboro Four, were celebrated and championed, their humiliation and arrests put on the front page of newspapers. Yet, as historian Danielle McGuire chronicles in her foundational book, *At the Dark End of the Street: Black Women, Rape, and Resistance—A New History of the Civil Rights Movement from Rosa Parks to the Rise of Black Power*, it was the sexual violence inflicted on Black women by authorities, many of them police officers, that truly propelled the civil rights movement. On March 27, 1949, Gertrude Perkins was walking home from a party in Montgomery, Alabama. Two white police officers arrested her for "public drunkenness," but they never took her to the police station. Instead, they drove her to a dark area near railroad tracks, forced her out of the police car and behind a building, and raped her at gunpoint. After they'd violated Perkins repeatedly, they abandoned her there. When she reported the rape to Reverend Solomon S. Seay Sr. and he took her to the station to report the crime, authorities called her claim "completely false" and said that bringing charges against the officers would violate their constitutional rights. No charges were ever filed. However, Rosa Parks, an investigator for the NAACP, was dispatched over and over to investigate these incidents of sexual violence, record the testimonies of victims, and work with local activists to push for justice. As McGuire told NPR in 2011, the Montgomery Bus Boycott, which forced the city to integrate public transportation and is considered the official start of the civil rights movement, was only possible because of the organizing Parks had done around sexual violence. "I think that historians have always been focused on civil rights, voting rights, desegregation, access to public accommodations, and they've left out some of the larger things that people were worried about, particularly human rights," McGuire said. "And they ignored some of these stories. I mean Black women have been testifying about these crimes for years. They're on the front pages of black newspapers throughout the 1940s and the early 1950s, but mainstream historians never really picked it up, because I think they were really just focused on major leaders, major campaigns, and the very simplistic idea of civil rights."

Another example is activist Fannie Lou Hamer's run-in with police in Mississippi in 1963. She was arrested in Montgomery County, Mississippi, after leading a voter registration workshop in South Carolina, along with June Johnson, Euvester Simpson, Rosemary Freeman, and Annelle Ponder. They were tortured under the guidance of Sheriff Earl Wayne Patridge. Patridge forced two Black inmates to beat Hamer with a blackjack, which left her with permanent kidney damage and a limp. During the beating, her dress rose up, and when she attempted to pull it down, a deputy yanked it back up—further humiliating and violating a Black woman. When Hamer spoke for the first time about the abuse during the 1964 Democratic National Convention, she was working to show how police brutality was used against voting rights activists, regardless of gender; nevertheless, there is still a persistent belief that Black *men* are most likely to be targeted by law enforcement.

For decades, police officers used their positions of authority to brutalize and sexually violate Black women while second-wave white feminists viewed law enforcement as an integral part of protecting white women from sexual violence at home, in the workplace, and from strangers. These divergent political commitments, which mirror the centering of white women in the current #metoo movement—a term created by Tarana Burke, a Black woman activist—influenced the mainstream feminist movement's understanding of police violence. When police violence is solely considered a Black man's issue that's irrelevant to the feminist movement, Black girls and women are deprived of the resources needed to save us, particularly as it relates to sexual violence. When we don't have conversations about the relationship between sexual violence and police brutality, we lose sight of the trauma that's often inflicted on Black women and women of color. Overlooking that trauma makes us more vulnerable to life-threatening violence, as we've seen in the Daniel Holtzclaw case. Between December 2013 and June 2014, the Oklahoma City, Oklahoma, police officer purposefully targeted, assaulted, sexually abused, and in some cases raped at least thirteen poor Black women with criminal records and outstanding warrants. Like the Montgomery officers in 1949, Holtzclaw intentionally preyed on the most vulnerable people in his purview, those he thought would never find the courage to come forward and would never be believed if they did. Most of the women had criminal records, were addicted to drugs, and engaged in sex work— characteristics Holtzclaw believed would discredit them among his fellow officers. He also behaved as if assaulting them were part of his duties as an officer, acting like he was performing a standard search while stripping them, groping them, and then, in exchange for their freedom, forcing them to engage in sexual acts ranging from oral sex to intercourse. He'd coerce the women into having sex with him by telling them that he'd drop warrants and charges if they did so.

When poets Grace Franklin and Candace Liger united in 2014 to create OKC Artists for Justice, a collective that addresses injustices committed against women of color, their primary motivation was supporting Holtzclaw's victims. When I spoke in 2017 with lawyer and activist Andrea J. Ritchie, who has spent twenty years documenting police violence against women of color, she said that the OKC Artists for Justice were rebuffed when they approached feminist activists in Oklahoma City to gather support for Holtzclaw's victims. "The initial response was 'we can't really get involved because of our relationships with law enforcement,'" Ritchie said. "That's a snapshot of what's happened over the past thirty years. Our investment in police as a response to violence has deepened, especially around sexual violence and domestic violence. It has meant silencing the things that would call [that commitment] into question."

Many of the victims did not come forward because they believed Holtzclaw wielded power. "I didn't think that no one would believe me," one victim testified. "I feel like all police will work together and I was scared." Their fear is war-ranted: How many women of color since Gertrude Perkins have come forward against police officers only to be disbe-lieved or, worse, blamed for their assault? Furthermore, in a climate where, since 2005, only fourteen police officers have been convicted of murder or manslaughter in cases where they shot unarmed civilians, and the majority of victims who re-ceive sustained media attention are cisgender men, it's difficult to see a pathway forward. Eventually, Holtzclaw was con-victed on eighteen charges and sentenced to 263 years in prison, but that was greatly influenced by the activism of Black feminists who wanted to secure justice for his victims. The mainstream feminist movement, however, wasn't invested in the case and didn't lend resources to bring him to justice.

In 2015, sixteen-year-old Dajerria Becton was attending a pool party in McKinney, Texas. When authorities were dis-patched for an alleged disturbance, officer Eric Casebolt was videotaped pointing his weapon at a group of teenagers be-fore slamming Becton to the ground and straddling her back. Casebolt slammed her face on the ground while he pinned her; she was dressed in swim attire the entire time. Inflicting pain on Black women and women of color seems par for the course for police officers, but holding them accountable is still not considered a priority for white feminists. Though more white people are killed by police officers than Black people and people of color, feminists still understand police violence as an issue that only Black people must grapple with. That's the privilege of whiteness. Being pulled over without worry-ing about leaving the encounter alive and calling the police for a domestic disturbance are privileges associated with whiteness, an overlooked spot that white feminists still hav-en't fully grappled with. When the Women's March, the sin-gle largest demonstration in American history, popped up on January 21, 2017, media boasted about the lack of arrests at the protest. White feminist writers, including Jessica Valenti, highlighted the fact that not a single protester was arrested. Their ignorance belies the fact that police aren't going to use the same tactics against large swaths of white people as they did against Black protesters in Ferguson, Cleveland, and Baton Rouge. "White women and white bodies can hold space on streets and shut down cities 'peacefully' because they are allowed to," wrote blogger and author Luvvie Ajayi in a Facebook post soon thereafter. "Black and brown people who march are assaulted by cops. In a world that doesn't protect women much, when it chooses to, it is white women it protects." Many white feminists failed to recognize—and still fail to recognize—this privilege.

Compare the peacefulness of the Women's March to the now-iconic photo of Ieshia Evans, a Black nurse and mother, who was arrested during a protest in Baton Rouge in 2016 after the police killing of Alton Sterling. She stands stoically, her hands out limply in front of her, as police officers swarm and arrest her. Evans's arrest was later mocked in a controversial Pepsi commercial that featured Kendall Jenner giving a police officer a soda in the middle of a protest.

The trivializing of police violence in general underscores a lack of feminist commitment to the issue. Putting police violence at the center of feminism will require a reckoning that can't solely be facilitated by Black feminists, who understand how Black women and women of color are marginalized at the intersections of race and gender.

The Rise of #SayHerName

It is unsurprising that Kimberlé J. Crenshaw, the legal scholar who originally theorized intersectionality, is also one of the forces behind the #SayHerName movement. Initially, intersectionality was posited as a tenet of Black feminist theory, and it called attention to the erasure of identities at the intersection of race and gender in domestic violence narratives and resources. While intersectionality is often applied from person to person, as if it's an identity that can be tacked onto a Twitter bio, the term as originally intended actually takes a macro look at how identities are systemically targeted, particularly when they intersect. Police violence offers an intimate portrait of how racial justice often fails to account for intersectional marginalization.

Crenshaw-Williams, who teaches at both Columbia University and the University of California, Los Angeles, cofounded the African American Policy Forum (AAPF), and coauthored the report *Say Her Name: Resisting Police Brutality Against Black Women* with attorney and activist Andrea J. Ritchie. The report's goal was to "shed light on Black women's experiences of police violence in an effort to support a gender inclusive approach to racial justice" and "serve as a tool for the resurgent racial justice movement to mobilize around the stories of Black women who have lost their lives to police violence."

"The failure to highlight and demand accountability for the countless Black women killed by police over the past two decades," the report observes, "leaves Black women unnamed and thus under-protected in the face of their continued vulnerability to racialized police violence." The AAPF's commitment to both highlighting and centering Black women, women of color, the elderly, LGBTQ people, and people with disabilities and mental illnesses in anti–police violence activism has led to a radical shift in how we collectively discuss the issue. Their sustained activism resulted in #SayHerName becoming a mobilizing hashtag on social media, used to amplify the lives and deaths of female victims, and the organizing of a vigil to honor those women. In 2015, the first #SayHerName vigil was held in New York City's Union

Square, and the second event was a national day of action to end state violence against women and girls, which spread across several major cities, including New York, Chicago, and Los Angeles.

It was, as Ritchie told me in our August 2017 interview, the first vigil she'd ever participated in that felt like home. "There are many vigils and events that I've helped organize over the years where I left feeling angry and frustrated because they didn't mention, center, or focus on Black women and girls," she said. "For years, it was hard for me to get people to say Black men and women when they were talking about police brutality. So it was life changing for me to walk away from a vigil feeling whole."

Much of that foundational shift can be credited to the Black women and queer people who have been integral to making the Black Lives Matter movement inclusive and centered on women and trans people. Similar to the civil rights movement and the Black freedom movement, the Black Lives Matter movement, along with its ancillary organizers who are unaffiliated with the organization, is primarily mobilized and orchestrated by women. In this moment, however, they're refusing to be sidelined or pushed aside in favor of a patriarchal narrative that deifies a man as the singular leader. While Alicia Garza, Patrisse Cullors, and Opal Tometi are considered the originators of the phrase itself, those who were integral to the uprising in Ferguson—Johnetta Elzie, Brittany Packnett, Ashley Yates, and others—have purposefully refocused attention on the impact of police brutality on Black women and others from marginalized communities. Watching our daughters die and then be erased has been of central concern, and they've fought to stop that erasure.

That careful dedication to those whom history tends to forget is surely a departure from the male-dominated lens through which we tend to see the civil rights movement and the Black freedom movement. Yet, the work is not done. Since the original #SayHerName vigil in 2015 and the subsequent day of action, there hasn't been a replication of the event. There hasn't been a sustained national focus on Black women and women of color who are subjected to police violence. The greater narrative still centers Black men at the expense of those who are equally vulnerable, and the brunt of the work to center Black women victims still falls primarily on Black feminists. As *intersectionality* becomes a buzzword, white feminists must turn inward to figure out what has allowed them to build comfort with police officers, and who that comfort has come at the expense of. They must grapple with how their whiteness shields them from state-sanctioned violence, and how they can use that access to power and privilege to raise awareness and work to dismantle systems that target Black people and people of color.

If I could return to the classroom, I'd balance that male-dominated police violence curriculum with the lives and tragic deaths of Black women, but seeing as time doesn't allow us to move backward, I'll end with this: We will say their names, no matter the cost.

NO DISABLED ACCESS

Frances Ryan

IT'S NOT ONLY steps that shut disabled women out of feminism. I think of this statement every now and again, more frequently of late. The resurgence of feminism in the mainstream political and cultural agenda in recent years has been liberating, from the ease with which younger women choose to identify as "feminist" to the vocal campaigns for abortion rights, female representation—from political bodies to statues—and ending male violence against women, such as the Counting Dead Women project in the UK (which names each woman killed by a man each year) and NARAL Pro-Choice Ohio (one of many groups across the United States fighting state legislation restricting women's reproductive rights). But at the same time as I celebrate this resurgence, I'm increasingly aware of a discomfiting thought: It's widely happening without the faces and lives of disabled women.

I've identified as a feminist since I was a young teenager. I had always been interested in politics—or rather, in using politics to make society more equal—and I wanted to be part of a political movement fighting to alter the unequal structures that result in women being underpaid, unrepresented, raped, and murdered. But as a disabled woman growing up in the UK in the early 1990s, I didn't feel represented by feminism as it was being presented to my generation. The Spice Girls' cries of "girl power" and the "ladette" culture of the era—in which female celebrities gained notoriety in the media by taking on supposedly "male" characteristics of drinking, swearing, and partying—were held up as examples of female empowerment, but there was a dearth of politicized feminist campaigns. What's more, I grew up at a time when it was still rare to even see a disabled woman in the media. I became almost used to the fact that, on the few occasions I saw women's concerns featured, disabled women were nowhere in sight. This is hardly a new phenomenon: There has never been a point in history in which the feminist movement significantly addressed the needs of marginalized women. But in recent years, during which the faux empowerment of the nineties made way for a revival of feminism for a new generation of young women, I've felt this more strongly still. While I watch vast progress being made in putting feminism on the mainstream agenda, there seems to be little advancement in terms of the inclusion of any marginalized women—and that includes disabled women. As feminism as a whole makes astonishing gains, I'm left with the aching feeling that many women are being left behind.

"Feminists are grappling with issues that disabled people also face in a different context," the leading disabled feminist philosopher Susan Wendell wrote, as far back as the 1980s. Diagnosed with chronic fatigue syndrome in 1985, Wendell used formative texts such as *The Rejected Body: Feminist Philosophical Reflections on Disability* to question the nature of disability and argue that feminist theory as it stood was skewed toward healthy, nondisabled experience—and incomplete because of it. Almost thirty-five years later, this is still the case, despite significant progress in the fight for sex and disability equality. Both feminists and disability rights campaigns are grappling with a battle to acknowledge that oppression comes from a socially constructed inequality, not from biology. Both campaigns are routinely concerned with the problem of idealized human bodies. They both fight the power and social structures that control them in sex, work, and reproduction. Yet instead of this building an affinity between disability and feminist concerns, campaigns for women's equality still appear achingly separate from concerns about disabled people's inequality. As a disabled journalist working primarily on disability and women's rights, I've often been struck by the way these two areas are routinely kept separate. Issues labeled as "disability"—say, cuts to disabled people's social security—end up rarely being seen as feminist, and feminist campaigns—for example, those against domestic violence—largely exist without mention of disabled people and disabled women in particular. This exclusion of disabled women's lives from mainstream feminism creates the danger of a movement that simultaneously aims to achieve female equality while actually cutting out the experiences of vast numbers of women. A feminism that fails to be inclusive is, of course, in many ways a hollow version of feminism—cutting out the color and complexity of a myriad of different women with a variety of experiences, priorities, and perspectives. But perhaps most worryingly, it means there's a very real risk that as the current feminist resurgence fights for progress in women's equality, disabled women's inequality will not be addressed.

This is true even at a time when the rights of disabled women are in many ways freshly under threat. When disabled activists staged a "die-in" in the US Senate in June 2017 to protest proposed cuts to Medicaid services, the resulting police action—which included a disabled woman being ripped from her wheelchair—was largely viewed as a grotesque metaphor for "Trumpcare." But as I read the coverage of the event, I couldn't help but think—why was this not being recognized as a feminist issue? After all, the women among the campaigners were more likely to be in poverty due to being both disabled and female, and any health cuts that threaten disabled people's support to live independently would be an assault on their dignity and their right to work and raise a family. In the United States, the original Senate bill the campaigners were protesting would have reduced federal Medicaid spending by almost $800 billion. Similarly, ever since the 2008 global crash, the UK has undergone vast cuts to health care and social security that are predominately affecting women and disabled people: As of 2017–18, austerity has cost women a total of £79bn, versus £13bn for men, with disabled people losing a minimum of £28bn. In addition to cuts in social security and care packages, women and disabled people in the UK have been hit by public sector cuts and vast changes to eligibility for legal aid (affecting anything from a young woman's ability to take her employer to court for firing her for getting pregnant to a cancer patient challenging the government's decision to remove her sickness benefits).

These measures go to the heart of both disability and feminist concerns—from cuts to social security to the closure of domestic violence shelters—but have widely been spoken of as two separate political issues: on the one side, the disabled; on the other, women. This goes to multiple other realms beyond austerity—something as fundamental as equal access to lifesaving health care. In 2017 the Million Women Study by the University of Oxford and Cancer Research UK found that disabled women in the UK are a third less likely to attend breast cancer screenings than other women, due to anything from limited transport to not being able to use a mammogram machine while sitting in a wheelchair. This is part of the larger picture of disabled women being shut out of health care related to women's biology:

Women with mobility problems routinely tell me they've been unable to have a pap smear because they couldn't physically get on the table, or that they were discouraged from using contraception because their doctor assumed that, as they were disabled, they weren't sexually active. Yet like austerity cuts, these issues haven't been picked up by either large-scale disability rights groups or mainstream feminist campaigns. At best, disabled women—our needs, our lives—are left to float on the outside, ignored as neither one nor the other. At worst, we are not part of feminism; we are considered someone else's problem.

This reluctance to bridge the gap perhaps stems in part from the fact that despite their common ground, there are seemingly conflicting goals between disability rights and women's rights. As Rosemarie Garland Thomson, academic and author of the foundational text *Extraordinary Bodies*, puts it, when it comes to disabled women's exclusion from mainstream feminism, it isn't only that feminism can fail to take into account their situations; it's that some of the differences that disability provokes can complicate feminism's understanding of female bodies and the oppression they experience. While caring for disabled family members, for example, can represent liberation for disabled people (in enabling our independence from institutional settings), in still falling predominately on wives and mothers, this responsibility is strongly associated with the oppression of women (locking them in traditional gender roles and often poverty—particularly for women already in low-income families who can't afford to give up a wage to take on a caring role but nonetheless have to).

This tension between women's rights and disability rights is rarely more evident than in the case of abortion campaigns. In the fight for reproductive rights, disabled fetuses are often held up as an example of "justified" abortion—the argument being that if a woman's pregnancy will likely result in a disabled child, it's a legitimate reason for her to end it. Along with cases of rape, the right to abort an abnormal fetus is often the first stage of any pro-choice campaign, while in the media, women's stories of anguish over their decision to raise a disabled child are routinely used as a means to convince even the most ardent antichoice thinkers that in some cases, abortion should be permissible. Creating a hierarchy of abortion rights—disabled fetuses can be aborted legitimately; "normal" babies cannot—is ultimately damaging to the wider aim of gaining full abortion rights for women, as it promotes the idea that some reasons for abortion are more valid than others and that a woman's choice over her body should not fully be her own. It also perpetuates harmful beliefs around disability that still largely associate it with negativity, failure, or something to be avoided at all costs. It falls into an ableist trap: In a culture in which disabled people's lives are often said to be worth less, disability becomes the "nightmare consequence" of a lack of abortion rights—as if the downside of restricting abortion is the possibility of having to raise a disabled child (rather than, say, being forced to give birth against one's will or having to raise a child in poverty). As a disabled woman, I've long found this discomfiting, but as a pro-choice feminist, I can feel conflicted even admitting it. It can feel as if I'm being pulled in two directions: a concern when hearing disabalist justifications for abortion and a desire to defend a woman's right to choose at all costs.

These concerns are real and complex, but I don't believe that they're insurmountable. Difference, after all, is not something that needs to be shut out of mainstream feminism, but rather something that needs to be embraced and understood if feminism hopes to represent more than white, wealthy, heterosexual, nondisabled women. Besides, the sexism and misogyny that surround disabled women—our circumstances, our choices—are rarely, if ever, entirely foreign to the issues facing all women. Rather, sexism and disability simply meet to mark our lives in particular ways. Take something as fundamental as the workplace. The recent surge in conversations around women at work—from a Sheryl Sandberg Lean In–type of focus on women's increased stake in leadership roles to campaigns for the unionized rights of migrant women enduring low-paid, insecure labor—is a vital change. But for disabled women, the workplace presents other inequalities, such as employers refusing to adjust the workplace to accommodate our disabilities (either through physical adaptations or measures such as flextime), and large-scale unemployment levels. While the gender pay gap continues to gain the attention of feminist campaigns, little is said about the disability pay gap, or the way gender impacts this; disabled women, after all, have to face two pay gaps at once. This lack of attention is despite the fact that in the UK, the pay gap between disabled women and nondisabled women is double that of disabled and nondisabled men (22 percent compared to 11 percent), while in the United States disabled women working full time are typically paid 73 cents on the dollar compared to nondisabled men (or 76 cents for disabled men). This inequality can be even worse if you're a disabled woman who also happens to be a from an ethnic minority background. While the intersection of disability, sex, and race is not clear-cut—for example, research by the Equality and Human Rights Commission in 2017 found most female ethnic minority groups in Britain had a pay advantage over white women—being female, disabled, and/or from an ethnic minority background increases your likelihood of being stuck in a low-paying job, as well as insecure or agency work.

This intersection of disability and sex is as relevant for cultural issues as it is for economic. Take objectification. In the past five years, campaigns against sexual objectification of women have gained fantastic attention—from Badger & Winters's ad campaign #WomenNotObjects in the United States to the UK's "Lose the Lads' Mags" and "No More Page 3" campaigns targeting the images of naked young women on tabloids in supermarket checkout lines. But for disabled women, objectification alone rarely reflects our own experience with sexism. Rather than being overly sexualized, disabled women are widely ascribed an asexual identity, battling a culture that assumes having a disability means a person lacks both sexual desire and desirability. A central challenge we face is how to carve out our own positive sexual identity in the face of this culture, while responding to a feminism that often infers that sexualization is the main issue for women. Growing up with a disability, I found it hard to identify with my nondisabled friends' concerns over being catcalled on the street. As a disabled teenage girl, you feel fear and degradation from learning that being out in public can lead to men whistling or calling at you—but if that doesn't happen, you may also experience the disturbing feeling we are not even female enough to be harassed in traditional ways. Of course, for those whose bodies, in addition to being disabled, do not fit the supposed ideal of the white feminine figure—for example, trans or Black women—this can be considerably harder still. For disabled women, caught between sexism and ableism, the message is one of failure on patriarchy's terms: Unlike those of "normal" women, our bodies are not even sexually useful. Crucially, this attitude toward disabled women's sexuality permeates care provision itself, with young disabled women and girls routinely excluded from sexual health education and access to suitable contraception and cervical cancer tests. These experiences are specific to the lives of disabled women, but they are clearly relevant to the concept of body shaming and further evidence of a sexist culture that seeks to police and shame all women—nondisabled and disabled alike.

Similarly, domestic violence can affect any woman, but the threat increases dramatically with disability. In the UK, disabled women are twice as likely to experience domestic violence as other women, meaning almost one in two disabled women will be abused in their lifetime; in the United States, there is a 40 percent greater chance of a woman being abused if she is disabled. The power and control common in other abusive relationships can be exerted with particular ease with disabled victims, particularly because the abuser is often the person being relied upon for care. Disability can become part of the abuse: removing a woman's wheelchair just as she's about to sit down; throwing a hearing aid across the room, leaving the victim unable to communicate; forcing a woman to sit in soiled incontinence pads. Even the struggle to escape is altered by disability: Disabled women are more likely to endure abuse for longer before leaving. This is partly due to the inaccessibility of wider society. Women's charities have told me of Deaf women who have left their abusers, only to have to return home because of a lack of accessible refuges or suitable public transport—and partly because of cultural prejudices. For example, the "white knight" myth— the belief that disabled women are less appealing as partners, and therefore any man with them is uniquely caring and selfless—can make it much harder for disabled women to be believed, while the infantilization of disabled people means it appears normal for a disabled woman to be accompanied by a caretaker (and abuser) in spaces that are often considered safe, like a doctor's office.

Recognizing the connection between our disability and sex is a matter of belonging for many of us, a sense of identity. When we see feminism and disability rights as separate campaigns, we shape political movements that cancel out the lives of certain women. It can feel as if our identity as disabled women is being split down the center: "too disabled" for one political movement, "too female" for the other. To watch mainstream feminism gain ground in popular culture, media, and politics without any reference to disability rights builds a version of feminism that does not speak to our own lives—that shuts millions of women out of the fight for our own equality. This results in not only a sense of exclusion for countless disabled women but also a weaker, less nuanced understanding of the key issues facing women for all. How can domestic violence truly be tackled unless the endemic level of abuse against disabled women is acknowledged? How can sexist depictions of women be addressed unless asexualization is recognized as well as objectification? Similarly, disabled women themselves will gain full equality only if all parts of our life are recognized—when, say, the struggle of a woman with multiple sclerosis to get adequate health care or a Deaf woman's sexual abuse is understood in terms of her being both disabled and female. A political movement that addresses the needs of disabled women must acknowledge the particular way in which being unequal in one affects being unequal in another.

The first stage of creating this movement—like all things, I think—is an awareness of the women who are currently missing. Part of this is banally practical. Yes, it's not only steps that shut disabled women out of feminism, but there's little hope of including disabled women if we're not even physically able to get in the room. Being vigilant in terms of literal access to events, protests, and campaigns at the local and national level is the foundation for including disabled women's voices (and insuring that access not simply for wheelchair users but also for Deaf women, women with sensory disabilities, and many others). At the same time, there's a real need to acknowledge the value of nontraditional forms of activism disabled women may adopt to accommodate our disabilities—say, calling political representatives, Twitter chats, or research. #CripTheVote, an online movement encouraging the political participation of disabled people in the US and UK, is one recent example. There's some snobbery around less physical forms of campaigning—epitomized in the phrase "keyboard warrior" (a term coined to signify someone who wishes to use the power imbued by anonymous internet commentary but who lacks conviction or effort in so-called real life). But not only are these methods effective, they also enable the participation of women disabled by their health, lack of mobility, or inaccessible transport and buildings who would otherwise be excluded.

The next stage, I think, is considering familiar issues—domestic violence, abortion, unpaid labor—from a disability perspective, just as we should for race, class, and other marginalized groups. It's the political equivalent of living in black and white and switching to Technicolor: Where once you were only able to see parts of the picture of female oppression, you can now envision multiple angles. For abortion rights, for example, this can mean not only including disabled women's concerns in abortion debates but also addressing the fact that concern for reproductive rights is almost exclusively about abortion. A full feminist campaign for reproductive rights would go beyond abortion rights to the coerced sterilization of disabled women, the rights of disabled women to raise children, and—in a climate of austerity and conservative small-state ideology—shrinking support for parents of disabled children. Unpaid care work, meanwhile, is an ideal subject for both women and disabled people to tackle, as the ones predominantly doing the caring and receiving the care. The International Wages for Housework Campaign of the 1970s—a feminist global social movement founded in Italy—aimed to challenge the gendered division of labor that painted caring roles as not "real" work, while pushing the idea that such responsibilities should be collectivized; a modern mainstream campaign could focus particularly on women caring for disabled relatives and the lack of state support for disabled people seeking to live independently.

Finally, great progress will come from expanding the definition of what is considered to be a feminist concern. The problem for some branches of marginalized feminism is often said to be the way their work is overshadowed by mainstream feminism. For disabled feminists, the problem is routinely not having their work or lives seen as feminist issues. Whether it's wheelchair users on the floor of the US Senate fighting for health care or women with depression and anxiety facing cuts to mental health services, some of the most pressing social and economic issues of our times are deeply feminist in that they disproportionately affect women. That disabled women are at the core of these issues—fighting for basic rights to health, independent living, work, and family—means the time has surely come for such struggles to be seen in feminist terms.

The ideas that I've discussed here are only a small contribution to an ongoing project. Countless disabled women are already working to bridge disability and women's rights globally, from grassroots activists to local charity workers to academics to online campaigners. Life, of course, and with it inequality, does not come with neat borders—disabled one day, female another—and neither can the political campaigns that we create in response. This struggle for an inclusive feminism is for us, the disabled women who are of value in and of themselves, who deserve a political movement that not only represents but also embraces us. To use the words of the famed disability rights slogan: "Nothing about us without us." But progress toward a more inclusive feminism will also, of course, be beneficial for all women. Mainstream feminism will only become stronger when it strives to embody the complexity and nuance of different women's lives—when it routinely thinks of disability, chronic illness, and mental health as crucial pieces of women's realities, along with class and race. There is something deeply apt about a feminism that has at its center women who are ignored, patronized, and excluded by society as a whole, who throughout history have been denied an education, put in institutions, and shut out from motherhood and employment because as both women and people with disabilities, they are deemed weak, incapable, or freaks, yet nonetheless survive, battle, and flourish. Disabled women, who have long been bearing the brunt of injustice and inequality, belong at the forefront of the fight against it.

A HUNDRED SMALL REBELLIONS

Eishar Kaur

"Go and make some chaa," my mother said.

The order to make tea for our guests came at the end of a stressful day for fourteen-year-old me. Exams were fast approaching, I'd had a fight with my best friend, and I'd left my purse on the bus—combined with a hefty dose of teenage hormones and a simmering resentment, it was enough to push me over the edge.

"You make it."

I will never forget the argument that followed after our guests left. My parents were adamant that I'd embarrassed them by committing the cardinal sin of "answering back." I raged about how I was always being asked to do chores while my brother got off lightly (an exaggeration, but I was a teenager and I was furious).

Recently, ten years later, I asked my parents if they thought they'd treated my brother and me differently as we were growing up. They requested an example.

"Well, I was asked to make the tea, and, y'know, chores and stuff."

"You don't make tea! Your brother always makes it!" Said laughingly, but it was the truth.

They weren't wrong, but I wonder now if they realized that this was my own form of rebellion, which began with that single refusal and slowly escalated over the years, until it became normal for my brother to cater to guests—ever the peacekeeper, he embraces making the tea to this day. They often feel selfish, but in the intensely patriarchal Punjabi culture, it's the seemingly trivial acts that keep girls in the diaspora sane; balancing Western life with your culture requires a hundred small rebellions.

The incremental progression of these rebellions is what led me to feminism. A few years after my first small rebellion, I moved six hours away to go to university. At the time, it was the biggest upheaval I'd caused in my family, who held the traditional view that girls should stay at home until marriage, but I felt the need for distance from the rigid cultural expectations I'd spent my teenage years challenging. After several battles and a trip to the campus that persuaded my parents it was the best academic option for me, I went, and there I learned about feminism. By that I mean I read the Western feminist canon included in my syllabus: Germaine Greer, Simone de Beauvoir, Andrea Dworkin, all considered necessary to any feminist education, and all white. I came home with bite-size quotes tripping off my tongue in response to any situation I perceived to be oppressive. I came home arrogant. My culture chafed against my newfound knowledge, and I found it harder to accept that certain things remained as they always had been.

As I argued against my culture, I began to pick holes in my own understanding of feminism. I found myself relating to cultural concepts that weren't covered by the theories I'd learned; for example, the complex ethics of arranged marriages, and uncovering issues that weren't even acknowledged by white feminism, such as cultural appropriation. Eventually I saw that I was inflicting this theoretical feminism, white feminism, onto my family and onto my culture—and that it was lacking. Even the term itself seemed distant from our daily lives—I hardly know anyone in my circle of Punjabi friends or family who would readily refer to themselves as a feminist. Is that because feminism is inaccessible, a concept far removed from the concerns and realities of the Punjabi diaspora? Or is it because the term is inadequate? Does "feminism" fail to encompass the challenges specific to our culture?

THE UK IS home to the largest Punjabi diaspora in the world, and as of 2013, Punjabis (the ethnic group hailing from the state of Punjab in Northern India and Pakistan) accounted for 45 percent of Indians living in the UK. The first significant migration, and the beginning of the Punjabi diaspora in Britain, was recorded in the 1940s and 1950s. Much of my generation, the diaspora of twenty-somethings referred to as "British Indians/Pakistanis of Punjabi heritage" by UK census data, can trace this migration back to our grandparents, making us third-generation immigrants.

At first glance, the different perceptions of feminism between generations of Punjabi immigrant families can be explained easily by historical context. Western feminism in the 1960s was a movement seen as militant, framing feminists as outspoken, rebellious, and even riotous to the general public. The media portrayal of feminism continued in this vein well into the early nineties. For the insular Punjabi immigrant community in the UK, the most pervasive and consistent image of a feminist was as a "bra burner"; for that reason, "feminism" remains inaccessible to the wave of second-generation Punjabi immigrants who grew up in the seventies and eighties, as the term itself recalls this image. The next generation is further removed from the judgment of these rebellious women as immoral and even "wild," but nevertheless has a watered-down distaste for the word itself that is gradually being unlearned. Still, the initial recoil at the term *feminism* persists across generations.

My father, a second-generation immigrant, would not refer to himself as a feminist. When pressed, he says that he "believes in equal rights," but doesn't "hate men." After I explain the dictionary definition of feminism (i.e. the belief in the social, political, and economic equality of the sexes), he retracts—of course he supports the equality of the sexes. This misconception isn't restricted to one generation, though. It's trickled through the Punjabi consciousness—every male friend and relation of every age I ask rejects the term. It's safe to say that this is indicative of the patriarchal nature of the culture. *Feminist* is associated with "angry" and outspoken women, which is contrary to the expected nature of a woman in a culture that strictly dictates her behavior, from what she wears to whom she marries. But this rejection of the term, the inaccessibility and occasional ignorance of it, doesn't mean the men of my culture are anti-feminist. It only demonstrates that the term doesn't resonate.

My father and uncles, my brother and my cousins would all be considered progressive by traditional Punjabi norms. Like much of the diaspora, they have broken boundaries, and have supported their daughters, wives, mothers, and sisters as they did the same. But by the rules of Western feminism, they would not be considered feminists (even if they wanted to be). The traditional values they uphold, and the roles women are assigned, seem outdated—a few steps behind the issues Western feminism is focused on. There are no markers of feminist progress in our short history; we have no reach into the issues of our homeland, and can't challenge the patriarchal framework in Punjab—we can only tackle the issues faced by the diaspora. The obstacles faced by daughters trying to change their families' perception of what it means to be a Punjabi woman are numerous, spanning everything from living away from home to dressing less conservatively to dating (especially with no intention of marriage) and sexual orientation. Moreover, the patriarchal nature of our culture prevents open discussion in many families, leading to the normalization of secrecy. At the top of this long list of ways we, the men and women of the diaspora, surely fail according to the standards set by Western feminism is one key, unavoidable point. We are brown, and feminism here is white.

Western feminism is white feminism. It is rooted in the concerns of white women, and its parameters are set by said women. British journalist Reni Eddo-Lodge posits that "whiteness positions itself as the norm" in feminism, and that this "becomes a problem when its ideas dominate— presented as the universal to be applied to all women." With this context, it comes as no surprise that *feminist* is an exclusionary term. It instantly invokes white feminist issues, and thereby becomes unrelatable to other cultures. White feminism is excellent at projecting issues onto other cultures as it sees fit, prioritizing the "big" issues over the day-to-day realities. For example, over the years there has been a consistent focus on rebuking the system of arranged marriage, but the conversation excludes the South Asian women who exist on a broad spectrum of challenging and supporting this cultural concept. Progress is determined according to the white feminist values imposed on these issues, and judgment passed on the culture accordingly.

As much as a large percentage of the Punjabi diaspora rejects the term *feminist*, feminism in this country rejects us. There is no room for gray areas in white feminism—and the feminism of Punjabi women in the UK resides almost exclusively in this undefined area between Western rebellion and the traditional Punjabi patriarchy.

"I WANT TO call myself a feminist but my experience is not just through the lens of being a woman, it's through race as well. That narrative doesn't really include me."

I am sitting across from my friend Amandeep in a Pret, both of us nursing overpriced coffees. We have different family backgrounds and we're from different parts of London, but our shared culture transcends our differences. Her experience of the patriarchy that forms the basis of Punjabi culture mirrors mine in many ways. Talking with her, I realize that the historical context for this patriarchy is, counterintuitively, more static here than it is in Punjab.

"Our reference point is stuck in the past," she says. "Music, clothes, Bollywood movies: I've got this locked version of Punjabiness in my head from my grandparents."

In an effort to preserve a culture left behind, progress in the British-Punjabi diaspora has slowed down. Feminism for us doesn't seem as pressing as India's issues, where the feminist movement is currently fighting extreme sexual violence and an all-pervasive rape culture, and it won't while our culture exists in this separate bubble, and our feminism has minimal benefits for women in India. Simultaneously, white feminism can't work as a framework for dismantling the patriarchal norms of Punjabi culture. We face issues that aren't given airtime in the Western feminist movement, such as limited sexual freedom, intense homophobia, colorism, and constant pressure to marry.

The misogyny running through many of my cultural experiences, and those of my female cousins and friends, is hard to ignore. Punjabi women are expected to be "good Indian daughters," who stay at home until they marry and are "pure" and "chaste." The historical idea that the family honor rests in the hands of the daughter is inherently misogynistic, and is now visibly threaded through everything from expectations of dressing "respectably" to so-called honor killings. The patriarchal nature of South Asian families often results in female voices being silenced. I'm lucky that this overt misogyny was absent from my upbringing, but the twelve to fifteen so-called "honor killings" per year in the UK attest to its continued presence in South Asian (including Punjabi) diaspora families.

When I asked Naadia, the only other girl in our UK-based contingent of cousins, if she thought she'd been treated differently than her brothers growing up, she instantly said yes. My brother and her brother were, a tad surprisingly, also quick to acknowledge that we were treated differently. My parents and aunt were just as quick to say no to the same question. They, optimistically, hoped to raise us all equally, and find it hard to acknowledge that the culture we were raised in is not so accepting. These cultural expectations are pervasive, and can be visibly pointed to in matters of household chores, dressing "appropriately," and many other small, surface-level irritations that you learn to traverse quickly. Until you can't.

"The Punjabi male gaze is exhausting." Amandeep puts the lid on her coffee cup. "I'm trying to be less afraid of confronting Punjabi men because I've grown up with that fear." Punjabi culture conditions us all to view sexual promiscuity as bad—and it associates this promiscuity with innocuous signifiers, like skirts above the knee, makeup, and even skinny jeans. If this isn't consciously unlearned by Punjabi men, a woman wearing any of these can be subject to sexual harassment at any time. White feminism provides a framework for defying catcallers and calling out sexual harassment, but it does so within the parameters of sexual freedom and acceptance that society affords white women. Punjabi women have no such luxury. In the diaspora we must tread the line between self-expression/freedom and fear/wariness.

It may seem surprising that we're not fighting for this sexual freedom, one of the cornerstones of Western feminism. But this is not only because, as Amandeep points out, we grew up in a culture where we fear confronting men. It is also because feminism in the diaspora has always taken a backseat to the bigger battle faced by generations of immigrants, from Punjab and elsewhere: racism.

When talking to my dad, he tells countless stories of cruel teachers discriminating against him at school, subtle racism at work, and overt racism from skinheads in the streets. In his own words, "racism was more of an urgent priority [than feminism] . . . one issue at a time." The visible difference of immigrant communities in the UK—the color of their skin—created an incendiary atmosphere for my parents' generation. In 1979, when my dad was fourteen, his friends and neighbors were caught up in the Southall race riots, when immigrant communities fought right-wing protesters and faced the daily threat of violence. It's easy to see how racism obscured all other causes, including gender equality.

The other predominant challenge at that time was economic equality, which is where feminism has made bold steps forward in the Punjabi diaspora community. Economically, women paved the way in both their families (for many families it was the first time women brought home paychecks) and their often male-dominated industries, such as IT and finance (as was common at the time). However, they were still taking these steps as brown women in mostly white environments, so the presence of race within their feminist moment can't be ignored.

FROM THESE PIONEERING women forward, feminism in the Punjabi diaspora—albeit barely acknowledged by white feminism—does exist. Speaking to women among my family and friends, I find that we are all pushing boundaries and flexing our freedoms. Our feminism takes form in ways that aren't covered by the term itself, or the Western framework behind it. Through a Western lens, moving away from home to go to university is not considered particularly groundbreaking. But in the context of the British-Punjabi culture, it is a distinctly feminist act. Many women of my mother's generation, my mum included, were prevented from pursuing higher education on the basis that moving away from home was unacceptable unless you were married. Your "honor" was expected to move from your father's house to your husband's house, with no stops (and no risks) in between. The fact that girls of my generation have gone to university in larger quantities year by year than any generation before us, many of those away from home, shows that boundaries are being broken by both daughters and their parents.

This feminist movement, though not referred to as such, has its roots, in fact, in second-generation immigrants, my parents' generation, many of whom are choosing to push back against traditional choices and historical expectations and raise their children, regardless of gender, in a more equal manner. My parents have spoken to me over the years of their biggest act of resistance against my grandparents' gendered treatment of me and my brother. It's a story I've heard many times, but each time their hurt and anger are palpable. There is a tradition that when celebrating the birth of a baby in the family, the heads of the family gift ladoos (Indian sweets) to family and friends. My paternal grandparents didn't do this when I was born, but three years later, they were immediately keen to—because my brother, a grandson, had arrived. Speaking of it now, my dad will talk of his anger, and his refusal to allow my grandparents to treat us differently. (Suffice it to say, my grandparents didn't take that very well.) My mum, on the other hand, had almost expected it. Gendered moments that directly affect men, like this one, can often elicit the reactions that women are constantly suppressing.

My parents were not alone in their dislike of this gendered tradition. Now there is a movement aimed at changing the perception of daughters in Punjabi families. The Pink Ladoo Project, started by Raj Khaira, encourages families to hand out pink ladoos to celebrate the arrival of daughters, in order to eliminate "the social ills stemming from patriarchy and misogyny by dismantling the sexist customs and traditions that hold them together." In the two years since its launch in 2015, the project has already become widespread in the UK and is slowly changing attitudes in the diaspora.

"IT IS CHANGING. Your generation is definitely changing," my mother says. We are sitting across from one another at our kitchen table. Serious discussions aren't out of place here—I grew up with conversation and debate over every family dinner—but this one has the express purpose of understanding the feminist who raised me.

"It's the evolution, isn't it, of having those roots. So for your grandparents' generation, having those roots meant being a certain way. For me and your dad, having those roots means having a foot in your grandparents' camp, and being our own selves, and having a foot in your camp. For you, you have a foot in our camp, and in your own, and then you'll have a foot in your next generation's camp. With each iteration, you get a bit further away from the thing that anchored it in the first place. We're already a step removed from how your grandparents view the world; you're a step removed from how we view the world. Your version of Punjabiness will be different from our version of our Punjabiness."

When I ask my female cousins and friends about their first encounter with feminism, they point to their mothers. Our second-generation Punjabi mothers introduced us to feminism in action before we read the criticism and learned the terminology and watched the world change. My mother points to her "feminist milestones" (a phrase she has begun to claim as we have learned about feminism together)—her own process of pushing against the patriarchal nature of her Punjabi culture. She mentions having a daughter while my aunts were having boys, and battling the family's heavy hopes I would be a boy. She talks about fighting for me— and as I look back, I see that she did. There was no "be seen, not heard" culture in my youth; I was always given the freedom to be as vocal and to have the same opportunities as the boys. Women's responsibilities were once seen as child caring and home keeping, but through being mothers to independent daughters, being working mothers, and being incredibly resilient, my mother's generation has shifted the culture. To white feminism this shift may be imperceptible, but to the generations that will follow it is vital.

Punjabi women are feminists in action even if not in name, and they are effecting change every day. But feminism itself is failing them; they are not equipped by current feminism as they should be. Evidence lies in the intensely complex relationship between the feminist movement in India and the feminism of the diaspora. White feminism loves to focus on an issue of another culture and turn it into a cause, despite the fact that it has no knowledge of said culture. While immensely damaging to women who live and survive in other cultures, this co-opting of issues also affects diaspora communities who are battling different issues that are much more pressing to them. No distinction is made between the issues that need to be focused on in India and the feminism that is needed in the British diaspora. British

Punjabi issues, like the high rates of domestic violence and honor killings, are overlooked by Western feminism, and thus also often ignored by the policy makers that can solve said issues. The issues we are assumed to face are conflated with the (very serious and real) issues faced by women in India, and while there is some overlap, this prevents a cohesive Punjabi feminist community from forming. How can we call ourselves feminists when the feminist movement does not know we exist?

If we were to lay claim to feminism and the ways in which we enact it, Punjabi feminists would first need to overcome a major hurdle. Our feminism exists at the crossroads between race and gender, by virtue of our existence as brown women. Our feminism must be intersectional—and we must dismantle the patriarchy across all cultures, not just our own. But to examine our own power structures reveals that across the generations, there is no sense in the Punjabi community of unity with other marginalized cultures. The phrase "woman of color" (used mostly by women of my generation) provides a new opportunity for affinity with other nonwhite cultures, but in order to seize this opportunity, we must overcome the rampant anti-Blackness in the Punjabi diaspora. This anti-Blackness has several sources, making it all the more difficult to dismantle. First, the British Raj and colonization of India elevated whiteness in India and created a disturbing structure of colorism—to be white was to be in power, and to be valued. The first wave of immigrants from Punjab (as they reeled from the brutal destruction of Partition) carried this elevation of whiteness over to the UK, where they came face-to-face with other immigrant communities, many from the Caribbean or from African countries such as Nigeria and Ghana (communities from both are interwoven with Punjabi communities in the UK, particularly in Birmingham). This aspiration to whiteness caused Punjabi immigrants to want to place themselves above these other immigrant communities, which over the years has developed into anti-Blackness in the form of stereotyping and offensive behavior. Until this anti-Blackness is unraveled and rejected, our feminism cannot be intersectional.

Our feminism is also in danger of becoming exclusive to the diaspora. Punjabi women in India and Pakistan face many challenges, and our feminism must support them, too. Punjabi feminists in the diaspora are closely linked to Western feminism, and this holds its own pitfalls. We mustn't inflict our feminist framework on the issues faced by non-diaspora Punjabi women. One example is cultural appropriation, white women who wear bindis and mehndi (henna)—a touchy subject for the Punjabi diaspora, but one that has little to no impact on the lives of women in India and Pakistan. While it should not be trivialized, it also shouldn't be projected onto other feminist frameworks. There is a culture of silence around discussing issues that has arisen in the UK diaspora, and it can have long-lasting effects (mental health issues are rampant and often ignored). The conversation does need to be opened here, while also protecting women of other nonwhite cultures and remaining sensitive to the ongoing feminist movement in India and Pakistan. White feminism needs to evolve to include these issues, and to advocate for women of color in a way that transcends its current focus. A more inclusive feminism can only have beneficial effects on both Punjabi diaspora women and Punjabi women in India, as well as nonwhite women across diasporas.

It's difficult to see where we go from here. From being an overlooked feminist movement to becoming incompatible with white feminism, feminism in the Punjabi diaspora isn't finished with its evolution and it shouldn't be. Though the steps taken are not seen as significant when measured against the milestones of Western feminism, they are hugely vital for future British Punjabi generations. Until white feminism evolves to include the concerns of nonwhite women, *feminist* isn't a word that will sit comfortably in the mouths of Punjabi women in the diaspora. Perhaps what is needed is a new word, one that encompasses this movement our mothers have started and the challenges we've faced since.

Looking forward, the next generation of Punjabi women will find a way to further this movement within the diaspora. My hope is that by then, mainstream feminism will look very different, and include space for the women who are changing a culture through many small rebellions.

ENDS, MEANS, AND SUBTERFUGE IN FEMINIST ACTIVISM

Emer O'Toole

IRELAND WILL HOLD a referendum on abortion in 2018. By the time you read this you'll know something I don't: whether the Irish electorate agrees that pregnant people should have autonomy over their bodies. It's going to be a tough couple of months of campaigning, replete with emotionally charged conversations tackling abortion myths and getting called baby killers. But we're feminists, right? We're used to this beat.

However, there might be something required by the campaign that we're less used to: namely subterfuge. The more I look at the lay of the land, the more I think that one of the most powerful feminist strategies in advance of the abortion referendum might be not to pose as feminists at all. And I'll do it. I'll do whatever it takes to win. I can't stand the thought of the next generation of Irish women and trans and nonbinary folk inheriting this mess.

And how did I inherit it, you ask? Why does Ireland need a vote on abortion at all? Well, you need to hold a referendum to change the bunreacht, or constitution, which was originally written in 1937. This ensures that a government can't wantonly dismantle the fundamental principles of the state, but also that the bunreacht is a living document, capable of reflecting society's evolution over time. For example, we needed a referendum to legalize gay marriage in 2015 because the bunreacht defined marriage as a union between a man and a woman. Over 62 percent of the Irish population voted in favor of recognizing same-sex relationships as equal to opposite-sex ones. There are pros and cons to this system of constitutional change, but with a population of 4.5 million, at least the Republic of Ireland is small enough to have a meaningful national conversation.

There was no mention of abortion in Ireland's original 1937 bunreacht. However, in the early 1980s, conservative Catholic lobby groups, frenzied by the Republic's recent legalization of contraception, pushed for a referendum to authorize a constitutional amendment giving the "life of the unborn" moral and legal equivalence with the life of the woman carrying it. Ireland in 1983 was still a deeply religious—I'd argue even theocratic—society; people voted overwhelmingly in support of the proposal. The resultant Eighth Amendment to the bunreacht reads:

> The State acknowledges the right to life of the unborn and, with due regard to the equal right to life of the mother, guarantees in its laws to respect, and, as far as practicable, by its laws to defend and vindicate that right.

With its passage, Ireland became the only country in the democratic world with a constitutional ban on abortion.

The Eighth Amendment is thirty-four years old as I write this, meaning that no woman of reproductive age currently living in the Republic ever had a chance to vote on it. Since 1983, Ireland has liberalized greatly: From 1985, you could buy condoms without a prescription; in 1993, homosexuality was decriminalized through parliamentary means; in 1995, after another divisive referendum, divorce was legalized by the tiniest electoral margin; 2015 brought the joy of the marriage equality referendum, and later that year the Oireachtas (parliament) passed an extremely liberal transgender recognition bill and struck down laws that allowed Catholic schools to discriminate against LGBTQ teachers. Hell, our current Taoiseach (prime minister), Leo Varadkar, is an openly gay person of color, which—while his politics often suck—would have been unthinkable thirty-four years ago. All of this would seem to suggest we're different now.

Yet when it comes to reproductive rights, Ireland can't seem to pull itself out of the church pews. We have some of the most restrictive abortion laws in the world; termination is permitted only to save the pregnant person's life. This is obviously a feminist issue—without full reproductive rights, women, trans folk, and nonbinary folk cannot exercise autonomy over their health, socioeconomic situations, careers, or families. And it's a class issue. Those who need abortions and have the economic means to do so can make the trip to England for the care they need. In practice, this means that middle-class women have abortions, while working-class women have babies. It's also a race issue. In Ireland, asylum seekers are housed in a dreadful system called *direct provision* while their claims are being processed. They're given less than twenty-five dollars a week to live on, and their accommodations and meals are provided in substandard institutions. The vast majority of those in direct provision are people of color from Africa and Asia. Of course, without the proper documentation, pregnant asylum seekers can't travel to get an abortion. Finally, abortion in Ireland is an ability issue. Pregnancy can affect those with physical or mental disabilities in dangerous ways. Getting to England or mainland Europe for a termination is simply easier for the abled. Some folks are more at risk of hemorrhaging on the plane home than others. Some folks have more need of medical aftercare, and many people who travel to England for abortions never tell a doctor in Ireland, out of shame or fear.

Abortion in Ireland is clearly an intersectional issue. Intersectional feminism compels us to think about the ways in which multifaceted burdens interact, rendering some more vulnerable than others, and to work from this awareness in our feminist activism, rather than assuming the category of "woman" as a one-size-fits-all measure of disadvantage. What happens to an asylum seeker with severe depression who wishes to terminate her pregnancy? To a working-class woman in a wheelchair?

The American pro-choice writer Katha Pollitt recently puzzled over the fact that LGBTQ rights have advanced so profoundly while reproductive rights won by feminists during the 1960s and 1970s remain under attack. Her exploration of why this is the case is nuanced and multifaceted, but one problem she identifies is that cis men can be gay, but they can't be pregnant. In a 2015 article for *The Nation*, she writes:

> Reproductive rights are inescapably about women. Pervasive misogyny means not only that those rights are stigmatized . . . but that men don't see them as all that important, while women have limited social power to promote them. And that power is easily endangered by too close an identification with all but the most anodyne version of feminism.

This is such an important observation to apply to the context of the battle for reproductive rights in Ireland, because even though reproductive rights are clearly a feminist issue, and very much an intersectional feminist issue, flying a feminist flag might well endanger women's rights in the upcoming referendum.

The idea that identification with feminism won't win you any popularity contests probably isn't news to many of us in the movement. If you believe what the daily papers have reported across a century of women's activism, the suffragettes were destroying the very fabric of society; the second-wavers were angry, man-hating witches; and contemporary feminism (which I understand as the third wave) is currently coming for your freedom of speech and then kidnapping your children to raise them in gender-neutral conditioning camps where the boys are only allowed to play with dolls and the girls are trained in state-of-the-art castration techniques. Hillary Clinton's feminist platform did her no favors in 2016, while Donald Trump's pussy grabbing did him no harm. And this is par for the activist course. When feminism is a majority movement—when the preponderance of people in a society recognize men and women as equals, are disgusted by misogyny, and work toward eradicating women's historically inscribed disadvantage—we won't need feminism anymore.

The suspicion of feminist rhetoric that Pollitt positions as endangering reproductive rights is absolutely evident in the polling information we have about attitudes regarding abortion in Ireland. As of late 2017, polls consistently show a strong majority in favor of liberalizing Ireland's laws to allow for termination in cases of rape, incest, danger to the health of the mother, and fatal fetal abnormality; however, the polls also indicate that most Irish people are not on board with the idea that women should be able to choose to terminate. This is telling. Folks who believe that abortion is permissible in the case of rape, but not permissible in the case of accidental pregnancy from consensual sex, are not actually condemning abortion; rather the moral axis here is the sexual behavior—the blameworthiness—of the pregnant person. While tragic stories of women as victims of male sexual violence or of wanted pregnancies with fetal abnormalities have managed to make inroads against the conservative Catholic logic that life begins at conception, the moral principle of women's bodily autonomy has not. The feminist ethos that we should trust women to make their own reproductive choices remains the Achilles' heel of Ireland's abortion debate.

Against an aggressively antichoice culture, feminists have pushed the abortion issue to the forefront of public consciousness; feminists have done the hard work of bringing the violence caused by Ireland's antiabortion regime to light. Yet, at this juncture, identification with feminism might kill the cause. And so I ask, in all earnestness: Is it time to suck it up and purr at the patriarchy? Might we achieve feminist ends through less-than-feminist means?

Before Ireland's marriage equality referendum, LGBTQ rights organizations did a whole lot of sucking it up. The primary campaigning group, Yes Equality, carried out intensive market research on the best way to win over the middle ground. They found that homophobic fears about gay people damaging children were the soft underbelly of the debate, and that images or talk of children should be avoided. They also found that their campaign materials should avoid images of gay couples as well as openly gay spokespeople. Middle-ground voters were more likely to be convinced by someone like them—parents of gay people, for example. Guided by this research, Yes Equality created posters and leaflets that were largely text based, or used images in which you had to look hard at a group of people to tell who might be gay or straight. In the campaign for marriage equality, gay couples and families were most conspicuous by their absence. Far from shouting, "We're here! We're queer! Get used to it!" LGBTQ groups got to know their audience, and played to the crowd. You might call their campaign strategically homophobic. But does it matter, if they won?

Some might say that the framing of the debate matters as much as the result, that the ends do not justify the means. There might certainly have been a concern that the subterfuge involved in winning would mean that LGBTQ couples and families would be expected to remain hidden after the referendum. But this doesn't seem to have played out in reality: Children of gay couples now have significantly more legal protections, and in the immediate aftermath of the referendum, rights for LGBTQ folks expanded beyond access to marriage. What seems most realistically at stake in adopting what I will term "strategies of subterfuge"—in which the fears of the powerful are assuaged (or suavely omitted) in situations where there is much to gain from doing so—is the personal integrity of activists who want to be of their word, who want to speak their truth. I get this. But I also think the record can be set straight later—after we've won.

Without militant activism from groups like the Sexual Liberation Movement in the 1970s, LGBTQ rights would never have been on the agenda in the first place; still, at a certain vital juncture, activists played Mr. Nice Gay. I'm as wary of tone policing as the next woke gal. But there's a difficult logic that dictates that sometimes the best feminist tactic is to be no feminist at all; to become, rather, someone to whom the word is irrelevant, even anathema, someone to whom the basic tenets of feminism—remedying female disadvantage, ensuring bodily autonomy and equality of opportunity—are suspicious demands.

It's not difficult to put myself in those nonfeminist shoes, because I wore them once. I grew up in the West of Ireland, the most conservative part of a conservative island. I was at university before I heard the word *feminism* uttered in a positive context. I never heard anyone describe themselves as a feminist. My answers to questions regarding gender inequality involved terms like *choice* and *merit* and *hard work*. I had no access to feminist ideas, vocabulary, or community, and espousing feminist views would have made me super uncool at school (okay, *more* super uncool). I was very certainly not a feminist. How could I have been?

One of the difficulties in achieving progressive social change in Ireland is that approximately 92 percent of state-funded primary schools and 66 percent of state-funded secondary schools are managed in full or in part by the Catholic church. Students in most of these schools take classes on Catholic doctrine several times a week. I remember a classroom debate on abortion in which there was no pro-choice side. Rather, we took it in turns to adumbrate the different reasons abortion was wrong. Was it wrong because it killed an innocent unborn baby? Or because the murderous pregnant harlot should have kept her legs together in the first place? Through the power of balanced discussion, we would figure this moral quandary right out!

Pre–widespread internet, all of our information was gathered from pro-life materials distributed at stands in Galway city; they alternated between the aggressively grotesque and the childishly schmaltzy. We passed around pictures that purported to be of aborted fetuses (which I now know could not have been of aborted fetuses). One girl read a poem in which a fetus talks to the woman who is aborting it, emotionally manipulating the fuck out of us with something subtle like:

> Help me, Mammy!
> They're tearing me apart,
> My little face, my little feet,
> My baby hands, my baby heart.

The teacher at one point left the classroom to cry. At the time, I considered this an expression of piety in accordance with our morally impregnable message. But knowing now that at least 168,703 Irish women have gone to the UK for abortions since 1980, I can't help but reassess this assumption. In that classroom, we were participating in and reaffirming a culture of misinformation, stigma, and shame, though we didn't know it. How could we?

Everyone left that classroom *knowing* that abortion was wrong. When we went home to our parents that evening and told them about the day's emotionally charged religion class, we received confirmation of our beliefs. I hope that many of the girls and boys in that classroom have grown into women and men with more scientifically sound and morally compassionate views on abortion. But if I'd stayed in the West of Ireland, there's little prospect my feminist politics would look like they do now. Equally, it seems highly unlikely that most of my former classmates are pro-choice. And millions of people indoctrinated just like us at the Republic's ubiquitous Catholic schools will be voting in 2018's referendum.

These are the systems of power and control in which we are operating. We can ignore that reality and speak from our hearts with an intersectional feminist message, centering the importance of reproductive rights to women's full participation in society. It would feel good. Our Jiminy Crickets would chirp happily on our shoulders. But we might lose. And the stakes are high.

In Ireland, if you need an abortion, you call a clinic in England. You find the money for a flight or ferry, for a hotel room, for a medical procedure in a foreign health system. Unless—due to your class, your asylum status, your disability— you can't. In a culture of silence, you create excuses, tell lies about where you're going, always wondering if some suspect. You travel hundreds of miles. When the procedure is over and you so badly want your bed, you must bleed your way back to a country that thinks you're a criminal. You can't go to your doctor for follow-up care. In the unlikely event something does go wrong and you get an infection, you need to be very careful about the medical practitioner you choose to consult. Then you spend most of your life pretending it never happened, listening to armchair ethicists muse over the personhood of zygotes, argue about gestational limits. When you switch on the radio, you hear politicians and activists theorizing about your body, your life, your rights, your sins.

This has happened to too many friends of mine. It is happening to ten women today. It makes me so angry that Irish people reserve their empathy for zygotes and embryos that can't feel or think, and care nothing for women in crisis. I want to shout about bodily autonomy, about the abortion regime as a simple extension of Ireland's historical church-endorsed persecution of women, as a symptom of women's second-class citizenry in the Irish republic. I want to scream about the women who can't leave the country because they don't have the money, or the documentation, or the physical ability.

Yet when I'm home and looking into the faces of folks I know, folks I love, for whom a woman who has an abortion is a murderer, for whom a twelve-week-old fetus is a baby, I realize that—practically speaking—none of these feminist modes of analysis or argumentation are worth anything. I can't talk in feminist principles. I have to speak to the dominant ideologies that exist in my society. But how?

Historically, framing abortion as a rights issue that affects men too has been successful. In 1992, a Supreme Court judge ruled that a suicidal fourteen-year-old rape victim (known as Miss X) had the right to an abortion. The girl had been abused by a neighbor and was suffering severe mental health repercussions. Her parents planned to take her to the

UK for an abortion, but inquired first with the Gardaí—Ireland's police service—whether they should keep a DNA sample of the fetal remains to serve as evidence in the rapist's trial. As a result of the Eighth Amendment, the Irish government issued an injunction against the girl procuring an abortion overseas. Her parents appealed and the Supreme Court found that the threat to the girl's life from suicide was sufficient grounds for abortion. The girl miscarried, but the legal precedent remained.

Irish politicians were left in a jam—they needed to create legislation based on the Supreme Court ruling but they did *not* want to. Instead they put three abortion referendums to the people in 1992. The first asked the electorate to overturn the X case ruling by removing risk of suicide as grounds for abortion. The people said no. The second asked if pregnant women should be allowed to travel freely, even if they planned to have an abortion. The people said yes. The third asked if information about abortion in other countries should be legally available. The people said yes. Go people! All of these newly liberal attitudes were a product of the X case.

Having received their answers, the politicians still did nothing to legislate. The country acted in accordance with the referendum results, but no solid legal framework as to how doctors should proceed in the case of suicidal pregnant people was provided. Then, in 2002, the government wondered if perhaps they'd heard wrong the first time, and they put another referendum to the people, asking if they were *sure* they didn't want to remove suicide as grounds for abortion. The people again said that a suicidal woman had the right to a termination, but by a significantly smaller margin this time. Time to legislate, one would think! But the government did not seem to be able to hear the will of the people inside the echo chamber of the Dáil. They didn't legislate.

Then, in 2012, a woman died. Her name was Savita

Halappanavar. She was an Indian dentist who had been living with her husband, Praveen, in Galway, my hometown. She was thirty-one years old and it was her first pregnancy. At seventeen weeks she began to miscarry and, knowing the fetus could not survive, she requested an abortion. If she had received one, according to Dr. Peter Boylan's expert testimony at her inquest, she would be alive today. However, because of the Eighth Amendment, medical professionals would not abort while there was still a fetal heartbeat unless there was a real and substantive risk to Savita's life. They had to wait until either the heartbeat stopped or Savita had life-threatening sepsis to do anything—a situation devoid of logic, governed only by misogynistic ideology, that resulted in great tragedy. Her family, in particular her husband, took the case to the Irish press and courts. I think that the Halappanavars' immigrant perspective is part of why the case made the papers at all. They dared to question the orthodoxy. Savita, a highly educated woman from a medical family, requested an abortion when she understood she was miscarrying, and when it was explained to her by a truthful midwife (who was viciously scapegoated by the Irish media later) that the reason she could not have one was that Ireland is a Catholic country, she protested that she was neither Irish nor Catholic. This element of the tragedy was reported in news sources around the world.

The public outcry over Savita's death—over the horror of monitoring the heartbeat of a second-trimester fetus that could not be saved while the woman carrying it deteriorated—forced the Irish government to legislate for the X case. It had taken twenty years and a woman's life for them to do so. Sadly, the resultant legislation is so restrictive that in the four years since it passed it has been proved entirely unequal to its intended purpose. When it was passed, the Abortion Rights Campaign said that it was doubtful that the act would grant a pregnant suicidal teenage rape victim access to abortion. This turned out to be not only true but prophetic. In 2014, a pregnant suicidal teenage asylum seeker—Miss Y— was forcibly hydrated when she went on a hunger strike, compelled to carry until twenty-five weeks, and then C-sectioned.

Ireland's antiabortion regime is responsible for a litany of abuses. There are Miss A's, B's, and C's—an alphabet of victimization. And of course there's the mundane reality of all the women who choose to make the journey to the UK and mainland Europe every day. There's the desperation of those who can't—who self-administer illegal abortion pills, or worse. But these two cases—Miss X and Savita—are the ones that made the biggest impact in terms of public opinion and political action.

Let's think about who we're asked to empathize with in both cases. If the Yes Equality campaign for marriage equality found that Ireland's middle ground was best convinced by someone "like them"—the parents of a gay person, for example—the X case and Savita indicate that for abortion, something similar is true.

The public were not simply asked to empathize with a suicidal pregnant teenager. They were asked to empathize with the mother and father of an abused child. What parents would force their little girl to carry her rapist's child to term? These were ordinary people, like us. We couldn't let this happen again.

When Praveen, Savita's heartbroken husband, spoke to the press about his wife's senseless death and the Catholic ideology informing the care she received, the terrible spectacle of his bewilderment and misery made people listen in a way that no woman describing her victimization by the Eighth Amendment could. I remember a conversation with my brother shortly afterward in which he said that Savita's death had changed a number of his male friends' minds on abortion. That could be their wives. That could be them. If men require obfuscation of the civil rights issues facing women in order to get on board with abortion legislation, then let's obfuscate. In Catholic Ireland, men have the power. If right now abortion needs to be not about women and trans folk, not about class, not about race, not about ability, but about men, let's make it about men.

In 2014, a brain-dead woman from the Irish midlands was kept alive against her family's will as a cadaveric incubator for her second-trimester fetus. The family had to go to court to have the life support switched off. The reaction of the Taoiseach at the time, antichoice politician Enda Kenny, was surprisingly compassionate. "Let anybody put themselves in the shoes of this family," he said.

In a country in which a woman needs to be dying before we can countenance her need for an abortion, it should come as no surprise that the way to appeal to public sensibilities is not to ask people to put themselves in the shoes of raped teenagers, women carrying fetuses with fatal fetal abnormalities, women in abusive relationships, women who can't afford another child, women with mental health issues, women for whom the pregnancy is a personal crisis, or women who simply don't want to be pregnant, but rather to ask them to consider the parents of raped teenagers, the husbands of women carrying fetuses with fatal abnormalities, the children of women suffering from abuse, mental illness, or poverty, the families of women in crisis.

Katha Pollitt says abortion is unmistakably about women, yet the cases that have moved public opinion and legislation forward in Ireland are ones in which that simple fact is obscured. The power that women do have to speak about abortion is, as Pollitt suggests, endangered by an association with feminism. So perhaps this is the time to seriously ask, "What about the men?"

Playing the strategic misogyny game is painful, even humiliating. It's in opposition to all of my feminist principles. But I remember back to that classroom debate, to how convinced everyone in that room—myself included—was of their moral rectitude. All of my former classmates can't be feminists, and to reach them, we can't be either.

The perfect is the enemy of the good, and in this moment, as I try to convince loved ones and strangers in Ireland of the moral necessity of repealing the Eighth Amendment, I am adopting a public and a private face. If we win (oh, please, *when* we win), I'll bring bolshy back. But a functional intersectional feminism must fight against the idea that strategic thinking makes us impure; it must acknowledge that neglecting to highlight intersectional narratives is in some very specific cases justified, that appealing to the needs of the most marginalized may sometimes hurt our cause, while appealing to the fears of the powerful may help it. This is likely true beyond the Irish case; so let's be cognizant of it as we strive in our own feminist communities and through our own feminist means to create a more just and equal world.

By the time you read this, you'll know something that I do not: whether the Irish electorate agrees that pregnant people should have autonomy over their bodies.

I hope you know something good.

AFRO-DIASPORIC FEMINISM AND A FREEDOM IN FLUIDITY

Zoé Samudzi

MY FIRST REAL understanding of my apparent poor grasp of my own culture—at least, beyond the painful self-consciousness of not being able to speak my mother tongue—came when a diaspora auntie made a joke about my poor etiquette, commenting that my parents had not taught me the proper way of engaging elders, and other everyday things like traditional ways of greeting. "What *did* your parents teach you?" I remember her asking me incredulously.

But my parents, even as immigrants to the United States and despite having been socialized into Zimbabwean traditions before they emigrated, are not the picture of upstanding cultural torchbearers. My father recently told me a story about what happened when he explained my parents' division of domestic labor to his family shortly after they were married in the mid-1980s. When he told them that he would wash dishes when my mother cooked and they would both take care of household chores, people in his house laughed, contemptuously referring to his willingness to share such responsibilities as "those feminist things." Their laughter confused him: He wasn't trying to embody a feminist politics; he simply rejected the idea that household work should be gendered. To him, it made sense that all of the household labor should be equally divided, rather than what was considered the "women's work"—responsibility for cooking and cleaning and childcare—falling solely on my mother.

Members of my extended family, some of whom were those very same conservative family members who scoffed at my father, have over the years commented in horror at my facial piercings, tattoos, and (sometimes) brightly colored hair. But my self-presentation is no longer a symptom of a "rebellious phase"; I'm an adult, and this is how I choose to express myself. My ability to do so is, at least in some part, the result of my parents instilling in me the importance of autonomy and a refusal to self-police to please others—a sense of freedom invaluable to Black women whose identities and fates are constantly defined by everyone and everything *but* themselves. Rather than teaching me to perform on-demand deference to elders, they taught me the things they felt were most important: independence and autonomy. There were contradictions, of course, as with all parents.

As immigrants often do—for unfortunate reasons, some of which are admittedly pragmatic—my parents tended toward assimilation. They pushed me to aspire to be just like everybody else (i.e. my white middle-class peers), which was their metric of success. We spoke only English at home, the rationale being there was no real reason for my brother and me to speak or understand Shona, our mother tongue. But despite this push for assimilation, my parents were not always so outwardly accepting of my desire to be "typically American." There was a strange dissonance in this: I was raised to reject certain parts of my culture and identity that they believed would potentially prevent me from becoming "fully" American, and yet it was made painfully clear that I was not American. My parents were strict; I went to academic camps during the summer and did extra math and book reports during the school year, and I wasn't allowed to do the things my "little [white] friends" in the suburban Midwest were doing, like hang out at the mall. I was never allowed to be complacent about getting *almost* perfect test scores. And I was always called from wherever else in the house I was to the living room to help my mother find the remote control—a cliché in African households.

As I got older, my identity and politics came into conflict with my parents' values. My mother did not respond particularly well to my telling her that I liked girls when I was in middle school. Though she was a progressive enough person, she lacked the language and tools to understand how to support me; she simply assured me, a tearful thirteen-year-old, that I would grow out of my confusing feelings. Later, both of my parents became nervous about my blossoming racial politics, which challenged the anti-Black exceptionalism they had subtly instilled within me. I was increasingly coming to understand that I, as a first generation American of African descent, was not special compared to other African Americans, no matter how many stereotypes I was pushed to believe. Though these reactions may have embodied stereotypes of "archetypal" African parents, they were nontraditional in so many ways. My mother made decisions on behalf of the household, and for the past decade, they have spent much of the year not living together because my mother spends half of each month on the East Coast. They have a relationship built on communication and a respect for one another's agency, which allows my mother to be largely independent, and travel whenever and wherever she sees fit. Neither of my parents saw a need to maintain a household grounded in the "tradition"-based patriarchal values that would require my mother's subservience and submissiveness to my father. I guess you can call that feminism, if you'd like.

————

I'VE GRAPPLED FOR a long time with what it means to be and to describe oneself as a feminist. Over time, I have toyed with a number of different descriptors, first "feminist," then "Black feminist," then "womanist," and so on.

Growing up surrounded by whiteness meant that my initial exposures to feminism were all through white women, specifically second-wave feminists. But as I came to understand more about the importance of domestic labor and care work, the uncomfortable empowered woman/oppressed woman binary of "working woman/housewife" frequently espoused by the second wave left me uneasy. The absence of anything vaguely resembling color, particularly given the gendered violence of chattel slavery, and the long history of Black women's reproductive labor in white homes in the United States (both forced and otherwise), did, too. It wasn't until college that I became familiar with Black feminism, a politics rooted specifically in understanding racial and classed and gendered experiences. I did not have to forcibly insert myself into an unyielding and exclusionary feminism because Black women were making their own. I didn't have to endure the silent discomfort and alienation of trying to use sets of theories that clearly weren't made with me, or women like me, in mind. I got to be Black and a woman at the same time, instead of jamming myself into the dominant but still ill-fitting notion of womanhood. Through Black feminism I also discovered, after my years of alienation as a Black (but "not really" Black, as I was reminded by white peers) intruder in lily-white suburbia, that there was a global community of Afro-diasporic first-generation women who also struggled with reconciling their class, cultural, racial/ethnic, and national identities.

I am still sometimes unsure about what it means to call

myself a feminist because of how often it seems that simply describing oneself as such is more important than the content of one's politics. I see, for example, women who refuse to validate the womanhood of trans women or the agency and needs of women in sex work celebrated as feminists. And because there seem to be public grappling with feminism that range from more radical ideas of gendered liberation to an idea of simply equality between men and women, it becomes unclear what it actually means to be "a feminist" depending on who you are engaging. But I am nonetheless appreciative of the Black women who have poured their hearts and souls into work that allows me to be affirmed and freed in my own right and not simply in proximity to white women.

As liberating as it was to gain access to feminist politics that were centered around my specific identity as a Black woman instead of a flattened idea of "womanhood" that was implicitly white, I began to increasingly and less comfortably grapple with other identities. My sense of self as a Zimbabwean woman, sowed by spending part of my formative years in Harare with my family in the late 1990s, when I was five, six, and seven years old, was growing, as was my sense of detachment from the very white American value system I had been taught was desirable by my parents. My sense of national identity can be best summarized by Toni Morrison: "In this country, American means white. Everyone else has to hyphenate."

When I returned to Harare for a conference in 2015, my first visit in nearly fifteen years, I found myself rediscovering and negotiating my identity in entirely new ways. When I checked in at the conference, the man at the registration desk saw my middle and surnames and said, "Welcome home." Clichéd as my grateful tears may have been, there was tremendous comfort in being somewhere that felt more like home than a white nationalist birth country that, at every opportunity, made me feel like an unwelcome alien, despite the sacred blue passport that was my birthright. "Home" is not always an easy place for Black people in the United States to locate.

After visiting Zimbabwe that following year for Christmas, I returned to the United States with a Zimbabwean birth certificate. In claiming my Zimbabwean citizenship (my birthright since the 2013 constitutional referendum), I was claiming a part of myself that feels less attainable for me in the United States because of my geographic distance from the land where my family is from. Zimbabwe is the home of my ancestors, a space of anti-colonial resistance, and a land of indigenous creation where, despite the legacies of African patriarchies and neocolonialism, I am able to gain an understanding of myself as a Black woman that I am less able to access in the United States because of how Blackness (and Black womanhood specifically) is often seen through the lens of white supremacist violence.

In the years of trying to learn more about the history and politics of Zimbabwe from non-Western accounts, I turned, first, to literature. Tsitsi Dangarembga's semiautobiographical *Nervous Conditions* is a coming-of-age story about a Zimbabwean girl named Tambu who, following the death of her older brother, has the opportunity to attend his mission school and stay with her successful British-bred uncle, Babamukuru. Babamukuru's children, Nyasha and Chido, were raised in England. While Chido is content with his colonizer's sensibilities, Nyasha, like her mother, yearns for a sense of independence beyond the Zimbabwean customs and her father's "traditional" authoritarianism. Tambu's navigation of traditional norms and expectations constructs something of a binary between customary values of antiquity and the newly opened door of opportunity that the apparently solely Western value of education could potentially offer. The book's title is derived from Jean-Paul Sartre's introduction to Frantz Fanon's *The Wretched of the Earth*:

> Our enemy betrays his brothers and becomes our accomplice; his brothers do the same thing. The status of "native" is a *nervous condition* introduced and maintained by the settler among colonized people *with their consent*.

Dangarembga's book examines the colonial dichotomy between tradition and modernity in the context of a postcolonial Zimbabwe. I identified in different ways with Maiguru (Nyasha's mother), Nyasha, and Tambu, all of whom are intelligent women whose education and ambition clash constantly with constraining gendered circumstances shaped by traditional patriarchal expectations.

I also discovered the work of historians like Alois S. Mlambo. I was struggling to understand my feminist politics within the context of Zimbabwean traditions because I sometimes found the two to be at odds with one another. In his comprehensive history of Zimbabwe (aptly titled *A History of Zimbabwe*), he describes, in the name of patriarchy-stained notions of traditional gender relations, how traditional leaders colluded with colonial administrators to stymie the increasing autonomy that native women had following the introduction of the migrant work systems in colonial Rhodesia. He writes: "Because of the absence of the men from the villages, women were forced to take over the duties and activities that used to be fulfilled by men, such as threshing grain, tending cattle and clearing and plowing the land." Women migrated to urban areas from the countryside and became engaged in capitalist labor markets, "working as domestics in white homes or as farm and factory hands." Other women entered the informal economy as sex workers or brewers of illegal alcohol, even engaging in never formalized and transactional *mapoto,* or "cooking pot," marriages, which freed women from traditional wifely obligations and duties—such as becoming a part of their husbands' families or extending the family line by bearing children—and allowed them to retain much of their agency. Under such arrangements men and women would cohabit so as to satisfy one another's sexual and economic needs, but women were not wedded to obligations imposed by the law or tradition. The result of these changes was that women became decreasingly reliant on a male breadwinner and on their traditional leaders for financial and social support. Members of the latter group were incensed at their loss of control and urbanity's corruption of *their* women, as well as the loss of supplemental income that accompanied the migration. (There were taxes paid to traditional leadership.) Their desire to shackle women to rural areas was shared by colonial administrators, who were more able to surveil and regulate native social and economic life in the countryside than in the city. With the thinly veiled justification of "tradition," this shared misogyny and collusion was put into a law that made "'African women into permanent legal minors' and [codified] 'polygamy and the system of bride-wealth payments known as *lobola.*'" In 1916, the Natives Adultery Punishment Ordinance was passed in an effort to control both women's migration and their "promiscuity." The ordinance was intended to "deter 'men from leaving their homes to seek employment out of fear that their wives will misconduct themselves during the husband's absences.'" If the men remained at home, they would be able to both pay taxes levied by traditional leaders and maintain traditional family structures.

Tradition, I'd later realize, isn't a single history that I

could memorize. Rather, it's almost entirely dependent upon who's recalling it. History often becomes a weapon because the notions of history that are shared and publicly remembered are usually steeped in patriarchy. This is a reality that I have had to continuously interrogate and reconcile as I seek to discover and embrace my roots.

Black feminisms, African feminisms, clearly described to me the structural links between my experiences as a Black woman in the United States and my subordinated identity as a woman in Zimbabwe whenever I return. Through European colonialism's imposition of value systems upon the African continent, European understandings of gender were also imposed upon African people. In *The Invention of Women: Making an African Sense of Western Gender Discourses*, Oyèrónkẹ̀ Oyěwùmí explains that for the Oyo-Yoruba people from what is now western and north central Nigeria, gender (i.e. the binary system that we understand today) was not an organizing social category until the colonial restructuring of Yoruba society. Her account has been contested, and isn't applicable to the entire continent, and of course it is irresponsible to conclude that no sex and gender divisions existed among any African peoples before the Europeans arrived. But it is still an important reading of colonial history that seeks to make sense of the creation of rigid gender constructs that were frequently adopted by colonized peoples, a project that has frequently been taken up by African feminists within their scholarly and other work.

In the tradition of existing African feminisms, I have had to create my own Afro-feminist politics, which has meant blending my own politics and value systems with my own understanding of traditions, taking into account the ways dominant interpretations of cultural practice can be harmful to young Zimbabwean women like me. This feminism is inclusive of all Zimbabwean people who have marginalized identities or engage in behaviors that mark them as "deviant": gay men brutalized by the state through the criminalization of "sodomy," lesbians subjected to harassment and "corrective" sexual violence, transgender women unable to self-express as they desire, and so on. This is critical for me as a bisexual woman.

However, I have to step back for a moment and contest the idea that being queer or trans is "un-African." In southern Africa, there has historically been more tolerance and allowance of sexually nonconforming behavior than is presently acknowledged. Within the context of an intimate friendship called *sahwira*, young men were, in the past, more able to share private details of their lives with one another (including about their wives' sexual performance) and were able to sexually experiment without any negative social consequence. What we might now describe as trans expression was socially acceptable if perceived to be caused by some kind of possession by a spirit of a different sex. Known as a *murumekadzi* or "man-woman," a man could occupy the public social role of his wife and do all of the chores typically attributed to a woman; the female counterpart was known as *mukadzirume*, "woman-man." Though the activity may have been justified by the desire to please a future husband, same-sex touching among young women was perfectly appropriate in the context of *kusenga*, the practice of manual labial stretching.

It has become necessary to create a feminism for myself that is fluid and open to change, because of the way my sense of self has changed over time, and also because my identity varies in all the different spaces that I occupy: Being a young Black woman in the United States is not the same as being a young Shona woman in Zimbabwe. The politics that I embody and espouse must account for that difference, because my navigation of gendered and ethnic/racial and social expectations are heavily dependent upon my location. One frequent shortcoming of mainstream feminism is its rigidity and oversimplification: We often create binaries dictating whether an act or some cultural production is "feminist" or not, with the answer often supplied by dominant feminisms, like those held by cisgender heterosexual and middle-class white women.

For example, feminists have long debated marriage, an institution that many women perceive to be "unfeminist" (particularly if you take your husband's surname) but that may afford other women the financial security they need to survive. While I might change my mind in the future, I have no present desire to get married. But if there were a person that I did feel I wanted to spend my life with, I think I'd insist on an updated traditional marriage practice, an adapted *lobola* consisting of our families gathering and exchanging things of sentimental value, rather than my partner paying my parents cattle or cash equivalent as tradition dictates. Patriarchal politics around marriage seem to revolve around our 'worth' as women and male ownership of our bodies (which is transferred from our fathers to our husbands). Our sexual politics, particularly for Black women, seek to liberate us from patriarchal controls over our bodies that span the diaspora. These politics center sexual consent, highlight the hypocrisy of unmarried women's virginity as praiseworthy (especially important in places that still practice virginity testing), and emphasize the importance of bodily autonomy and sexual agency. They combat social attitudes in which the threat or acts of sexual violence are received as acceptable indications of domination of men over women, of "cultural" ideas that our bodies and freedoms as women belong to our would-be husbands, and our actions as unmarried women should include or revolve around improving our prospects as future wives. My personal sexual politics are also contextual.

Embracing my queer identity is undoubtedly a feminist act, but my personal truth is an altogether different story from coming out to my extended family, which is, unfortunately, unlikely to happen. Queer visibility can be more harmful than it is beneficial or freeing, though conversations about visibility and representation as "progress" often dominate popular LGBTQ conversations in the Western world.

BEING BORN ACROSS the Atlantic does not weaken my claim to my Zimbabweanness, my identity as *mwana wevhu* (a nationalist expression meaning child, or daughter, of the soil, referring to indigenous Zimbabwean ancestry). My Black feminism and my queer identity, which have been described to me as "Western" things, are not antithetical to any notion of Africanness because Africanness is not in a state of arrested development, entombed at the moment of European arrival. That is a logic held by both our former colonizers and the masculine gatekeepers of tradition empowered by them. There's an irony in how so many Africans reject colonially imposed notions of who and what we are, yet cling tightly to systems of rigid gendered organization and oppression that Europeans forced upon colonized subjects. Our feminism as African women, and as women regardless of location or diaspora, can also reproduce these systems of oppression. This is why intersectionality is such a vital framework for understanding systems of power, because "woman" is not a catchall category that alone defines all of our relationships to power. If we rely on gender alone, we fail to engage in a struggle that is truly inclusive or liberating. Intersectionality allows me to understand how I, as a cis woman, can harm trans women by defining womanhood around certain biological functions—like childbirth or menstruation—or certain life experiences, such as a childhood where they were able to express themselves and be received as young girls, which many trans women did not have.

As I GRAPPLE increasingly with the idea of spending more time in Zimbabwe, I'm finding that while many of us young Zimbabweans share many of the same conservative values as our parents, others still are grappling with our African and diasporic identities in entirely different contexts. The continent contains histories in which we can ground ourselves, as well as creative precedents for the telling of new or resurrected less oppressive African stories that might lend themselves to the creation of more inclusive and expansive futures. White Western women did not export feminism to African women, as some anti-feminist African men might tell you; African women were resisting colonial violence and subverting familiar patriarchies even before white women began fighting for suffrage. It is in the legacy of those women—women like Nehanda Nyakasikana (who was a spiritual leader that inspired the Shona people to revolt against British colonization in the late 1800s), like my maternal grandmother (who taught my mother to refuse patriarchal demands)—that we understand ourselves and our gendered struggle. My respect for tradition—the ways I treasure and honor my ancestors, the ways I often defer to my elders, the way I love and respect the land itself (and by extension, myself)—need not come at the expense of my safety, my well-being, or my personhood. My Shona culture and the beliefs and practices therein are dear to me, but a self-annihilating sense of sacrifice to maintain each is not. For women like me, a fluid Afro-diasporic feminism can help us to embody our multiple identities and realities simultaneously, and to recognize that while we are knowers and interpreters of "tradition," we can also create new notions of culture and history and tradition that free rather than stifle us.

REPRESENTATION AS A
FEMINIST ACT

|||||||||||||||||||||||||||||||||||||||||||||||||||||||||||||||||||||||||||||||||||||||||||||||||||||||||||||||||||||||||||||||||||||||||||||||||

Aisha Gani

IN MY HOUSE, she is known by her first name: Nadiya. From my mum asking when Nadiya is on the telly, to my older sister mailing me a copy of her cookbook as a surprise and my teenage niece rustling up her version of cheese scones over a weekend, Nadiya seems like part of the family.

In my friendship circle, Nadiya Hussain—the thirty-three-year-old winner of the sixth season of *The Great British Bake Off*, the quintessentially British competitive baking show with millions of faithful viewers—has inspired intense discussion. This discussion includes what she means for the representation of women of color in the public sphere, for intersectional feminism, and for us personally when we see her on the cover of women's magazines (which still is a very white space). We have also discussed what it means to us to see her excel and do something she is passionate about, and how she handles gendered anti-Muslim comments on social media.

As a young British-Bangladeshi Muslim woman, watching Nadiya Hussain win Britain's much-loved baking show in 2015 was personal for me. In a victory speech that made millions of viewers tear up, she held a bouquet of flowers in her hands and said, "I'm never gonna put boundaries on myself ever again. I'm never gonna say I can't do it. I'm never gonna say 'maybe.' I'm never gonna say, 'I don't think I can.' I can and I will."

It was a moment of British television that spoke to me and reminded me it was time to lock away the doubt and impostor syndrome that so many women internalize. I remember thinking, *I can relate.* Here was a woman of color speaking honestly about the challenges of self-doubt in a society where women of color, in particular visibly Muslim women, and the children of immigrants, are often viewed only in certain roles. For me, her triumph also sent a bold message to white feminism: A brown woman can choose motherhood, can enjoy baking, and can go on to have a career in television on her own terms. Her win suggested that a successful woman does not have to look a particular way. Nadiya's winning speech was a feminist statement for me. It was a powerful expression. The very fact it was said out loud was self-actualizing and was an example of her leaning in on her own terms.

Going to work the next day, I remember hearing conversations about her at the national news desk where I was employed. My colleagues were ecstatic about the fact Nadiya had won. She had become a national treasure for her wonderful facial expressions and because she was likable. People were genuinely rooting for this hometown heroine, albeit for different reasons than I was. I had never seen anyone on British television whom I could identify with so strongly.

When Nadiya first walked into the *Bake Off* "tent," the studio where Britain's best amateur baker would be found, she was a stay-at-home mum with three children and a love of baking. Now, three years on, she is the winner of a major show and has released two cookbooks and a number of children's books. She hosted *The Big Family Cooking Showdown* and *Junior Bake Off*, filmed *The Chronicles of Nadiya* in Bangladesh, and baked the Queen a birthday cake. Nadiya has also become a columnist for the *Times* newspaper and made appearances on other British prime-time TV shows, including *The One Show* and *Loose Women*. It is brilliant to see a woman of color excelling.

Nadiya's achievements and choices demonstrate how important representation is. Many women will be inspired when they see a woman of color in a high-profile position doing something she loves. A brown Muslim woman on-screen helps bring an undeniable amount of social capital and, some may say, helps raise the profile of an otherwise underrepresented voice. And being unapologetic and proud of going places—while facing microaggressions from dominant groups—is a powerful feminist act.

For me, one of the most powerful motivations in being in the public sphere as a journalist is being reminded how a young person out there may just see you and be inspired to also chase their own particular dream. An intersectional feminist myself, I believe this is crucial. But at the same time, I see the ways in which representation can be a double bind. The way in which women of color are expected to explain themselves to white feminists, sometimes even reinforcing the dominant perception, is where representation for representation's sake becomes problematic.

When we do anything remotely different or are successful and perceived to be "breaking stereotypes," we are thrust into a spotlight, but these stereotypes are placed on us by someone else. We then have to be ready with answers for the dominant group, who never have to explain themselves or their existence. There is an expectation that we have an emotional story, with exotic embellishments, about overcoming cultural or religious pressures and trauma, which we will then recount for the benefit of the white gaze.

This burden of having to represent when there is no choice in it can sometimes feel like it is only for white feminist consumption. And that is why representation can sometimes look like a check-the-box exercise—a Band-Aid that masks the lack of structural change in feminism and elsewhere—and why it can look disingenuous. Like a show with one character of color in the background, who has little agency or speaking parts but is good for the optics. We want to speak for ourselves and do for ourselves without the burden of having to justify our existence or success, and without being a tool for anything else. That is real agency.

I HAD HOPED the focus on Nadiya on our screens would be about what she is good at, but that was hoping too much. As she was catapulted to fame she had to speak again and again about the fact she wears a hijab. Although I found Nadiya's candid responses refreshing, particularly when she told the *Times* that she put on a hijab at age fourteen probably to cover up her "bad hair more than anything else," I was frustrated; I thought we had moved on from this obsession—but evidently not.

In another interview, Nadiya dealt with the issue of representation, telling the *Radio Times* she had "struggled at the beginning" because she thought, "Am I the token Muslim?" She said in all her years she had never before been labeled as such, but during filming it was different: "I heard it constantly, 'Oh, she's the Muslim, she's the Muslim.'"

"I certainly didn't enter a baking show in the hope of representing anyone," she said. "Being a Muslim for me was incidental, but from the day the show was launched, I was 'the thirty-year-old Muslim' and that became my identity."

People may disagree, but I find her speaking out about forced representation important. The fact that anyone from a minority community who becomes successful is robbed of their individuality because they are expected to speak for a whole community is a huge issue. Minority groups are treated like monoliths, with brown and Black women especially treated as though they have no agency. A woman of color can represent, but only within the confines of the category or box she has been placed in.

In 2017, a review was published in the *Guardian* of Nadiya's book *The Secret Lives of the Amir Sisters*, which had been described by her publishers as a heartwarming and modern British Muslim take on *Little Women*. The review was by writer Jenny Colgan, an award-winning author of numerous bestselling novels. It posed the following question about Nadiya: "Does she really need to put her name to a novel, too, when there's only so much shelf space to go around?" I have worked in bookshops, and I can confirm that the charts are overwhelmingly filled with titles by white TV celebrities who have ghostwritten autobiographies and children's books. And yes, Nadiya is a celebrity whose book was also ghostwritten, but why had this particular criticism of taking up "shelf space" come into play here and not for the others?

As a journalist, I found the incident far too relatable. It demonstrated the way in which a woman of color in the literary world can be interrogated. And it felt like the epitome of white feminist privilege. It displayed an entrenched belief that entering that space was undeserved; there was only a finite amount of it and it was being wasted. The importance of representation counted for nothing in this instance.

I was taken aback by how Nadiya could be undermined in such a manner, when there was no actual literary criticism in the review. The criticism was not about her book; it was that she was doing too much. A brown Muslim woman taking up "shelf space." How dare she. A space that is usually very white, with an abysmal record of representation of Black and minority ethnic writers—figures from *The Bookseller*, a British magazine reporting on publishing news, show that out of thousands of titles published in the UK in 2016, fewer than one hundred were by authors who are nonwhite.

As a result, Shaheen Kasmani, an artist based in Birmingham, started the twitter hashtag #TooMuchSpace. Clearly that mantra of breaking glass ceilings, a phrase we are all too familiar with as a consequence of mainstream and white feminism, did not apply to the rest of us. So people such as Shaheen had enough and felt it was important to point out this disparity publicly. She wrote, "Dear black, brown and all women of colour. Please do take up as much space as possible, whether on screens or shelves or anywhere else." Other women joined in, sharing tweets and photos of literature written by women of color taking up space on their shelves.

It was really important for marginalized women to express themselves in the wake of this review, and to support one another. That support network, while digital, is where sisterhood exists for many women of color, because we are often excluded from spaces occupied by the dominant group.

When I spoke to Shaheen about the hashtag, she said, "It just made me feel everything we do and all our achievements become very tokenistic. Because this person has got this ticked off, that person has done that—we do not need any more." In terms of representation, even though Nadiya may be seen as the perfect role model—she cooks, bakes, has a family, a husband, children, she ticks all those boxes—she is still brown and Muslim and wears a hijab, so: "The minute she wants to step out of that and do something else, they start attacking her."

SHAHEEN THINKS THIS is a good example of why some people find feminism problematic—that for many people feminism means white feminism, and that is exclusionary. It is privilege.

Working at BuzzFeed News when this article came out, I

saw this discussion about shelf space as an opportunity to invite Muslim women writers to share their work and challenges. It may seem like a trivial incident, yet it felt like a sharp reminder of the everyday aggression that women of color can face from their white women counterparts. I tried my best to channel the disappointment and provide a balance to what was presented in the review. So I profiled Muslim women authors who are currently making waves, as well as some published by smaller publishing houses around the world. This resulted in an article titled "Here's What Muslim Women Authors Have to Say About Finding Their Voice."

In the article I spoke to Shelina Janmohamed, author of *Love in a Headscarf*, who said, "I think the challenge for both Muslim women and the publishing industry—and I include in that the media—is to create a space in which Muslim women can tell stories that are not about terrorism, burkas, burkinis, or niqabs, and instead can be about anything at all and don't have to be about being Muslim whatsoever."

Na'ima B. Robert, author of young adult book *She Wore Red Trainers*, told me writing was important for her as she had "always tried to push the envelope, when it comes to characters and people of colour as main characters, and particularly in opening the door to Muslims, Muslim lifestyle, and Islam through story-telling."

This point was significant for me, as it is not for others to judge the authenticity of marginalized women's work, including the writing and work of Muslim women, just because it does not fit within an orientalist perception of what Muslim storytelling looks and sounds like.

IN MY OWN REPORTING, I try to steer clear of a framing that reinforces stereotypes or depicts Muslim women as smashing them. This seems to be the media's way of determining whether Muslim women are newsworthy or content-worthy: They make headlines if it is a story about hijabs, FGM, or forced marriage, or by proving their humanity by breaking stereotypes that others have imposed on them in the first place. I am determined to resist both modes. A Muslim woman should not be newsworthy only if she is the first visibly Muslim woman in a particular field, or even if she is a Muslim woman in what is perceived by wider society to be an unusual field. She is more than that. A simple example of this is a video by *Elle* magazine that shows four Muslim beauty influencers wearing hijab. They are labeled as "breaking stereotypes" because they are wearing makeup. Who would have thought that such a thing exists? It is patronizing and boring. In an attempt to normalize, it only serves to other.

Amani Al-Khatahtbeh, founder of lifestyle site Muslim Girl.com, told me for my article about authors finding their voice, "I feel we haven't been able to have a space for conversations directly relevant to our lives," adding that she wanted a Muslim girl to be able to walk into a bookstore and see her identity emblazoned across the cover of a bestseller, her name in neon letters.

"I think when it comes down to marginalized communities, what's personal for us is political. Inherently political," she said.

THIS IS HOW representation can be a feminist act. When marginalized women face oppression from white feminists and traditional patriarchal structures, reclaiming such a space is a powerful act. And it is about amplifying and giving that space to other women at the other intersections, too, forming those networks, creating those platforms where nurturing and mentorship can happen. For me, to practice intersectional feminism is to disrupt, to firmly plant your ass in a seat at the table. It is also knowing when to vacate a space, allowing others to shape their own narratives, and acknowledging your privilege. The idea of taking too much shelf space made me reflect on how our very existence and representation is seen as taking space from others—whether that's demanding rights, asking questions at a college seminar, or appearing on the cover of a magazine. This is how demanding representation and the power this brings can be a feminist act.

As a brown and visibly Muslim woman working in liberal spaces where being a practicing Muslim and a feminist is seen to be antithetical, my existence is trouble. But I will own that trouble, and for me that means channeling it every day in my reporting and including marginalized narratives, because this lack of inclusion is problematic in what is meant to be a pluralistic society.

There is a quote by Nora Ephron that sticks in my mind when I think of the need to be a tenacious journalist. In her speech at Wellesley College's commencement in 1996, she said, "Whatever you choose, however many roads you travel, I hope that you choose not to be a lady. I hope you will find some way to break the rules and make a little trouble out there. And I also hope you will choose to make some of that trouble on behalf of women."

THERE IS SOMETHING to celebrate in the places where representation is changing, and Muslim women are making waves and creating that change, so much so that advertisers and the media can no longer ignore them. It is joyful for me to see the rise and rise of Halima Aden, born in a refugee camp in Kenya, who became the first Somali-American to compete and become a semifinalist in the Miss Minnesota USA pageant. She was also the first hijab-wearing model to walk international runways and to be signed to a major agency, and has graced magazines around the world, including *Vogue Arabia*.

When Halima was unveiled as a face of Rihanna's Fenty Beauty campaign, my social media feed was full of support and appreciation. People could not get enough of Fenty Beauty's diverse campaign, with its forty shades of matte foundation. This is something to celebrate when it is taking up space in an industry that is still selling to a white audience, thinking they can get away with slight variations of beige products while missing whole markets. The traditional model does not make business sense, but more important, it does not cater to many women.

At the same time, I wonder: Is representation in and of itself the end goal? Companies are now well aware that diversity is a commodity. One example is that many more designers are targeting wealthy Muslim women in the Middle East. Brands such as DKNY, Oscar de la Renta, Tommy Hilfiger, and Mango now produce collections featuring flowing gowns and wide-leg trousers, often sold around Ramadan. Dolce & Gabbana debuted a line at the beginning of 2016 featuring hijabs and abayas.

Wokeness, or being aware of social justice issues, is itself becoming commodified—we can see that on the runways, with models holding aloft FEMINIST posters. Chanel's spring 2015 runway show was staged as a feminist rally, with models carrying signs that read: HISTORY IS HER STORY, FEMINISM NOT MASOCHISM, WE CAN MATCH THE MACHOS, and LADIES FIRST? We are now in an era of feminism as a buzzword, which is tokenistic and minimizes the struggle and everyday oppression that women face.

———

THIS CAN GO horribly wrong for multinational corporations, none more so than Pepsi's controversial ad in 2016 featuring model Kendall Jenner at what looked like a Black Lives Matter protest, which sparked global outrage. Jenner is depicted as leaving a photo shoot to join a demonstration; in the process, she takes off her blond wig and tosses it to a Black woman on her way out. Not only was it embarrassing, trivializing demonstrations aimed at tackling social justice causes and suggesting that protesters and police would get along better if we just handed out a soft drink; it also tokenized that woman, making her an accessory to the white leading lady.

There was also the tone-deaf use in the ad of a visibly Muslim American woman photographer wearing a hijab. I have become so used to the hijab being used as a prop to signify diversity, but given the timing of the ad in spring 2017—with the backdrop of anti-Muslim discrimination, surveillance, Donald Trump's "Muslim ban," and silence in the wake of attacks on mosques and the rise of supremacist groups—it felt particularly jarring.

In its apology, Pepsi admitted it "missed the mark." But it is awful to realize that perhaps no one had pointed out some of the issues highlighted here earlier in the process, which suggests there was little representation from underrepresented communities among those working on the campaign. As this example so clearly demonstrates, visibility itself is not the end goal.

How CAN IT be the goal, when Muslim women have a triple disadvantage when it comes to employment opportunities: being a woman, usually being a woman of color, and being Muslim?

Though the UK government's social mobility watchdog, the Social Mobility Commission, in 2017 found a strong work ethic and high resilience among Muslims that resulted in impressive results in education, it is just not translating into the workplace, with only 6 percent of Muslims breaking through into professional jobs, compared with 10 percent of the overall population in England and Wales.

The study found 19.8 percent of Muslims aged sixteen to seventy-four were in full-time employment in the UK, compared with 34.9 percent of the overall population.

Representation in places of work is hugely important, and when a significant minority is underrepresented we should pay attention. Eight percent of Muslim women in the UK aged sixteen to seventy-four were recorded as "looking after home and family," compared with 6 percent of the overall female population. One of the reasons given for Muslim women staying at home in the study was that it was assumed there are cultural reasons and pressure. When I see these reports, I keep asking myself, where is the advocacy for economic equality between the sexes for marginalized groups of women? And while cultural reasons play some part, with further research by the commission we now know Muslim men and women are being held back in the workplace itself by widespread Islamophobia, racism, and discrimination. Their recent study (the Social Mobility Commission) finds that Muslim adults are far less likely to be in full-time work.

There is a neat line in US comedian Hasan Minhaj's show *Homecoming King* when he recounts the time he went for an audition at *The Daily Show* and saw the photos of the correspondents on the wall who came before him. He says, "You know we don't end up this far. You know the way it is. Middle management till we die. We're not on that stage, ever."

It is a line that may have cut deep for many, as in the United States, 29 percent of Muslims are underemployed—meaning they are either employed part time but would prefer full-time work, or are looking for work. By comparison, 12 percent of US adults overall are underemployed in this way. Meanwhile, three in ten US Muslims have college or postgraduate degrees, equivalent to the number among US adults as a whole.

If we are feminists, the representation and economic equality of marginalized women in professional contexts must be something we speak out about and seek to address. As Audre Lorde, the civil rights activist, said, "I am not free while any woman is unfree, even when her shackles are very different from my own." This is a wonderful way of saying that the fight for women's rights must be intersectional in its approach. While there has been some progress in terms of popular representation for women from underrepresented groups, mainstream feminism is not doing enough to promote economic equality for all women. As intersectional feminists, it's not just about breaking glass ceilings, but also breaking the concrete ones for marginalized women. That would be true advocacy of economic equality among the sexes. How have we turned a blind eye to the women who take care of the children—we read the memoirs of CEOs as they shatter their own ceilings, but are often left wondering how they build a ladder to bring others up also.

And how can representation be the goal when violence against women persists? When anti-Muslim hate crime and gendered Islamophobia exist? It is not unusual for a Muslim woman in public life to be met with threats, to receive hate-filled e-mails calling her a "raghead," sent images of acid-attack victims on social media. I hate to think what Nadiya Hussain's Twitter notifications look like—one look at her timeline reveals the daily abuse she has to endure, from gendered Islamophobia, to racism, to colorism, to comments about the way she ties her hijab. That is why we need to fight back against disingenuous representation.

IN SEARCH OF GENDER TROUBLEMAKERS

Juliet Jacques

As a GENDER-DYSPHORIC teenager in a small English town in the mid-1990s, I struggled to find a way to understand myself, let alone to form a basis for political action. The internet had not yet become a ubiquitous source of information and exchange, and Section 28, passed by Margaret Thatcher's government in 1988 to ban local councils from "promoting homosexuality" through schools and public libraries, remained in place. The way I gradually found my way to transgender people, feminism, and transfeminism was through film: first, a wave of popular 1990s films that featured trans characters, such as *The Crying Game*, *I Shot Andy Warhol*, and *The Adventures of Priscilla, Queen of the Desert*; and then through older, underground films that starred and were partly written by trans people, who brought the realities of cross-gender living, including their relationships with feminism, into the scripts.

During the 1990s, I wasn't aware of any writers, directors, artists, or activists who referred to themselves as feminists, let alone the long-running and hot-tempered debates about whether feminist movements should accept transgender people, and most of the films from that time, mentioned previously, were written and directed by men. In the newspapers my parents bought and the comedy shows I saw (and otherwise enjoyed), feminists were portrayed as humorless, dungarees-wearing man haters who didn't even bother to shave their legs. Mainstream media was where I saw people like me: I found TV documentaries about people who'd had a "sex change," and especially "the surgery"; newspaper or magazine articles about "transsexuals" and "transvestites"; and films that featured characters whose gender was ambiguous, or different from the one assigned at birth.

Most of these portrayals of trans life were frustrating and alienating—even terrifying. My parents' paper of choice, the *Daily Mail*, ran endless stories about "transsexuals" stealing resources from the NHS, often accompanied by a cartoon of big, burly people in dresses who didn't even bother to shave their legs. Many articles made it clear that to break the rules of gender was to isolate oneself, losing family, friends, lovers, and jobs. (I didn't realize it back then, but this was a backlash against the feminist idea that biology is not destiny as much as against transsexual people; the fact that feminism and trans activism had not always been on the same side didn't matter.) Even sympathetic interviews emphasized appearances, with before and after photos to heighten the abnormality of transition; only those who "passed" perfectly in their chosen gender, usually as a conventionally attractive woman, were presented as acceptable. Documentaries focused on the social, physical, and mental difficulties of cross-gender living; their desperate chase for ratings often peaked in lurid and gratuitous surgery scenes.

The wave of 1990s films about trans people felt more inviting—partly because they avoided labels such as "transvestite" and "transsexual" and instead showed the challenges of being a gender-variant person in the wider world, dealing with hostile responses from families, friends, lovers, and strangers. Though they never cast trans actors in trans roles, they did at least move beyond portrayals of transsexual women in conventional, heterosexual suburban marriages toward depictions of trans people in queer circles, giving a sense of not just community but also a common history. I didn't see a path for myself in these films' characters, exactly—I couldn't picture myself in a drag act like the performers in *Priscilla, Queen of the Desert*, nor getting caught in political intrigue like Dil in *The Crying Game*—but I could at least envision a future where I could be "out," with a language to express my identity and discuss my experiences, both with a trans community and outsiders who wanted to support us but didn't know how.

The only film I saw as a teenager that explicitly addressed the relationship between trans people and feminism was *I Shot Andy Warhol* (1996), directed by Mary Harron and based on a true story. Set around Andy Warhol's Factory—the studio he owned in New York, where he and his friends made art and films and held parties—it depicted a radical feminist, Valerie Solanas, attempting to assassinate Warhol in 1968 (he survived). The film showed how Solanas became angry with Warhol for not producing and then losing the manuscript for her play, *Up Your Ass*. It also depicted her commitment to overthrowing the government, abolishing capitalism, and ending male dominance over society by using any force necessary.

What interested me, though, wasn't her growing resentment of Warhol, but the rising tension between Solanas and Candy Darling, the transgender *Superstar* actor who appeared in some of Warhol's films (including *Women in Revolt*, a satire of the "women's lib" movement made three years after Solanas's assassination attempt). In a scene in *I Shot Andy Warhol* where Solanas talks about how much she hates men, someone asks if getting men to have "a sex change" is a solution. No, says Solanas: "Look at Candy Darling. He is the perfect victim of male oppression." I didn't see it like that—I thought Candy was defying expectations of how men should behave, rather than conforming to expectations of how women should. Just before she shoots Warhol, Solanas breaks into Candy's room, shouts, "Andy likes you because he hates women and you're an effing freak," calls her Jimmy (her "dead" name) and hits her, and then leaves. To me, it looked like Solanas's hatred for Candy was a personal grudge, rather than a reflection of a wider trend, though the film did not make feminism look inviting to me.

I only learned about feminists like Janice Raymond and Mary Daly, who attacked transsexual people and the medical model of transition from a supposedly radical viewpoint, when I was a university student, and the responses I read were exclusively by North American trans-identified authors who had been around in the 1990s but couldn't be found in my parents' *Daily Mail* or in the library of my small Surrey hometown: Kate Bornstein, Leslie Feinberg, and Sandy Stone. In particular, I was inspired by Stone's idea (in "The Empire Strikes Back: A Post-Transsexual Manifesto") that we should openly discuss our experiences of life beyond the gender binary to break down stereotypes, but it took me some time before I found a film that delivered on Stone's suggestion.

I wish I'd been able to see *Gender Troublemakers* when it first appeared in 1993. The twenty-minute documentary was made by Canadian artist-activists Xanthra Phillippa MacKay and Mirha-Soleil Ross, with an 8mm camera and their "last two hundred bucks." Lovers at the time, MacKay and Ross interviewed each other about their sexual histories and political ambitions, using the lo-fi aesthetics of 1960s underground filmmaking and 1980s zine culture to create a film that was both hard-hitting and tender: a celebration not just of their relationship, but of the possibility of sharing it with the world.

The film opens by insisting on the terms on which its makers are seen with a series of title cards, one of which reads, "We are two gender queers / gender outlaws / trans dykes / gender troublemakers / who don't look like Tula" (the pseudonym of model-actor Caroline Cossey, who appeared in a James Bond film and became an activist after the *News of the World* outed her as transsexual). MacKay and Ross are at their most defiant in these inter-titles, which flash up on the screen before and after important scenes and make direct attacks on transphobia, in the media and the wider world: "We have the right / to be proud of our backgrounds / to be proud of our heritages / without having them slammed in our faces / by gender bigots."

I can imagine myself as a fifteen-year-old, having never been told this by anyone, let alone reached this conclusion by myself, and thinking: *Yes!* Although *Gender Troublemakers* made it clear that the video did not "pretend (nor can any other) to be a universal statement for transsexuals' issues and experiences," my own life, either side of transition, has made me familiar with the themes it explores: misogyny in gay communities; "passing" and public ridicule; sexual objectification, especially by "straight" men; and the search for a language to understand how it feels for trans and gender-variant people to be attracted to other trans and gender-variant people, in a way that avoids binary conceptions of gender and sexuality.

The most touching points in *Gender Troublemakers* come when MacKay and Ross share their love for each other with the audience. They talk about how they had both wanted to meet "somebody of [*their*] own gender" (i.e. a transgender or transsexual woman) before they got together. This is understandable after Ross explains how a gay man touched her in front of his friends, laughing at the idea that a transsexual woman could be attractive, and they explain how, in each other, they have found not just love but a sense of sanctuary. Boldly, the film lets us into the bedroom. The scenes there form a stark contrast to the moment in Neil Jordan's film *The Crying Game* (1992) when the male hero, Fergus, sees that Dil, the woman he is dating, has a penis, and then vomits. The visible tenderness and humor when MacKay and Ross have sex demonstrates the power of showing trans people together, and the possibilities that come with community.

Another underground film that featured trans people in dialogue—if not as lovers—that particularly inspired me was *City of Lost Souls*, by the often-controversial German director Rosa von Praunheim. Made nearly a decade before *Gender Troublemakers*, in 1983, it was a musical about a group of American outsiders living in West Berlin, loosely connected by living in a residence owned by Angie Stardust, the first Black transsexual woman to perform in New York. Unlike *Gender Troublemakers*, *City of Lost Souls* is a feature film, but only nominally; its thin plot barely makes sense. What is interesting about the film is not its scripted scenes, but the many improvised, documentary-style conversations between cast members, who mostly played themselves, that made the final cut. Importantly, these conversations allowed them to get beyond crude stereotypes about trans people and set the terms for discussions about their lives rather than have them dictated by outsiders. This would give them the power to define their own identities, and generate a new language to express those identities; they would be able to understand each other better, and they built a stronger sense of solidarity that could allow them to form a community.

Like MacKay and Ross, Angie shares crucial parts of her personal history. She tells us how her father tried to beat her youthful femininity out of her, and how she was initially turned away from Club 82 (New York's biggest drag revue before the Stonewall riots of 1969) because she was Black. She also talks about moving to Berlin only to find that many of the generation who voted for Hitler and supported the Nazis throughout their twelve-year rule have passed their prejudices down to their children and grandchildren, who sing racist songs at her in the street.

Angie tries to create a safer space around her by hiring sympathetic people at the Burger Queen restaurant she manages, and renting rooms at Pension Stardust to the open-minded. She finds herself feeling old-fashioned, however, next to Tara O'Hara, who keeps bringing men back to her room to "teach them English" (and more). The best scene in *City of Lost Souls* is when Angie and Tara, who are both playing themselves, have a long argument about the different ways in which they express their gender identities. The voice-over sets up the conflict: Tara is a "transvestite" who "wears women's clothes but wants to remain a man," while Angie is a "transsexual" who wants to change her body using hormones and surgery, but "her only problem is that she has a penis that she wants to have removed."

Tara briefly undermines Angie's identity, first with the kind of question that Angie (like me, and countless others) has often heard from hostile outsiders, and which echoes Valerie Solanas's attack on Candy Darling in *I Shot Andy Warhol*—"Do you think a sex change will make you a woman?"—insisting that physical transition is no longer necessary. Tara's "transvestite" ideal anticipated the gender-queer and nonbinary identities that have become more prominent in recent decades, but Angie angrily insists that it is "because of the old school that you can be what you are. . . . We pumped the hormones, we put up with people calling us "faggot" and "drag queen." . . . Now it's easy for you [*younger trans women*], you get tits, your hair grows, you're a woman. It was harder for us, we had to act over-feminine . . ." By doing all this in the face of widespread social disapproval, Angie suggests, her generation were pioneers, gradually opening possibilities not just for people to move from one gender to another, but to find space beyond them.

This conversation shows the importance of generational dialogue, understanding, and respect. Knowing nothing of the postwar gender identity clinics that gave hormones and surgery only to those who met their (often unattainable) standards of femininity, or Angie's struggles against racism, Tara thinks Angie's whole way of being is outmoded. Gradually, she realizes how people like Angie paved the way for her, and eventually, they reach an awkward compromise. Angie refuses Tara's imperative to "accept yourself as a transvestite" and the insistence that "we're the third sex"—a position rarely explored in feminist texts before Sandy Stone's "Post-Transsexual Manifesto," which was first published five years after *City of Lost Souls* was filmed. Instead, Angie prefers to say, "We're the New Women." In the next scene, when we see Tara persuading a man that sleeping with a "transvestite" doesn't make him gay, insisting, "I'm a different kind of woman," we get a sense of the challenges they have both faced, with Angie constantly having to justify her existence even to other trans people, and Tara worrying that any moment when she fails to "pass" will result in violence. We also see how the wisdom of the older generation can help the next to navigate the world safely.

Tragically, that inherited wisdom wasn't enough to save Tara O'Hara. When I first saw *City of Lost Souls*, in 2010, I wondered what had happened to this captivating, free-spirited person, who seemed to be showing a way to live joyfully, beautifully, without restraint. Like several of the film's cast, she contracted AIDS, but that isn't what killed her. In 1983, soon after the filming was completed, Tara was found in a restroom in Tiergarten in Berlin. She had been attacked and had suffered serious head wounds. She spent a few weeks in a coma, after which doctors decided to turn off her life support. Her name appears on the Transgender Day of Remembrance website as one of thousands of names of trans people worldwide known to have been murdered. Many of those—mostly trans women—have been people of color or sex workers, highlighting the way transphobia acts as an intensifier of misogyny and other prejudices.

In May 2014, *Time* magazine announced a "Transgender Tipping Point"—a moment when trans people were no longer something to ridicule or ignore, though their struggle for respect and recognition was not over. Their cover star was Laverne Cox, an American trans woman of color who stars in the Netflix series *Orange Is the New Black*, playing a trans woman in prison. As the show—and internet-only dramas in general—achieved mainstream recognition, Cox had become a spokesperson for the trans community, and she reflected intelligently on the pressures that came with that. Asked if she was a "role model" for trans people, she replied, "It's presumptuous to think that anyone should model their life after you, but I do like the term possibility model.

I mention this for two reasons: first, because it makes me reflect on the possibilities denied to Angie and Tara O'Hara; and second, because it reminds me of a film that was being made as Cox was taking on the burden of celebrity: *Tangerine*, directed by Sean Baker. Like *Orange Is the New Black*, *Tangerine* was a breakthrough hit, meeting with a surprising level of critical and popular acclaim when it premiered in

2015. It had plenty in common with "underground" films such as *Gender Troublemakers* and *City of Lost Souls*, and those that Paul Morrissey made with the Andy Warhol Factory's trio of gender-crossing *Superstar* actors: Candy Darling, Jackie Curtis, and Holly Woodlawn. Vitally, *Tangerine* featured two trans women of color, Kitana Kiki Rodriguez and Mya Taylor, playing trans sex workers named Sin-Dee and Alexandra. Neither were professional actors; instead they were chosen from the Los Angeles LGBT Center. Neither needed to spend valuable screen time putting on makeup, taking hormones, or seeing doctors about surgery, as cisgender actor Felicity Huffman had to do in *Transamerica* (2005), in order to establish that their characters were trans.

Tangerine brought Rodriguez's and Taylor's experiences, and particularly their slang, into a script that was partly prewritten and partly improvised, and—like the works mentioned previously—shot very cheaply, using three iPhone 5 cameras. (Using such everyday technology, as well as being inexpensive, allowed Baker to shoot on the streets of Los Angeles without obtaining a permit.) In the film, Sin-Dee (Rodriguez) is released from prison after twenty-eight days to find that her boyfriend and pimp, Chester, has cheated on her with a cisgender woman; she literally drags the woman, Dinah, through an underworld of motels, strip clubs, and all-night diners as she tries to track him down and confront him. But the revelation that Chester has also slept with Sin-Dee's friend Alexandra only makes things more complicated, and tests their friendship to the limit.

The plot of *Tangerine* is more structured than *City of Lost Souls*, which was central to its breaking out from the festival circuit into mainstream cinemas, unlike the underground trans films that came before. The storyline, however, is not the most important aspect. Rather, it turns ideas about the "authenticity" of trans people upside down. Sin-Dee and

Alexandra seem like they are expressing themselves, or simply *being* themselves without restraint in a city where everything is false, or as one character puts it, "a beautifully wrapped lie." As a result, it becomes easy to identity and empathize with them, even when they are behaving badly. It feels like the characters are not representing anyone other than themselves, which gives them real freedom: Sin-Dee and Alexandra do not have to be role models, but they allow actors Rodriguez and Taylor to become two new possibility models.

Tangerine's popular success could also be attributed to the "tipping point" described by *Time*. Decades of work by trans activists, academics, and artists, as well as intersectional feminists who had long stressed the need to fight racism and transphobia alongside misogyny, had paved the way for a film like *Tangerine* to be enjoyed and understood by people outside trans communities. Digital technology has been important, too—not just in allowing *Tangerine* to be made on a shoestring budget and still be palatable to theatrical distributors, but also in eroding boundaries between mainstream and underground cinema. Now that the internet has made it easy to find a film like *City of Lost Souls* alongside big-budget films like *Transamerica*, perhaps there is no mainstream/underground divide anymore—just things that we, individually, know about, and things we don't.

Certainly, an open conversation about trans lives and experiences will allow our language to keep evolving, and with it our communities and political movements, as well as our relationships with other struggles—against sexism and misogyny, racism and fascism, inequality and exploitation. If trans actors, writers and directors can be prominent in these discussions, in mainstream and underground spaces, then they could open all sorts of new possibilities—which the likes of *Gender Troublemakers* codirector Xanthra Phillippa

MacKay and *City of Lost Souls* star Tara O'Hara could only have dreamed—and create a feminism that is more inclusive, more persuasive, and more aware that the fights against misogyny, homophobia, and transphobia are linked, part of a vision for a better world in which difference is respected and celebrated, rather than a defensive struggle against prejudice and discrimination.

BODY AND BLOOD

|||||||||||||||||||||||||||||||||||||||||||||||||||||||||||||||||||||||||||||||||||||||||||||||||||||||||||||||||||||||||||

Brit Bennett

TEN DAYS AFTER a white supremacist carried a gun into a Black Charleston church, I was in Los Angeles, listening to a Black minister preach about the end of the world. A coincidence of timing, maybe, although the message seemed apt. What could be more apocalyptically evil than a racist massacre within the hallowed walls of a church, an angry young man sitting through a Bible study before slaughtering the nine strangers who had invited him in to pray? Yet on that Sunday, when the pastor talked about the end, he did not mention Charleston or the seven Black churches that had been burned throughout the South in the immediate aftermath. Instead, he spoke about fornication. "M-hm," a woman behind me chimed in, "and gay marriage." The ladies beside her murmured their assent. Just the day before, the Supreme Court had legalized same-sex marriage, a decision that seemed to disturb the congregation more than anything that had happened in Charleston. I didn't understand it. How could marriage equality be a sign of the impending apocalypse, but not a church shooting? How could the evils of fornication be a more pressing topic than the wave of racial violence affecting the very congregation sitting in the pews?

The Christian church has a problem with bodies, which

is ironic, as sociologist Michael Eric Dyson notes in his 1982 essay, "When You Divide Body and Soul, Problems Multiply." "After all, the Christian faith is grounded in the Incarnation, the belief that God took on flesh to redeem human beings," he writes. "That belief is constantly being trumped by Christianity's quarrels with the body. Its needs. Its desires. Its sheer materiality." Within the Black church, this quarrel with the body becomes even more complicated. What does it mean to be at war with your own flesh within a culture that already hates the Black body? And what does this mean for Black women, whose bodies are doubly despised?

I SPENT MY childhood split between two churches. Though my parents were, and still are, married, my sisters and I went to catechism and mass at my mother's mostly white Catholic church. We spent Christmas and Easter services at my father's mostly Black Protestant church. At my mother's church, I learned about transubstantiation, the belief that the bread and wine become the actual body and blood of Christ. The figurative body becomes literal; as a particularly imaginative child, I felt there was something wonderful about this, the idea of words transforming into flesh. My father's church was less mystical, more pragmatic. It was almost disappointing. I'd grown up watching emotional Black church services in movies—bombastic ministers spontaneously breaking out into song, flamboyant organists leading praise breaks, church mothers fanning sinners at the altar. But my father's pastor disdained this emotionalism—it made your flesh feel good in the moment, but what about when you left the sanctuary? What good was an emotional sermon once you had to face the troubles of life?

"God's people are destroyed for lack of knowledge," he

liked to say, quoting Hosea 4:6. And feeling God was not the same as knowing him. It seemed strange to me that church itself could cater to the flesh, but this, apparently, was the strong hold our bodies have over us. The body distracts from higher things—holier things—which is why we cannot let our bodies govern us. As a girl, I heard this mantra over and over: You are a spirit; you have a soul; you live in a body.

In a way, this language is liberating. You are not your body. You are not your torn skin, failing organs, broken bones. You are not decaying flesh that will be dropped in a hole someday to rot. As a Black woman, there's something additionally comforting about the idea of transcending your body. Our history in America is written in bodies that have been stolen, mutilated, tortured, raped, beaten, exploited, and killed. Not only this, but we have suffered violence because we have the wrong bodies, the wrong skin, wrong lips, wrong hair. Our bodies are erased and mythologized and fetishized, declared inferior by scientists and artists and politicians. Why wouldn't you want to believe that you are more than that body?

Still, I've always been troubled by the idea of separating myself from my body. In a 1968 speech to the World Council of Churches, James Baldwin argued that this self-repression had split Christianity into two. His debut novel, *Go Tell It on the Mountain*, also plays with this idea: The coming-of-age story follows teenager John Grimes as he struggles to reconcile his family's expectation that he follow his father to the pulpit with his own lack of faith. In the opening pages, John watches as Elisha, a seventeen-year-old pastor, is filled with the Holy Spirit.

> At one moment, head thrown back, eyes closed, sweat standing on his brow, he sat at the piano, singing and playing; and then, like a great, black cat in trouble in the jungle,

he stiffened and trembled, and cried out. *Jesus, Jesus, oh Lord Jesus!* . . . Sometimes he did not stop until he fell—until he dropped like some animal felled by a hammer—moaning, on his face. And then a great moaning filled the church.

With erotic, feverish language, Baldwin focuses on all the physical details: the sweat gliding down Elisha's face, his thighs quivering underneath his suit, his fists clenching. Witnessing Elisha's spiritual rapture also serves as a moment of sexual awakening for John, who nurtures a secret attraction to men. But shortly after this moment, Elisha is censured by the church elders for growing too close with a young lady in the church. Although they had not yet sinned, "sin was in the flesh," and in order to avoid temptation, Elisha could no longer spend time alone with her. By playing with both carnal and spiritual language, Baldwin depicts a Black church divided against itself, trying in vain to separate the flesh from the spirit.

"From my point of view, it seems to me the flesh and spirit are one," Baldwin said in his 1968 speech. "It seems to me that when you mortify one, you have mortified the other."

As a girl, I learned to fear my body. Not only its wants or needs, but its power. A girl's body is uniquely vulnerable and uniquely dangerous. I remember taking a road trip with my family, my mother making me change my shirt because she said the neckline dipped too low and some trucker, sitting up high in his big rig, might be able to look down it. I may have been twelve; I argued with her before finally changing, irritated, convinced she was overreacting, but still disturbed to know that while I sat in the backseat of the family minivan, filling out crossword puzzles, some trucker could be staring at me.

My mother has always been wary of strange men. Even now, nearly seventy, she won't wait alone in a movie theater with a strange man, always sitting outside until more people filter in. I, on the other hand, was still learning all the ways to fear men. In a way, my naïveté was a gift. According to a study by the Black Women's Health Imperative, 40 percent of Black girls are sexually abused by the age of eighteen. I was still learning what many girls like me already knew.

In church, nobody talked much about how to protect young girls from sexual violence. I did, however, hear sermons about how oral sex was wrong. I heard about a young female employee who'd been fired by the church after she'd gotten pregnant out of wedlock; in an act of compassion, or so it was framed, the church paid to help the young lady travel back to her family on the East Coast. I'll also never forget hearing a pastor say that women impregnated by rape should not have abortions because "you have to make the best out of a bad situation." In other words, when life hands you rape, make lemonade. Even my Catholic mother was appalled by that one.

From that car ride on, I continued encountering new ways my body would be policed. A friend's mother who said to me, after I'd gained weight, "Something must've tasted good this summer." A music teacher who commented, in front of the whole class, on the length of my miniskirt. A family friend who called a flirty girl in my class "fast." There was no parallel term for boys. No one clocked the speed at which their bodies flew.

Although we often talk about intersectionality as a combination of identities, Kimberlé Crenshaw originally coined the phrase to describe the interaction of multiple forms of oppression. In her groundbreaking 1989 essay, Crenshaw argues that the tendency to treat gender and race as mutually exclusive categories erases the experience of Black women, who are "multiply burdened." Black women experience not only both racism and sexism but also racism that is gendered and sexism that is racialized. To live in a Black female body is to be caught within both racialized and gendered violence, to occupy a body that is both scared and scary. So I learned to police myself. I never walk into stores with my hands in my pockets. I always follow traffic laws because I've mourned Sandra Bland and Philando Castile, and I know a routine traffic stop does not always end so routinely for us. I've watched my sister straighten her hair before a job interview, my mother move aside on the sidewalk for a white neighbor to pass. As girls, my sister and I whispered about how embarrassing that was, to be so deferential; now, thinking about my mother's childhood in segregated Louisiana, I realize maybe she's not even thinking about it—maybe stepping aside for a white person is muscle memory, embedded deep in her body. The same way that, in Michigan, white students would command the dry patches of sidewalk, expecting me to walk in the slush.

Perhaps this is one of the biggest problems with separating the body and the spirit: Flesh is not neutral. Different bodies carry different cultural and political meanings. In *Go Tell It on the Mountain*, John Grimes oscillates between self-loathing and sexual repression. He feels shame for feeling same-sex desire and he feels shame for being Black. Within a religion that symbolically frames darkness as evil, John sees "the hand of Satan" on his own dark face. He hears a voice asking whether he believes that all Black people are cursed. By the novel's end, John experiences conversion, allowing him to finally join his community fully. But his conversion only seems like a vehicle for his sexual shame and self-loathing. In the world of the church, hating his Black body becomes holiness.

———

THROUGHOUT HIS WRITING, Baldwin criticizes Christianity's avoidance of sexual desire, from the virgin birth to the condemnation of homosexuality. To him, anxiety about same-sex desire stands in for a general anxiety about physical intimacy. "It's not a fear of men going to bed with men," he tells Fern Marja Eckman, the author of his 1966 biography *The Furious Passage of James Baldwin*. "It's a fear of anybody touching each other." Although he finds this anxiety especially pronounced in America, he locates it more specifically within the crosshairs of race. "If you're a Negro," he says, "you're in the center of that peculiar affliction because anybody can touch you—when the sun goes down. You know, you're the target for everybody's fantasies. If you're a Negro female whore, he comes to you and asks you to do what he wouldn't ask his wife to do—nor any other white woman. But you're a Black woman! So you can do it—because you know how to do dirty things!"

To Baldwin, Black women are uniquely vulnerable in a repressed culture because whiteness projects its sexual desires onto our bodies. Historically, Black sexuality has always been viewed through the warped lenses of white fantasy. In the *African American Review*, literature scholar Aliyyah I. Abdur-Rahman describes how Europeans believed that Africans were sexual savages: Scientific investigations in the nineteenth century argued that Black people had abnormally large genitals, which gave them "predetermined illicit sexual propensities," including promiscuity, rape, interracial lust, bestiality, and homosexuality. During slavery, fantasies about deviant Black sexuality served as justification for white owners to exploit their unfettered legal and personal access to Black bodies. While strict, monogamous heterosexuality predominated the rest of American culture, on a plantation, "non-conformist sexual attitudes and behaviors found flagrant expression unlike anywhere else in society." You can be as dirty as you want toward a body that is already dirty.

After slavery, the white imagination continued to frame Black sexuality as deviant. Historian Winthrop Jordan argues that the myth of the Black male rapist—"You blacks are raping white women every day," the Charleston shooter said, before killing mostly older women—served as a smoke screen; white men, who for centuries had turned the routine rape of enslaved Black women into financial gain, projected onto Black male bodies an image of violent, uncontrollable, interracial lust. They also framed Black female bodies as inherently lustful. In this calculation, the innocence of white women needed to be protected at all costs; Black women, already gone in their own lust, were incapable of being raped. This is the history of Black women in America, not a small feature but the single definition: Your body does not belong to you. Anybody can touch you. Your body is both the location of violence and the result. How could we not fear a body like this?

IN THE BLACK CHURCH, I learned self-control.

How to wake up early on the weekend. How to wear uncomfortable clothes that I hated. How to pinch myself to stay awake during a long sermon. How to report to service, week after week, even when I didn't feel like it—especially when I didn't feel like it—because if nothing else, learning how to show up regularly, in spite of tiredness and doubt, prepared me for the writing life. You are a spirit; you have a soul; you live in a body. You bring your body under subjugation. You do not allow your flesh to control you. Black thinkers have often criticized Christianity's hold on the community, arguing that it makes us passive; instead of fighting to improve this life, Christianity lulls us while we wait for the next. But my experience in the church is the opposite: I grew up in a church that imports agency. If you want to be healed, you have to ask for it. If you want good things, you have to speak positively, because death and life are in the power of your tongue. I see the strength of this, especially for a Black congregation to hear that they are in control of their lives, when our experience in America has meant anything but.

In a 2008 *American Quarterly* article, scholar Thaddeus Russell traces this strand of the Black church—a theology that prioritizes disciple and control—back to the civil rights movement. In the 1950s, he argues, Black activists "launched the greatest and perhaps most effective campaign" to replace the freedom of Black culture with "obligation, discipline, and rejection of the self." Civil rights leaders realized that to gain full citizenship, they needed to present a Black culture that affirmed the traits valued by white America: responsibility, productivity, and heterosexuality. This campaign gained traction in the church; in 1951, Adam Clayton Powell Jr., a prominent minister and NAACP leader, penned an essay in *Ebony* railing against the "increasing trend of homosexuals parading" through the streets of New York and criticizing the "fantastically high percentage of worshippers who blatantly and openly flaunt their sex perversion." He declared homosexuality one of the forces that debased the Black race. As the civil rights movement gained steam, other black leaders sought to distance Blackness and queerness. Dr. Martin Luther King Jr. publicly instructed Black people to shun immoral forms of sexuality, including homosexuality. "We must walk the streets every day," he told one audience, "and let people know that as we walk the streets, we aren't thinking about sex every time we turn around."

King also identified laziness, gambling, materialism, and

drinking as issues that were destroying the Black community. He criticized churches that only "whoop and holler . . . merely to get people to shout and kick over benches" and advocated for "a gospel that will make people think and live right and face the challenges of the Christian religion." To prove ourselves worthy of citizenship, to prove that we were more than flesh that acts on its most primal urges, we needed to control our bodies, even within the confines of the church. A controlled body is a safer one. The Black church has inherited and propagated this idea, which is as understandable as it is tragic. The white imagination defined our sexuality as deviant, so we worked harder to distance ourselves from any sexuality that deviates. To prove our humanity, we deny our flesh, when flesh is what makes us human.

ONE OF MY favorite scenes in the 1985 film *The Color Purple* is when Shug Avery, blues singer and fallen woman, leads the sinners from the juke joint to her disapproving father's church, where she sings along rapturously with the choir. I always love watching Shug and her army of wayward souls burst through those church doors, a moment that manages to be both reconciliatory and rebellious. So much of my favorite music exists on that long march between the church and the juke joint. Ray Charles and the Raelettes, moaning back and forth like a preacher and his lascivious choir. Kendrick Lamar meditating on salvation after violence on *Good Kid, M.A.A.D City*. Preacher's daughter Aretha Franklin crooning about her do-right, all-night man. In *Respect: The Life of Aretha Franklin*, when asked whether the spiritual or the blues came first, legendary gospel singer Reverend James Cleveland calls that question a riddle that can't be solved. "How do we know whether someone out there picking cotton didn't first start moaning about how tired he was, or about how much he wanted a woman?" he asks. "Then maybe a God-fearing woman heard that song and switched it up where she was praying for God to save *her*. The fleshly needs and the godly needs are very close." The holy, the profane, the flesh, the spirit. Which did we first learn to worship?

In the preface to her Pulitzer Prize–winning novel, Alice Walker writes that she is surprised *The Color Purple* is so rarely identified as a book about God. After all, the first words of the book are "Dear God"—for most of the text, Celie addresses her diary to God, a type of written prayer. Not only that, but Celie experiences profound spiritual transformation throughout the novel. In the beginning, she sees God in a traditional, masculine image, "all white, looking like some stout white man work at the bank." By the end, she recognizes the divine as transcending the body altogether and residing in nature itself. Shug gives Celie the gift of a God who creates beauty and delights in our ability to recognize it. "I think it pisses God off," she tells Celie, "if you walk by the color purple in a field somewhere and don't notice it."

Celie also finds God in her love for Shug. The 1985 film is coy about this relationship; Celie and Shug share only a single, quick kiss. In 2011, Steven Spielberg admitted to "softening" the lesbian relationship between Celie and Shug in order to ensure the film received a PG-13 rating. "I basically took something that was extremely erotic and very intentional, and I reduced it to a simple kiss," he told *Entertainment Weekly*. "I got a lot of criticism for that." Because I'd seen the film first, I was surprised by the eroticism of the novel, and how significant Celie's sexual awakening is. Celie has suffered a lifetime of physical and sexual violence. As a girl, she's raped and impregnated by her father and forced to give the baby away. She's married off to Mr., a cruel man who views her more like a beast of burden than a wife. She labors away in fear of him, and at night, she endures sex, waiting for it to be over. She has never experienced any sexual pleasure until her relationship with Shug, who teachers her how to love a body that has only caused her pain. In the novel, their sexual relationship is the catalyst for Celie's eventual spiritual liberation. Salvation is physical.

"I wash her body," Celie writes in her diary. "It feel like I'm praying."

LIKE CELIE, I search for the divine outside stained glass and wooden pews. I try to unlearn a theology that splits me into two irreconcilable halves: the spiritual and the physical. I look, always, to Black women artists. Beyoncé at a plantation, surrounded by fire, belting "Freedom" while the mothers of Trayvon Martin, Oscar Grant, and Eric Garner look on. Zora Neale Hurston's ability to capture the beauty of Black joy in *Their Eyes Were Watching God*. Toni Morrison's *Beloved*, in which an old woman with a twisted hip dances in a clearing. In the woods, surrounded by former slaves, Baby Suggs exhorts her community to love their flesh, down to their "beat and beating hearts." Loving the body becomes a final act of liberation; to accept its desires and vulnerabilities is to embrace the full scope of a denied humanity.

I turn, always, to books because reading is the ultimate act of leaving your body, writing the ultimate prayer. You send words into the world and hope that someone is there listening, someone willing to leave their body to meet you halfway in the space between language and air. I have always found hope in this space, even as a little Black girl in a church dress and white tights, daydreaming during a long sermon, amazed that I could be anywhere.

LOVING TWO THINGS AT ONCE: ON BISEXUALITY, FEMINISM, AND CATHOLICISM

Caitlin Cruz

IN MARCH 2017, I started to come out to my friends as bisexual. It started with a text to one of my best friends, whom I've known for fifteen years, and after that, it started to just tumble out. Once I told one person, I started telling everyone. It was a long time coming. But I found that being honest about my sexuality stopped being easy when I started trying to reconcile it with my relationship with God and Catholicism.

As a Mexican-American woman raised by parents who were married in the church, I grew up a cultural as well as a practicing Catholic. Faith was deeply important to my family. I was baptized at a parish in Arizona and received two other sacraments at our parish in Nebraska. Our home was decorated with multiple crucifixes and crosses, and we went to mass every weekend.

Going to church is one of my favorite memories of my childhood. When my sister and I finished Sunday school and transitioned into Wednesday night catechetics classes, we started going to Saturday night services. We would have dinner as a family, attend mass, and then go to the bookstore.

We'd get coffee and pastries for dessert and browse the stacks; it was my weekly opportunity to catch up on the latest gossip in *J-14*, or find a new novel to get lost in. Once a month, this ritual would include a trip to the confessional. Looking back, the sins of eleven-year-old Caitlin and even eighteen-year-old Caitlin—the worst of which were not doing my chores, or saying I was going out with friends and instead peeling off to hang out with my boyfriend—seem wonderfully naive and even funny.

I sometimes wish I could go back to that time. It's not that I want to be an adolescent or teenager again—because who could handle the emotional ups and downs of those ages a second time?—but I do wish it were possible to have a less complicated relationship with God.

I've never believed there was an inherent conflict between being queer and loving God. But in the past year, as I've accepted that both of these labels apply to myself, I've begun to really struggle with my relationship to the Catholic Church—and by extension, with my faith. Stating my truth, announcing my differences, made it impossible not to confront how I relate to religion and to God. It meant I could no longer exist in that wishy-washy space where the Church's treatment of queer people and women bothered me but I could still go to mass unscathed if I tried hard enough; it meant that I couldn't continue sitting in the comforts of ally-dom. Putting up blinders to policies I didn't wish to support had felt like the simplest solution. It didn't require tough questions for a bishop or priest, or the potential loss of a community. It worked okay for me, until I found myself part of a group the church maligned.

It's not that the churches I went to were openly homophobic. By the first decade of the new millennium, the message was "Hate the sin, love the sinner." Though it's more subtle than hating them openly, the assertion that queer people are sinners any worse than other child of God is just as insidious. It's hard to continue to support an institution that sees you and people like you as irredeemable when we're taught that we are equally deserving of love and forgiveness.

LONG BEFORE THE NEED AROSE to reconcile my Catholic faith with my queer identity, I struggled to reconcile it with my feminism.

I've been a feminist as long as I can remember. Feminism, I think, is a praxis many of us come to at a young age, before we have the language to describe what we believe. I mean, we believe in equal rights, duh. When this long-held belief in equality collides with feminist theory and writing, we develop ways to better articulate our political beliefs and take political action to advance the cause of equality. Thanks to my parents' continuous assertion that I could be anything I wanted, I always saw myself as equal to members of the opposite sex, but I first learned about certain feminist principles from my high school speech coach. She insisted on being called Ms., not Mrs., and was one of the few teachers who treated the queer kids like, you know, *people*. It's something you notice, even before you're ready to admit certain truths. A few years later, reading bell hooks introduced me to the radical politics of feminism. Through hooks, I learned not just that feminism is a belief in the equality of the sexes, but that these beliefs carry with them a political imperative to fight for things like reproductive health care and racial equality. hooks taught me that feminism is about building a class-conscious system that lifts up the least among us. In her feminism, intersectionality is a given.

Intersectionality describes overlapping systems of oppression based on a number of factors including but not limited to gender, race, ethnicity, educational attainment, incarceration, immigration status, and socioeconomic status. hooks showed me that feminism is meant to take up all of these mantles in the fight for equality for all. Despite Christianity's emphasis on kindness and service to others, this fight isn't something with which the Catholic Church seems to concern itself.

My feminism has always centered on believing in reproductive rights and health justice for all women. When people are allowed to decide if and when they reproduce, they're able to take control of the trajectory of their lives. A just feminism advocates for the right to birth control and abortion without requiring that women publicly justify their choices. Health access and justice, I believe, have a significant role to play in bringing about racial and ethnic equality, and dignity for all people. Needless to say, the Church's attitude toward reproductive health care hasn't been favorable in my lifetime.

In 2015, Pope Francis announced the Year of Mercy, to run from December 8, 2015, to November 20, 2016, during which time women could seek reconciliation for the grave sin of abortion. To his credit, at the conclusion of that year, he decided to allow rank-and-file priests to absolve the sin of abortion indefinitely. Of course, he has yet to say—and likely will never say—that abortion is not a sin. It was a small step, but since tiny steps look like miles when held up against thousands of years of dogma, Pope Francis is hailed as a progressive.

He again made headlines when, according to the *New York Times*, he told the press, "If someone is gay and he searches for the Lord and has good will, who am I to judge?" The reporter noted that he spoke in Italian, except for the word *gay*, which was said in English. Again, a tiny step that appears to be miles ahead of the church tradition. But it's not progressive to think gay people are deserving of respect. It should really just be your default position after reading the edict to love thy neighbor as thyself.

Further troubling policies are pretty standard critiques of the Catholic Church, including the stance against same-sex marriage. It's preposterous to me that the Catholic Church continues to take a moral stance against queer people and same-sex marriage. Marriage is a beautiful sacrament that brings together your families (chosen or otherwise) and your community before God. It's incredibly sad that a portion of Catholics miss out on this opportunity because they choose to marry someone of the same gender.

My family's commitment to faith is not uncommon among Latinos. In 2014, the Pew Research Center found that 48 percent of Latinos identify as Catholic. It was still the largest religious affiliation among us, despite a growing number of people who chose to be unaffiliated.

In theory, I could simply take the parts of Catholicism that resonate with me and move to a more progressive sect of Christianity. In past years, before I came out, I drew false comfort from the idea that queer people who were unwelcome in the church could still seek God with other sects and faiths. Your relationship with God can be as solitary as you like it, I thought. But how do you transfer your belief in God and an institution—a belief that feels like a cultural act as much as a spiritual one—to another institution, or to no institution at all? Can you really just pack up and leave? I worry about what I risk leaving behind. Does the Virgin of Guadalupe hear our prayers if we aren't going to Holy Days services?

In the days before Christmas, my family sets up luminarias, small paper lanterns, to show the way to safe passage for the Blessed Virgin and Joseph. The luminarias are an incredibly important tradition in New Mexico, where my father was raised. They're also a part of Las Posadas, a nine-day religious observance of the story of the birth of Jesus, which is observed in Mexico and by Latinos in America and beyond. It's a beautifully simple thing to do during the holidays to connect you to the start of a new year. This tradition is as much about being a Mexican-American as it's about connecting with the birth story of Christ. Can I still participate in this ritual welcome if I leave the Church? It is very difficult to untangle the religious and the cultural. Because at the end of the day, my love for the Virgin is equal parts biblical and reverential. She will always be a port in the storm and I hope I can always help guide her home, even if our homes may not be the same.

Beyond such complicated questions, I struggle with the idea of letting go of the communion with others that you feel in a big church. I crave the fellowship of the apostles that we duplicate when we attend mass. Religion imposes order on a life that we have very little control over; Catholicism imposes even more order if you so choose. There's comfort in that routine.

Attempting to undertake a solo faith, one separate from my family and my heritage, is daunting. But it seems to me that refusing to confront the intersection of religious tenets and the beliefs that women and queer people are less than equal is what got us here. We must continue to demand more from our religious leaders and doctrines. So I continue to try to be true to my own duality, even if church officials cannot. This means I've mostly stopped going to mass, attending only on holy days like Ash Wednesday and Easter. I am still working out what my faith looks like when separated from the motions of weekly mass, monthly confession, and seasonal devotion. How do I build a belief system, within or outside my deeply ingrained Catholic faith, that unites my steadfast belief in equality with my steadfast belief in God?

How do I continue to seek grace? I'm not sure it's possible to seek grace within an institution so devoid of it, but I'm praying that I still may.

There's a moment in the film *Spotlight* when a reporter is on the phone with a sociologist and former priest who studies the sexual and celibate practices of Catholic bishops and priests. The reporter asks the sociologist how he keeps his faith alive in the face of the abuse he's studied. He replies, "Well, the church is an institution, Mike, made of men. It's passing. My faith is in the eternal. I try to separate the two." But how, exactly, do you separate your belief in the eternal from the people called to represent it? I wish I knew. What I do know is that my faith in the institutions of man is waning.

IN EARLY 2018, I attended mass with my parents at their awesome (in the awe-inspiring sense), ornate church in the Dallas suburbs. It was the feast of the Epiphany, when the magi visited Mary, Joseph, and Jesus in the manger—the last weekend of the Christmas season according to the Catholic calendar. It was my first mass outside of Christmas in almost a year.

The feast of the Epiphany is meant to be a time of celebration, the closing bookend to a joyous time. But for me, it fell flat. Reading about multiple "pro-life" fund-raisers in the church bulletin made me unbelievably sad. Of course, I should have been prepared for this, given that when you walk into a Catholic church, especially in Texas, the belief in reproductive freedom rarely follows.

Nearly two years after coming out, I still haven't figured out how to leave Catholicism, or even if I want to. I still don't know how to separate my devotion and beliefs in God from the rituals ingrained in me after years of kneeling at pews and at my bedside. What I do know is how uncomfortable I feel at mass, knowing the men leading and the people following (myself included) are either explicitly or tacitly okay with discriminatory beliefs and policies that don't allow women and queer people like me to live fully realized lives. I can't help but return again and again to the fact that these policies and beliefs are directly in violation of the teachings of Christ.

But just as the church fails to meet my standards by denying women bodily autonomy, feminism sometimes fails at taking up issues many churches support, like anti-poverty campaigns. Both could be more inclusive of LGBTQ persons. Both could be better at fighting for the least among us. The belief in kindness, unconditional love, and the importance of good works is what guides my relationship with God. This is not at odds with the belief in equality that guides my relationship to feminism. I wish I could find a way to reconcile the two.

I will never regret being honest about being bisexual. It feels so natural and *normal* to live in this identity, and it's a relief to enjoy it every day. I have no idea if I'll remain in the Catholic faith, or eventually seek something outside its doors. But there's always the chance to begin again; that's what the church teaches us. To try harder, to fight stronger, to forgive, to love more deeply. There is supposed to be another shot at redemption. Starting over can be a deeply intoxicating choice. And a new beginning doesn't have to forget the past, especially when it includes the Lady of Guadalupe.

IMPERIAL FEMINISM

Afua Hirsch

SOMEWHERE IN AFRICA, a dream is alive. It begins with a fluorescent white orb rising above the savannah, staining the wide sky with light. Clouds prostrate themselves haughtily above the earth, drawing slowly toward the horizon. On the shadowy land below, gazelles shift in sleek streams, elephants stride, and the sun appears again—a red disk rising raw out of the night. A beautiful white woman appears, her hair silky, her pale skin radiant against siren-red lips. She gazes wistfully into the distance as attendants powder her neck and arrange her delicate, loose curls into an image of perfect glamour.

She is the pop star Taylor Swift, and in her video for the song "Wildest Dreams," she has commandeered this landscape of time immemorial, a place where prehistory has survived in all its natural glory. Like many artists before her, Swift borrows the crudest clichés of Africa, but dispenses with the need to depict any of its people. Instead, she sits at her dressing table in the wilderness, a single giraffe lurking nonchalantly behind her, a clapboard revealing the imagined date in this southern African wilderness as 1950—the era of apartheid. The dream world she creates with such stunning effect is one where white landowners played out their love stories uninterrupted by the inconvenience of interacting with Black Africans, except for the servants. She films love scenes with her sandy-haired leading man—and sings of white love: rosy cheeks in the sunset.

This is Africa, after all—as the Kenyan writer Binyavanga Wainaina reminds us, famously satirizing common perceptions of the continent—"the Land of Wide Empty Spaces." It's the "dark continent," a place that Swift, a generation far removed from the colonial architects who built such falsehoods, similarly depicts as "hot and dusty with rolling grasslands and huge herds of animals . . ." It is onto this blank canvas that the pop star, like so many other white artists, politicians, and business tycoons, projects her own images of greatness, beauty, and might. Her depiction of herself as a one-woman colonizer, transforming the landscape with her pale beauty, is a feminist one, of course. Swift considers herself, and frequently stages social media interventions as, a feminist activist. She has surrounded herself with a "girl squad" of supermodels and singers, almost all of them white, mobilized a vague notion of "girl power," whose actual meaning is hard to pin down. In 2017, Swift was one of the Silence Breakers who were collectively named *Time* magazine's Person of the Year for speaking out against sexual assault.

Strip away the private jets and sold-out international tours and Swift's feminism isn't so different from the kind I was first exposed to, growing up in the 1980s and 1990s as a middle-class Black child in a well-educated and liberal corner of suburban London. The white feminists in my orbit were concerned with things like their career options, women's representation in politics, the extent of the gender pay gap, and the division of domestic labor. In their own struggles to meet the unrelenting ideals of white, blond thinness and "having it all," they were indifferent to or unaware of the otherness and degradation of nonwhite women in which they were complicit. It's not surprising, then, that my mother, a Ghanaian woman who has lived all her adult life in a community populated with highly educated, middle-class white women, identified as a feminist but lacked enthusiasm for the movement around her—an ambivalence I inherited without knowing its source. The arenas of social injustice in which white feminism battled may have affected us, but they were not our primary struggle.

My primary struggle as a Black child in a white environment was related not to my gender, but to my identity as the daughter of a mother who had come to the UK from Ghana and a father with Jewish German and English heritage. As a young girl, I absorbed messages about Africa and what it meant to be African from images similar to those in Taylor Swift's video; from nature programs, which always focused on Africa's wildlife but never on its people (save anthropologists or adventurers occasionally examining life within what they regarded as "primitive tribes"); and from films like *Out of Africa*, *Zulu*, and *Ashanti*, which were frequently the only viewing options on our four-channel TVs. They depicted the African continent as a primal space devoid of any civilization, except the white people who came to exploit its wildlife and natural resources, and to twist and contort it into a flattering backdrop for their whiteness. Africans were irrelevant; Blackness was primitive. It was this dismissal of my Black heritage that led me, in my vulnerable and impressionable teenage years, to deny my association with the African continent altogether.

Rejecting Africa meant fully exposing myself to the reality of a society dominated by norms of whiteness. The tyranny of white beauty standards, by which measure my afro hair, brown skin, and ample flesh were exotic and other, triggered self-loathing and self-harm. The perpetuation of myths of Black hypersexuality and delinquency reflected in the media I consumed tempted me to fulfill this caricature of Blackness. I took hip-hop videos as a literal guide to Blackness: To be Black and female, in the contemporary images available to me, was to be raunchy, feisty, and seductive—dangerous messages for a girl going through puberty. The white feminism around me remained silent about these struggles.

It is from this perspective that I watch today's iconic self-proclaimed feminists, like Taylor Swift, continuing the erasure of Blackness, even when—remarkably—they situate their work on the African continent. African women and their experience are invisible in Swift's video, which has more than half a billion YouTube hits at the time of this writing.

The fact that the messaging I found so damaging as a child three decades ago is being renewed and refreshed for another generation, especially by someone who self-identifies as a feminist, points to how little progress has been made at the intersection of feminism and race consciousness. It also points to another disturbing trend, which the cultural anthropologist Renato Rosaldo has called "imperialist nostalgia," in which the "agents of colonialism long for the very forms of life they intentionally altered or destroyed." While few would now openly call for an actual return to the British Empire, a powerful nostalgia that romanticizes its lifestyle benefits has become a mainstream sentiment—as evident in Swift's music video as it is in the rhetoric of political leaders. Britain's decision to leave the European Union has shown the sheer force of this nostalgia for a time of unquestioned white supremacy, changing the entire sociopolitical future of a nation, with potentially profound consequences for the equality, progress, and opportunity of the people within it, especially the people of color.

I came across Rosaldo's work in a seminal essay by bell hooks, "Eating the Other: Desire and Resistance." Writing long before Swift was to become a pop star, hooks—one of the greatest Black feminist intellectuals—anticipated the imperialist nostalgia so evident in "Wildest Dreams," linking it to a crisis of white identity and desire. Imperialist nostalgia, hooks explains, is the gloss that glamorizes a gruesome reality in which white culture seeks to "eat the other."

I'm sitting in a small refrigerated radio studio, talking too loud because of the deadening earphones muffling my hearing. I'm contributing "down the line," from another location, so I can't see the other guests on the show. But I can certainly hear my opponent—an academic known for defending the idea that the treasures looted by Britain and other colonial powers should remain in the museums of London, New York, and Berlin—on the other end.

The debate is the latest installment in a long-running row over cultural appropriation. It began with a discussion of the fact that the Braid Bar, a braid service at one of London's most exclusive department stores, has been marketing cornrows to white women. The models they have chosen for the campaign are Lila Moss, daughter of the eponymous Kate, and Stella Jones, daughter of Mick Jones, the guitarist from the 1970s British punk band the Clash. Their images are synonymous with the privilege that comes with being a second-generation model or rock star. The second-generation immigrants who pioneered the look, on the other hand, have been airbrushed out, along with any other references to its African roots.

The ensuing row follows the usual pattern of discussions with the predominantly white deniers of cultural appropriation. My opponent claims white women adopting the hairstyle is an example of cultural and creative exchange, and that in attempting to police the boundaries of Black and white culture I am enforcing a Jim Crow–era segregationist ideology. This goes both ways, she claims. If people cannot borrow ideas from other cultures, then we must equally condemn Beyoncé for appropriating Hindu art, and Bob Marley for taking his dreadlocks from ancient Egyptian culture.

I respond by explaining the difference between such exchanges—which are an inevitable and intrinsic aspect of humanity's social evolution—and cultural exploitation, which is self-explanatory. Appropriation: the act of taking or using things from a culture that is not your own, without an understanding of or respect for that culture. The context is so significant a factor that this is not even about the hairstyles themselves, or Jamaican jerk chicken, now commonly served in restaurants with no Black owners or staff, or African print clothes, so often seen on the catwalk of European designers who continue to show little interest in using Black models. "Ethnicity," bell hooks reminds us, "becomes spice, seasoning that can liven up the dull dish that is mainstream white culture."

This type of rampant appropriation is a symptom of a commodity culture within a capitalist system, with implications that are predominantly based on race and class. But it is consumption that has special consequences for women. "When race and ethnicity become commodified as resources for pleasure," writes hooks, "the culture of specific groups, as well as the bodies of individuals, can be seen as constituting an alternative playground where members of dominating races, genders, sexual practices affirm their power-over in intimate relations with the Other." In a world in which imperial nostalgia has new gravity and seismic political force, old, gendered patterns of oppression against the women located in this imperial narrative are as dark and sinister as ever.

That mainstream feminism does not recognize the need to embrace the battle against these evolving forms of oppression. hooks wrote about eating the other in 1993, when I was twelve. I was not yet familiar with the phrases "cultural appropriation," "imperial nostalgia," or the host of other tools with which feminists are able to define daily acts of oppression: othering, microaggressions, exoticization, and so on. But 150 years after Sojourner Truth's famous "Ain't I a Woman?" speech noting the dual oppression of race and gender faced by Black women, and four years after Kimberlé Crenshaw coined the term *intersectionality*, I, too, was experiencing the patriarchy first and foremost as a power structure centered on whiteness.

It was only through the work of Black and intersectional feminists like hooks that I was able to unlock my inherent feminism, and allow it to manifest in a politically activated identity I felt I could own. Yet years later, advanced in my own feminism, I continue to witness how the phenomena that pose some of the greatest threats to Black women— imperial nostalgia and cultural appropriation—are divorced from feminist discourse.

For example, each Halloween I am hauled onto national radio stations to answer the question of whether it's okay for children to dress up as people from other races and cultures. A small town in southern England, Lewes, is still debating in earnest whether it is acceptable to follow a tradition in which white participants dress as Zulu warriors, complete with blackface, on Bonfire Night, an English fireworks celebration held each November 5. I do not find feminists rallying en masse behind those who, like me, speak out against the practice of partying in blackface, just one of so many ways in which mainstream, white culture seeks to "eat the other" as a manifestation of patriarchal white supremacy. Feminism is still blind to racial injustice, and in its blindness is undermining its very integrity as a movement centered on dismantling structures of oppression.

Advertising is another area feminism fails to speak out against. Take, for instance, the advertisement by the cosmetics company Nivea in 2017, which sought to cash in on the estimated $10 billion skin-lightening industry with a cream that promised Ghanaian women it would bring out their skin's "natural fairness." Reaction to the message united Ghanaians, Nigerians, African Americans, British, and other European communities of African heritage in a stance that unequivocally rejected the beauty industry's propagation of a self-loathing of Blackness. Those speaking out against it linked the commodification of anti-Blackness with imperial nostalgia, because "solving Blackness" through European manufactured cosmetic products was one of the most enduring legacies of European colonialism. But this was not framed as a feminist debate, nor was it owned as a feminist cause. In this separation of feminism on the one hand and the battle to overthrow the propaganda of empire on the other, women of color are still pulled in separate directions by movements that should represent the totality of our struggle.

Because it is women of color who have been the loudest—and sometimes the only—complainants against recent acts of cultural appropriation. When white feminists have sought to problematize practices of cultural mockery—as parenting blogger Sachi Feris does in her post "Moana, Elsa, and Halloween" on the blog *Raising Race Conscious Children*, in which she criticizes the practice of white children dressing up as Disney character Moana—they have not been met with support from other white feminists. The message still appears to be that this is a problem for people of color, a burden that we alone are expected to carry.

Because white feminism refuses to take a stand on the ways in which white capitalism continues to encourage consumers to commodify Blackness, I am constantly asked to comment on the issue, with the result that I find myself having to explain again and again that I am not the police, and these are not my borders to patrol. The ignorance that leaves people believing, unthinkingly, that cultural exchange happens in a fair context and on a level playing field, is not something my advocacy can overturn. We should all concern ourselves with the structural injustices that pervade our attitudes toward art, history, heritage, and beauty; it is a question of intellectual and social integrity. It is all of our responsibility to teach a new generation a fact-based version of past events, and not the propaganda that still persists, airbrushing past exploitation.

For people whose own stories lie in that history of exploitation, it is a useful reminder that for too long, we have shared our cultural resources in the same way we have our oil, gas, gold, and labor, trusting others to use it with respect and affection. It's time we invested more in the intellectual property, rights, and custodianship of our own inventions so that in the future, respecting our contributions is a necessity, not a choice.

Debates about cornrows, dreadlocks, or braids are not really questions of hairstyle, but of power relations in our society—a concern that is feminist at its core. It cannot be exposed, let alone dismantled, by Black feminists alone, nor should it be seen as our problem. Change starts with disrupting the narrative—something only an inclusive and intersectional future can do.

THE MACHINERY OF DISBELIEF

Wei Ming Kam

"WHY IS THERE a separate box for 'same-sex partner'?"

"What?"

Liz points at the options underneath the question "Under which category are you applying for leave?"

"Spouse or partner, unmarried partner, spouse/partner of someone with refugee leave, civil partner, fiancé, same-sex partner, child of partner, etc. We've been able to get married since 2014, why is same-sex partner still a separate category?"

I stare at the page. "We're both unmarried and same-sex partner. For God's sake. We could tick both boxes?"

"I think only one option is allowed. I don't know."

We're going through the form that Liz has to fill out to apply for a UK family visa. It's seventy-nine pages long. We're on page eleven.

"Who the hell wrote this f-ing form?"

"Straight people. Racists. *Theresa May.*"

There's a faintly hysterical note to the laughter that follows this, the kind of laughter that comes from knowing that it's either that or cry. Liz sticks a Post-it on page eleven as a reminder to come back to it, then ruffles her hair and looks at me.

"Do you know anyone who knows an immigration lawyer?"

———

Towards the end of my teens, as I became more interested in politics, immigration started to rear its head as an issue of importance once again in the UK, but I'd never really sought to understand why. But since my partner, Liz, had made the decision to move to the UK, it had become impossible to ignore. As I learned more about the details of each visa that might allow her to stay and the policy decisions behind it, it became clear that despite mainstream feminism's general neglect of it, immigration is also a feminist issue.

How could it not be when the majority of immigrants arriving in the UK on much-sought-after Tier 1 category and Tier 2 work visas are mostly men? How could it not be when those on the overseas domestic worker visa are mostly women?

The disparities in numbers of men and women immigrating in different categories matter because these visas differ hugely in terms of the rights that they give to their holders. Tier 1 visas are given to immigrants who are considered either leaders in their fields or entrepreneurs, while Tier 2 visas are for those who have been offered a skilled job. Those on Tier 2 visas can stay in the UK for up to five years (Tier 1 visa holders can stay for over three years, but can extend for another two years), are able to bring their families with them, can switch jobs and employers, and have the right to eventual settlement. In stark contrast, overseas domestic workers are not granted any of these rights, apart from being able to change employers. They are also only allowed to stay in the UK for six months, and the dependency on their employers that this denial of rights creates has led to "increased levels of exploitation and physical and sexual violence." Their visa is described as "a chattel visa . . . abuse [is] being facilitated by [this] immigration status."

A truly inclusive feminism would put an issue like immigration, which affects the most vulnerable women on multiple levels, at the center of its concerns, research, and campaigns. As Liz's application process for a family visa began and I looked further into how the UK's immigration policies affect people, what I saw instead were smaller groups at the forefront, like Lesbian Immigration Support Group, and Women Asylum Seekers Together, often led by women of color, working to help and fight for the most powerless.

I consider myself a feminist, but I understand why many women of color do not. I understand why they reject mainstream or "white" feminism as one that does not think beyond women who are not white, cisgender, straight, middle class, and able-bodied. This version of feminism dominates cultural and political thought when it comes to tackling issues of inequality and injustice in Western countries. Intersectional feminism, which deals with the many different forms of oppression and power, and the ways in which they interact with and affect women, seems to be an afterthought, albeit one that is finally, slowly gaining prominence.

The more research I did into how immigration policy affects women, the more I realized that mainstream women's rights organizations are mostly failing to support those impacted. It's the smaller groups with an explicitly intersectional approach who do all they can to help the migrant women who are affected, and who see how other issues such as gendered violence are, and have always been, affected by immigration.

IT'S HARD TO DESCRIBE the experience of applying for a UK family visa to anyone who hasn't gone through it. There's an emotional strain that fogs the background of everyday life: a cocktail of stress, financial anxiety, confusion, and anger that turns into a vague dread that's always lurking in the back of your head.

It's a natural reaction to the hostility toward immigrants that's embodied by the conditions set for the British sponsor and their non-EU family members, which reflect the fact that there are certain types of migrants the British state would prefer, and those they wish to exclude. The harsh financial and language requirements have received the most attention (since 2012 the British partner must earn more than £18,600 a year, and their partner has to pass an English test at a certain level of European language proficiency standards). Demands to satisfy opinions on the "genuineness" of the relationship reveal what type of families the UK prefers, and who escapes indirect discrimination.

Tying immigration status to a partner's income inevitably means disqualifying various sections of the population from bringing family to the UK; most notably, it automatically discriminates against women because of the gender pay gap. As of 2015, almost 75 percent of men earn enough to sponsor non-EU partners, while 55 percent of women do not. If you're an ethnic minority, in your twenties, or without a degree, the chances of meeting the threshold are also lower. If you're sponsoring a child as well as your partner, the income threshold goes up to £22,400.

It is telling that the Migration Observatory, where I obtained these stats, doesn't analyze data from people who experience discrimination in multiple forms. In failing to examine the nuance that would emerge from such research, they echo mainstream feminism's focus on white women as the default for all women, missing out on the fact that women of color would be even less likely to earn enough to sponsor non-EU partners.

We need to crack down on abuse of the family route [to British residency] . . . family migration must be based on a real and continuing relationship, not a marriage of convenience or a

> marriage that is forced or is a sham . . . they must not be a bur-
> den on the taxpayer.   —*Theresa May.*

As mentioned previously, the family visa is built for hetero-normative standards, but culturally specific proofs of "genuine" relationships—like previous cohabitation as well as the language requirement—also deliberately discriminate against practices like arranged marriages, which fall outside of what white British societal standards consider to be real. Great scrutiny is generally focused on South Asian women, consistently stereotyped as "passive victims of such [arranged marriage] practices." Since such traditions are not within white British society's expectations of what constitutes genuine relationships, they are implicitly used as one of the reasons for the difficulties of obtaining residency for non-EU partners, as they are closely associated (mistakenly) with forced marriages.

The shaping of immigration law to police what the British state deems to be the right type of family migrants isn't new: From 1983 to 1997, "the primary purpose rule required foreign nationals married to British citizens to prove that the primary purpose of their marriage was not to obtain British residency." This meant that any Home Office official dealing with such cases would be starting from the assumption that all marriages to foreign nationals were the result of foreign spouses wanting British residency; the burden of proof that the marriage was genuine and not for immigration purposes was placed on the people applying for a visa. In practice however, "the primary purpose rule was . . . discriminatory to the arranged marriage culture [of] the countries that make up the Indian sub-continent," while "men and women from white countries continued to enter unhindered."

The fact that some of the most violent consequences of policing immigration and immigrant families fall upon women of color is not new either. Back in the late 1970s, for example, it led to the testing of at least eighty South Asian women to determine whether they were being truthful about not having been married before (rules at the time meant that women coming to the UK to marry a fiancé did not need a visa if they were married within three months). Such invasiveness was based "on the stereotype of south Asian women as 'submissive, meek and tradition-bound' and on the 'absurd generalisation' that they were always virgins before they married."

Gendered discrimination enabled by the state continues to this day. Yarl's Wood Immigration Removal Centre, which hosts those waiting for the verdict on their immigration cases, is the most prominent example: It has frequently come under fire for allegations of sexual assault and mistreatment of its primarily female population. Another example is the policy for the family visa and the visa for overseas domestic workers, two visas for which the majority of applicants are women and that are arguably the most restrictive. Overseas domestic workers have few rights other than being able to work in the UK within the domestic work sector for six months, while the family visa ties people's migration status to a family member, creating an unequal power balance.

The Immigration Act of 1988 prevented spouses from getting immediate permanent residency when they arrived in the UK, making them apply for an initial temporary one-year residency before they could apply for permanent settlement. It also required the immigrant spouse's application be supported by the resident spouse.

This probationary period was justified as a means of making sure that marriages to non-EU partners were genuine and not sham, but as pointed out by many, the dependence this created risked women "being forced to stay in abusive relationships in order to escape deportation." Reinforcing this is the fact that non-EU partners have no recourse to public funds, making them potentially financially dependent on their partner as well.

Thanks to years of campaigning by women's activist groups, led by Southall Black Sisters, a South Asian women's group who campaign for and work with Black and Asian women, small concessions toward protecting immigrant victims of domestic violence have been gained from the Home Office. Those who entered the UK on a family visa (often known as a partnership visa) and can prove domestic violence can apply for permanent settlement, while the Destitution Domestic Violence concession allows them to claim public benefits for three months while their application for settlement is being considered. Despite these small victories, which Southall Black Sisters and others say do not go far enough, the overall attitude from the state remains the same: They assume that migrants are "seeking illegitimate access to the UK [and] the burden of proof [that they are not] is placed squarely on the shoulders of the immigrant." In 2003, the probationary period for those on family visas was increased to two years, and in 2012, it was extended yet again to five years.

The difficulties faced by immigrant women who suffer from domestic violence are huge, particularly in the past few years as cuts to shelter funding continue. Women's services, let alone specialist ones for children or BAME women (Black, Asian, and Minority Ethnic; terminology used in the UK for "people of non-white descent"), are struggling, but even without the added pressure of austerity, shelters need to cover the costs of the safe accommodation they provide, meaning that women who cannot work and have no access to public funds are usually refused places. Southall Black Sisters and Amnesty International's 2008 report on domestic violence and the consequences of the "no recourse to public funds" rule found that those affected were often point-blank refused help by police, local authorities, and shelters. Any attempts to help were severely limited by the lack of funds. If nothing could be done, the women, facing a choice between violence and destitution, usually returned to their abusers.

It was while researching the decades-long campaign against the "no recourse to public funds" rule led by Southall Black Sisters that I came across an intriguing pilot project that aimed to help women who had no access to public funds, run by an organization called Safety4Sisters, a Manchester-based grassroots feminist and anti-racist migrant women's rights organization. Safety4Sisters supports migrant women with an insecure immigration status who are experiencing gender-based violence. The group helps these women assert their most fundamental rights, and also raises awareness around the discriminatory practices that they face.

Hoping to learn more about the group, I Skyped Sandhya Sharma, one of the directors of Safety4Sisters. Earlier that day, a paper about Brexit was leaked to the *Guardian*, revealing that the government intended to apply much of its legal treatment of non-EU immigrants to European immigrants. The continuing hostility toward immigrants and increasing levels of hate crimes overshadowed our whole conversation.

I first ask Sharma to tell me about the history of Safety-4Sisters, and what their initial goals were. "We never intended to be a direct service provider; our role was really to support, through campaigning and other activities, other mainstream organizations to be able to support this group of migrant women. But we found that the will to do so was lacking," she says matter-of-factly. "So we wrote out a plan for the 'Migrant Women's Rights to Safety' project, and we applied for funding."

In November 2015, Safety4Sisters launched a pilot project that ran for ten months. They provided practical and emotional support (one-to-one advice and advocacy), which ran alongside a support group, a space where the women could "give voice to their experiences of both the impact of domestic abuse and the compounding effects of immigration control . . . of being located at the intersection of these systemic forms of control." They were also given travel costs to get to and from the group, a breakfast and a hot lunch, access to phone and internet resources, and basic toiletries for themselves and their children.

"We also just wanted evidence, that these women [escaping domestic violence who are affected by the 'no recourse to public funds' rule] exist, and these are the problems, and really go into depth."

There has been no UK-wide comprehensive research into migrant women who flee domestic violence who have no recourse to public funds. Southall Black Sisters estimates that six hundred women a year who enter the UK as dependents face violence from their spouses, but due to the difficulties of reporting and seeking help, this is believed to be a significant underestimation; the real number is estimated to be up to one thousand. There are currently very few statistics on the children affected, and there is little research on the effects of having no access to public funds on other victims of exploitation, such as overseas domestic workers and victims of sex trafficking.

There are various reasons for this, including the difficulty of collecting data when things like the criminalization of illegal work means many will avoid the authorities. But the "no recourse to public funds" policy has been in place for almost three decades, and so the scarcity of research around this particular consequence of it also speaks to the lack of care that society has for marginalized women. Feminism cannot be separated from the shelter movement (part of the women's liberation movement in the UK that started in the 1960s; focused on providing shelter for women who were victims of domestic violence), and yet those involved in recording and investigating data have largely failed to consider the women who are affected by multiple forms of discrimination and systems of power. It's another example of how mainstream feminism has left those most susceptible to exploitation and abuse on the fringes of concern and support.

I asked Sandhya about the estimate of migrant women who are victims of domestic violence, and she explained, "They [counted those on] spousal visas. We work with a whole range of women who have no recourse to public funds, not just spousal visa entrants, and migrants. We work with women on student visas, those who were undocumented, overstayers, we worked with women who were in the asylum process, pre-asylum, and once their asylum claims have been rejected."

Safety4Sisters has found that in addition to services being refused, there was a "toxicity of the immigration discourse . . . [and a] hostile and suspicious climate towards migrant communities." This, in addition to the tightening of immigration policies and the onset of austerity, meant that these women "often found their own immigration status scrutinized before, or instead of, the perpetrators' abusive behavior." Abusers frequently used the women's immigration status against them as another form of control.

"The emphasis is on disbelief: Prove you were fleeing such-and-such, and prove that you can't go back, and prove that you're a lesbian, prove the domestic violence, then we'll decide," Sandhya says exasperatedly. "It's [now also] nonstate actors, this is seeping into everyday life. At colleges, at doctors, there is this constant demand and emphasis on the immigration and the immigration status of a woman before anything else." Every woman they speak to experiences this disbelief and scrutiny, she tells me, and it comes up endlessly in the women's group meetings.

My first violent partner—I had to go into a women's [shelter] but he called the Home Office to say I was illegal so that I wouldn't get my residence. The state ignores or criminalizes you and the men know you are vulnerable so they can exploit you.

—Safety4Sisters group member

The police told me—you are illegal so we can't do anything for you.

—Safety4Sisters group member

I went to the Adult Education Centre to apply to do an interpreting course. I gave my ID and said that I had ILR [Indefinite Leave to Remain] and they said who gave you this and why? I said that this is not your business but he said how did you enter this country? They asked me too many questions.

—Safety4Sisters group member

"Unless we de-link immigration status from women seeking safety, [who have experienced] domestic violence, we can only provide a partial safety net at best," Sandhya says.

The camera on Sandhya's iPad isn't working properly, and occasionally the internet connection cuts out, but this does very little to deter her from answering my questions at great length. In spite of the distressing nature of her work, she is passionate and optimistic.

"I want to say something else," she says, in the middle of the conversation. "Racism is profound at the moment. Whilst you have the tremendous barriers of not getting into a [shelter], [there are also] the messages that we're sending out as a society—'You're not welcome, because you're a migrant, and you are different, your needs are different.' How it plays out in the women's lives is devastating."

If I could change one thing it would be for all these services; social, police, housing, job centre, legal aid, to stop thinking that domestic violence is the norm in different cultures. That domestic violence is to be expected in different cultures, and so they don't help the victims in the same way.

—Safety4Sisters group member

I ask her what she meant when she said at the start of our Skype chat that help for the women with no recourse to public funds wasn't forthcoming from mainstream women's organizations.

"What we were coming up against, what we still come up against, is a blanket ban—[shelters saying] we don't support women with no recourse to public funds—without actually looking at what recourse women do have. However, what you could say is, 'Well, we are aware of the Destitute Domestic Violence concession, what we will do is get her access to an immigration adviser quickly."

At this point, Sandhya's tone is becoming more vehement. "Which is what [shelters] were set up to do, wasn't it? We will provide that advocacy and support for women on all aspects of their lives, and their accompanying rights, whether it be housing or education, or immigration, or childcare, it's part and parcel of what [shelters] *should* be doing." She continues, "But because these women's experiences—as victims of crime and of domestic violence—[are] linked to immigration, their immigration status is looked at first, and not their needs.

"Part of the injustice is that we have lost our desire, and our ambitions for campaigning," she says, now more thoughtful. "I think that's what the [shelter] movement was set up to do. . . . I joined the feminist movement as a [shelter] worker because of that [partial progress on the "no recourse to public funds" campaign]. It was unrelenting, and very difficult work, but that was part and parcel of the principles of feminism, and part and parcel of the principles of justice." She sighs. "So, it is particularly sad to see that many [shelters] that we come across will not take women with no recourse to public funds, without at least pursuing the remedies that are available and are at hand."

The internet connection at this point starts to act up even more, and it is with difficulty that she answers my question about what else women's services and state authorities need to consider. "A lot of the gender-based violence programs that run up and down the UK are fantastic, but they don't necessarily reflect the realities of migrant women. And a lot of the support around migrant communities and displaced people doesn't necessarily reflect the gender-based violence in women's lives and realities. You really have to have an intersectional analysis," she continues, "because otherwise, you only get part of the experience, and you can't deal holistically with a person. You can't just deal with the poverty, you can't just deal with the immigration, you can't just deal with the gender, or the issues of race and racism, and being a migrant. They are all compounding identities for women. And they all intersect, and they all have an impact on each other."

I ask Sandhya what Safety4Sisters is doing now that the pilot project to support migrant women is over. "To continue to provide direct services to women on a casework level . . . that we couldn't deliver. But what we could deliver is the Migrant Women's Rights to Safety support group. . . . We've got fantastic links with the Greater Manchester Immigration Aid Unit; a lot of the women that come to us get legal advice and immigration advice," she says. They also raise funds to provide accommodation for women who can't access public funds.

At the time of writing, Safety4Sisters is funded until April 2018.

IN THE PROCESS of researching this essay, I became fully conscious of the gender discrimination that is an intrinsic part of immigration policy and the family visa. I had been so focused on the excessive conditions that gaining a family visa required that I had not properly considered the restrictions that would come with it. After a meeting with Claire Falconer, the legal director of Focus on Labour Exploitation, I realized—rather belatedly—that British citizens were being given power over their non-EU partners and spouses by Home Office policy.

Claire had emphasized throughout our discussion how exploitation and abuse were enabled by employers being given leverage against their employees by things like immigration policy. Towards the end of the conversation, I was suddenly aware that by saying I was legally and financially responsible for her right to live and work in the UK, the Home Office was treating Liz as if she was temporarily my property. When we were finished, I knew I had to talk to Liz, and pulled my phone out as soon as I was outside.

"I am really effing uncomfortable with how dependent you are on me . . . your immigration status is tied to me and our relationship for the next five years. I hate the power they give to British citizen partners," I texted, explaining how the meeting had led to my sudden self-awareness.

"I didn't even think about that. Guess I just assume the relationship will last?" she replied.

"I love you," I texted back, knowing even as I pressed send that it was an utterly inadequate response. Love did not remove the power inequality that this visa had placed upon us.

When I got home, I slumped on the sofa. She came and sat next to me. "I'm sorry, this is the worst," I said.

"I know," she replied.

IT IS IRONIC that current policy discriminates against people from non-EU countries partly in the name of making sure that marriages aren't fraudulent and exploiting vulnerable women of color, while the same policy in fact means that the immigration status and potential financial security of non-EU people are effectively subject to the whims of their British partners. It is no surprise, then, that the immense imbalance of power that it creates facilitates potential domestic and emotional abuse.

Irony aside, the Home Office is making it as difficult as possible for the most vulnerable women (the majority of family migrants are women) to stay in the UK with their partners. Once it approves visas, it strips back non-EU partners' rights as a condition of their probationary residency. Making British citizens responsible for their non-EU partners is a state abdication of social responsibility, a conscious decision from a country that views particular noncitizens as both threatening and less-than, and one that leaves the vulnerable open to destitution and abuse.

If the two of us—both middle-class, highly educated women whose first language is English—were not aware of the full consequences of the family visa rules, what hope is there for those who do not have our advantages? More urgently: Many, if not the majority, of women's rights organizations and shelters *are* aware of the potential repercussions for those migrating on the family visa (and the overseas domestic worker visa, which has similarities). They are aware of the impact of the "no recourse to public funds" rule, and that it disproportionately impacts poor women of color, especially those who are disabled. Why are women's rights organizations, with the exception of one or two that focus directly on the issue, still failing these women?

Southall Black Sisters and other organizations have repeatedly lobbied the government to extend the exemption from the "no recourse to public funds" rule to all victims of gender-based violence and exploitation, and to lengthen the number of months they can access public funds from three to six, due to the time it takes to process applications for permanent settlement. Despite this, there have been no changes since 2012.

THE UK IS far from unique when it comes to immigration policy and victims of domestic violence. There are similar policies in the United States.

The US restricts spousal visas to couples who are married, and if they have been married for less than two years, the migrant partner is subject to conditional residency of two years, after which they must apply to remove the condition from their permanent residence. Like in the UK, the application depends on the sponsorship of the citizen partner, and like in the UK, women "comprise the majority of marriage migrants" and "thus depend on their husbands for immigration status." Once again, the potential for marriage fraud is cited as a reason for the conditional residency, and once again, dependency and conditional residency is a powerful motivator for those suffering violence to stay with their abusers.

There are various routes to permanent settlement for migrant or undocumented victims of domestic violence in the United States, including the battered spouse waiver and the U visa (the latter does not require the couple to be married, and was created to encourage "immigrants to report dangerous criminals to law enforcement . . . a lifeline for victims of repeated violence"). Crucially, some of these routes allow the applicants to work, giving some of them a way to access safety and other resources.

However, since Donald Trump's executive order that considers "all removable aliens subject to deportation" and enlists police as partners of the Department of Homeland

Security, "training them 'to perform the functions of immigration officers in relation to the investigation, apprehension, or detention of aliens,' advocates are unsure whether to advise clients to cooperate with police regarding the U-category visa." Immigration and Customs Enforcement say that they will consider whether an individual is an immediate victim of or witness to a crime when determining whether to take action, but immigrants and their advocates are wary, and with reason. In February 2017, a transgender woman called Irvin Gonzalez sought a protective order in Texas against her ex-boyfriend, only to be arrested as she left the courtroom by ICE officers (she suspects her ex of giving ICE information on her whereabouts). She has applied for a U visa, but it is unlikely that deportation proceedings will last long enough for her to stay in the United States and see through her application process.

Many legal advocates are reporting a trend in clients backing out of bringing cases to court for protective orders against abusers, in order to stave off ICE's attention. It is impossible to say how many have simply decided to stay quiet and continue to live with violence for fear of deportation.

It is perhaps too early to see how this new round of hostility toward immigrants is affecting domestic violence shelters and other women's services, but the difficulties that many women of color and immigrant women have when dealing with domestic violence shelters in the United States has long been documented, leading some to state that "the anti-domestic violence movement is largely a white women's movement."

Language barriers are a major obstacle, as many shelters do not have multilingual staff; some have told women to seek help elsewhere because they could not communicate with women who did not speak English. It remains to be seen how women's shelters and other services are affected by and respond to a potential increase in the number of women (who will probably be largely women of color and migrant or undocumented) who decide to stay with perpetrators of violence.

The fact that women are willing to risk gendered violence in order to not be deported makes it clear that immigration is an urgent feminist issue, yet many mainstream feminist organizations over the past few years have done little campaigning on the matter. Just because immigration policy largely impacts the lives of poor women of color should not mean that mainstream feminism turns a blind eye to it, and yet it is still not seen by most as a subject of feminist concern. It is indicative of the failure to understand intersectionality and to embrace it as a fundamental part of feminism, and to really be inclusive of women of color.

At the end of my conversation with Sandhya, we talked about some of the conclusions that Safety4Sisters came to at the close of their pilot project. The first two key recommendations they had for shelter service providers (and indeed, for anyone who came into contact with migrant women who were at risk) were as follows:

1. Put the safety and rights of women ahead of immigration enforcement.
2. Women should be at the heart of the response.

I was struck by the fact that Sandhya thought it was necessary to recommend what seemed to be obvious considerations when dealing with women who are at risk of domestic violence, and I told her as much.

"Well, even if you think it's quite a simple and obvious conclusion," she responded, "so many people don't. If you work with the *most* disadvantaged, you will automatically be able to provide a service for all people. If you only work with those people who are deemed to have rights, you will only provide a partial service."

If women's services would apply an intersectional lens to their work and place the most vulnerable at the center of their support, the obstacles that migrant women face would decrease. But it is state policy that affects them the most.

"The barriers [to helping these women] are just overwhelming and they're manifold, and a lot of it is at top policy level anyway, Immigration and Home Office level, that can't really be entirely resolved by some group in Manchester," Sandhya said.

If you were to construct a family or partnership visa policy that does not facilitate abuse, it might look more like Canada's. Current policy is that the ability of Canadian citizens to bring noncitizen partners to the country isn't tied to an income threshold, and all noncitizen partners are given permanent settlement once their application is approved. Crucially, settlement isn't dependent on a probation period, and partners aren't barred from receiving public benefits.

However, there are still shadows of anti-immigrant feeling lurking. The Canadian partner is responsible for paying back any public benefits their noncitizen partner may claim, echoing the UK's principle that they must not be a burden on the taxpayer. In addition, from 2012 to April 2017, the Conservative government amended the rules for the family sponsorship route to permanent residency, making permanent residency for non-Canadian partners of Canadian citizens dependent on the partners residing with their Canadian partner for two years. If they did not comply with this probation period, they would be at risk of losing their conditional permanent residency, and ultimately could be deported.

The reasoning given by the Canadian Conservatives at the

time was that this was "in the name of curbing 'marriage fraud' or 'marriage of convenience'," but legal advocates stated that the Conservatives were making these changes "without offering evidence of the prevalence of these problems." It was one of several changes to immigration routes that Immigration Minister Jason Kenney stated were put in place to reinforce the "fairness and the integrity of the system." He said that "the abuse of Canadians and our immigration system by foreigners seeking to use marriage illegitimately as a tool to get into Canada" was what spurred him to make permanent residency for immigrants via family sponsorship dependent on cohabiting with their Canadian partners once they were in Canada. The two-year period was deemed necessary for immigration services to determine whether or not the relationship was genuine.

There was an exemption for those who could prove they were being abused, but as in the UK, often the women who needed to escape the violence enabled by the probationary period didn't know about the exemption.

Unsurprisingly, in the wake of the amendment being passed, "Immigrant Women Services Ottawa staff and child protection services report[ed] a spike in new [violence against women] cases." In 2016, the new Liberal government announced that they would remove the probation period.

I mention all of this recent policy history to illustrate how quickly and easily migrant and women's rights can be removed because of anti-immigrant feeling The Liberal government's reasoning for removing the probation period as a condition for permanent settlement reveals an understanding of why it enabled domestic and emotional abuse; an understanding that the UK Home Office apparently does not have.

The Government recognizes that, while cases of marriage fraud exist, the majority of relationships are genuine and most spousal sponsorship applications are made in good faith. Eliminating conditional permanent residence upholds the Government's commitment to family reunification and supports gender equality and combating gender violence.

As a result of the requirement for the sponsored spouse or partner to live with their sponsor, an imbalance between the sponsor and the sponsored spouse or partner could have been created, potentially making the sponsored spouse or partner more vulnerable.

The UK has long been outwardly committed to the protection of human rights. It has ratified international treaties such as the Convention on the Elimination of All Forms of Discrimination Against Women and the European Convention on Human Rights (incorporated into domestic law by the Human Rights Act 1998), among others. The Conservatives, led by Theresa May, claim "a strong record on tackling domestic violence," but cuts to shelter funding continue, with specialist services for ethnic minority women often being the first to go (at the time of writing there are no permanent LGBTQ-specific shelters in England). And yet, despite the government's awareness of the vulnerability of women under its immigration laws, none of the raft of laws introduced have even mentioned the difficulties faced by migrant women who suffer gendered violence, let alone included measures that would help them.

The simplest way of removing the power imbalance that enables domestic abuse as a consequence of the policy around family visas is to grant non-EU partners of British citizens permanent settlement, and to give them access to public benefits as a result of that settlement. There is an urgent need for victims of exploitation and abuse in general to be able to access public funds (or, in the case of the United States, receive public assistance). But the assumption that all immigrants are lying and that they will be a burden on the taxpayer, and the further conclusion that more immigrants will be drawn to the UK and the US by such benefits, is so deeply ingrained in immigration policy and societal thought that this cannot be contemplated.

There is a refusal, from the highest levels of government to on-the-ground services, to see migrant women as human beings instead of as merely stereotypes and their immigration status. To acknowledge that is to acknowledge that domestic violence policy is exclusionary, that gendered discrimination runs deeply through immigration policy, and that a cornerstone of feminism—the shelter movement—has failed those who are the most vulnerable.

It has been a difficult few years for the UK shelter movement and other social services under the austerity measures of the Conservative government. But much of their failure to help the most powerless women stems from multiple avenues of discrimination and the lack of an intersectional approach to providing help. Within women's organizations it is imperative that going forward any movement for justice or help provided must be explicitly intersectional, or it is inevitable that many more women will be left behind.

"OKAY. LET'S TRY this again."

Liz is staring at copy number two of the family visa application form. The first one is largely filled out, with question marks on certain pages and corrections in red pen on Post-its. Next to that is a stack of folders: our documentation, organized by theme (financial/employment, citizenship, living arrangements, proof of relationship). There are duplicate folders, because she's photocopied everything twice (the Home Office has occasionally lost people's original documents).

"So." She takes a deep breath, before turning page one of seventy-nine.

She goes through the form, double-checking everything. We've been extraordinarily lucky: After we put out a call for help with some confusing questions on Twitter, one friend volunteered to look over our answers on the form because they work for the Home Office, and another said they'd ask a friend who specializes in immigration law if they could offer advice.

Later that week, Liz types the answers into the online application form. She pays the £993 fee, the £200 per year immigration health surcharge for non-EU immigrants (£500 in total), and later, another £20-odd for biometrics. I transfer half the costs to her, and try not to think about how we will cover that month's rent. We have yet another minor panic over something small, and then suddenly, it's in the mail (£8.55, tracked). Everything is done. And then we wait for an answer.

THROUGHOUT THE APPLICATION PROCESS, I couldn't stop thinking about the many women whose circumstances would make their encounters with the Home Office, social workers, and women's services impossibly difficult, even traumatic. Women who don't have access to the middle-class networks that I have, who don't have friends who might know an immigration lawyer. Women who can't afford a lawyer or adviser, who find that legal aid cuts make it even harder to get good legal advice. Women whose first language isn't English, or who would find it hard to trust strangers with details about their abuser or about what they needed generally. I thought often about the impact of all of this, as well as poverty and other problems, upon their mental health.

Immigration is a feminist issue. If you consider how gender discrimination is affected and compounded by other forms of power and oppression, it is impossible *not* to think of it as a feminist issue.

The lack of willingness, training, and knowledge in shelters across the country to assist migrant women who have suffered gender-based violence reflects not just austerity cuts, but mainstream feminism's wider failings. Feminism that isn't intersectional in thought and action, and that mainly campaigns for the rights of a small section of women only, isn't really feminism. If it is going to move forward and really be inclusive of all women, giving platforms to explicitly intersectional organizations like Safety4Sisters to raise awareness, listening to them, campaigning with them, and allocating more resources, would be a step in the right direction. Political decision makers who claim to be feminists would do well to look at how policies across areas like immigration affect women. Prioritizing the most vulnerable women and the issues that affect them most is what will make feminism truly comprehensive.

BROWN ON THE OUTSIDE

Mariya Karimjee

I DO NOT remember when I first heard the word *feminist*, but I identified as one as soon as I was introduced to the concept. As a teenager, my definition of the word was simple: Women should be allowed the same things as men. This was as ingrained in me as breathing—in Karachi, where I lived until age ten, not every woman had the right to go to school, to work, to desire a career. I was aware that not everyone believed in the concept, but in high school in the United States, the playing field seemed so even. Everyone got to go to school. Everyone got to learn to drive. Everyone got to wear what they wanted. Girls could hope for higher education. Women could vote. Birth control existed. In the Houston suburb where I lived, these were inalienable facts. That anyone would argue that feminism wasn't necessary confused me. It had given us everything we had today, what women in the country of my birth did not.

My best friend in Texas was the first woman I met who didn't reflexively agree. We were juniors in high school, and I was editing an essay in which I'd inserted the word *feminist* as a qualifier for her. She slowly rolled her tongue around the word as though it were foreign. "I don't know, Mari," she said. She was answering a question I did not know I had asked. Something inside me cracked. This is up for debate? I wondered.

You believe that women are equal to men, I wanted to say. So what exactly is the problem? "I think it's pretty basic for me," I explained, trying not to squirm. "I think that a woman should be allowed to do anything that a man can do. If you believe that, you're a feminist."

But for my friend, describing herself as a feminist would take the puzzle pieces of her life and put them back together in a completely different shape. She'd grown up cosseted by whiteness and femininity, and she had what I now realize is a common worry that embracing feminism would mean that she couldn't wholeheartedly love her dresses or enjoy putting on makeup. She worried that feminism meant that she would have to hate women's traditional roles, when she didn't. She worried that feminism meant that the romantic comedies she liked would evaporate. She worried that feminism meant she'd stop loving her father with the boundless youthfulness that allowed her to see him as infallible.

I never had these concerns. For girls in Karachi, attending school was a privilege. I'd grown up knowing my younger brother was loved more simply because he was a boy. I'd grown up knowing that I did not have the same access to space as a man—in Karachi, whole sections of the city hummed with men, not one woman in sight. In those heady days of early adulthood, my friend's calculus of whether to call herself a feminist was so much more complex than my own. We talked it through, and she chose to include *feminist* in a list of adjectives that described her. I assumed that meant the issue was settled. I assumed the hurdle for her was not a basic belief in equality.

I CAN PINPOINT exactly the first moment in my life when I realized that whiteness is transactional, an ingrained unconscious power that is imprinted on all interactions. I was standing in the bleachers at a high school football game, maroon and white ribbons threaded into my hair and my T-shirt. I was in the eighth grade and every time I jumped up to clap my hands together, cheering for a team that I believed would be mine, school spirit literally jingling around me, little bells shaking on avid fans everywhere. It was a Friday, two and a half days since planes had flown into skyscrapers in New York City. It had been less than two years since my family had moved from Pakistan to the United States, and before allowing me to go to the game that evening, my parents had had a long phone conversation with my friend's parents. "Do you think it will be safe?" my mother had asked, and my friend's father comforted her by insulting me. "No one thinks of her as Muslim," he said. "To all of us, she's basically white."

Basically white. I mouthed the words, my lips pressing down on the *B* and rounding on the *W*. Two words and this man had managed ineloquently to sum up years of trying to fit into the United States. The accent I had painstakingly curated, the clothes I fought with my parents to wear, the types of after-school snacks I made sure my mother kept around for when I had friends over. "Basically white," I repeated in my head, when it was third and goal and the marching band started playing the jaunty slinging notes of "Proud Mary." My entire bleacher section stood up, swaying with the beat, and I noticed that every person around me was singing the song. Rollin', rollin', they shouted, and even though I didn't know the words, I pretended to sing along. With this constant struggle to make sure that no one recognized I was a fish out of water, I had somehow rubbed my identity off myself, transforming into something acceptable for the people around me. Basically white.

What I cannot remember is exactly when I learned that

convincing people that I was white was a form of power. I cannot remember that moment when I internalized that in order to be successful in a country that would always define me by my race, I had to convince everyone around me of my universality. I cannot remember the moment when "fitting in" came to mean "being white."

In high school, my friends joked that I was a chicken nugget. Brown on the outside, they would say, and white on the inside. I laughed with them, too scared of what they'd say if I tried to describe how confused and alone this made me feel. At home, I scribbled on a piece of notebook paper. "White on the Inside," I wrote on the top, then listed everything my friends thought was exclusive to their race. Liking American football. Scream-singing along to Kelly Clarkson. Having memorized the recipe for cookies on the back of Nestlé Toll House chocolate chips. Muttering "Jesus Christ" as a curse under my breath. Shopping at the same stores as they did at the mall. Running my fingers across the deckled edges of books. I'd worked so hard to fit in that almost everything I did fit under their umbrella of "white." They had a narrow definition of what it meant to be brown, and everything outside that, it seemed, was white.

The only things that didn't fall under this header, I realized, were those that were exclusively South Asian. My bangles. The Bollywood music my mother played in the car. The fact that I could slip in and out of three different languages. Whiteness had claimed every other part of my personality. The only way I would not be white in their eyes was to remain exactly like they imagined brown women. There was no space for nuance.

Then we left for college. I went to Mount Holyoke, the first college for women in the United States. It was there, absent the fight for gender equality, that I began thinking critically about race and class. I learned the word *heteronor-*

mativity. I learned about gender as performance. I learned that the world was expansive and incredible, and also that there was a long history of structural and systemic oppression, yes, even within the United States. I learned how to say, confidently, "I am a woman of color." It was not a statement I had ever known could imbue me with such power and knowledge—I wasn't alone, it said; there were people before me and people who came after me. I occupy a very small part of this country, my words reminded me. I am grateful. I am strong.

I was excited by how empowering this felt, and I was eager to discuss it with my best friend, both of us home for winter break after our first semester away. We were no longer simply women fighting for equality in a man's world. "Race is a social construct," I told her, driving together in our hometown. "That's dumb," she said. "We see it everywhere. How can it be imaginary?" The conversation fizzled out, but I thought about the list I'd made in high school. I wanted her to see that the ideas and stereotypes you attach to a race are entirely made up.

"If I had a son," this same friend texted me recently, "I would never put him in a shirt that said the Future is Female. I wouldn't want him to feel like HE couldn't be the future." Huh, I thought, but responded by ignoring it. Nearly ten years had passed since our first discussion of feminism. She was in Texas and I was in New York City, where it had just poured outside, turning the world into a rainbow. My Twitter feed seemed to have paused over this miracle. "Some sort of magic sky sunset is happening," I said, holding my tongue. If social media—the angry, buzzing virtual safe space I had created for myself—could be in harmony about the beautiful weather, maybe my friend and I could be, too.

Later that evening, while I was moisturizing my legs—my mind empty, my hands busy—her text popped back up in my mind. I had not successfully shrugged it off, I realized. I still felt a buzzing irritation at her words. I could not remember the context in which it was said, just the words themselves. "What?" I said out loud to myself, physically shaking my head and speaking to an empty room. *What on earth did she mean by that? Did the context even matter?*

Those two questions had become a sort of mantra, something I'd started repeating to myself every single time my friend said something I disagreed with, something that made no sense to me. "I watched twenty minutes of a documentary about ISIS," she had said once, from the comfort of her shockingly white Dallas suburb. "I'm home alone and I'm afraid to shower." What on earth does she mean by that? I asked myself, genuinely wishing to understand. Was there a context in which her comment could make more sense, give me insight into whatever had prompted her to text me this self-centering response to learning more about ISIS?

I listed every possible explanation I could come up with.

Maybe she meant: I have only just now realized that ISIS is dangerous, and it has scared me down to my core. Or maybe: I have realized that the world is dangerous, and even my shower is no longer safe. Or maybe: It has been easy for me to pretend that the world is not terrifying outside the comfortable environment that I am lucky to have as a benefit of my white privilege, and for a second I remembered it was not.

None of these hypothetical explanations would change the fact that she often said things she believed were innocent but that I could only see through the lens of her unexamined privilege.

I chose not to tell her that sometimes when we spoke, keeping silent felt like I was ripping my insides into tiny shreds and lighting them on fire. We had always been different. My brown skin next to her white skin, my black hair next to her blond. Her devout Christianity next to my Muslim upbringing, my current uncertainty about whether I even believed in a god. None of that had mattered when we were younger, but now it felt like these differences had propelled us into completely different lives. No longer interested in performing some kind of whiteness, I wondered what we had left except for a shared history—dissecting pigs in biology, loving the same kind of stationery, sharing books and trading camera lenses. Every time our conversations veered even slightly into politics or current affairs, I felt as though I couldn't even recognize the kind of person she was. Could one of my best friends truly be a person who responded to educating herself about ISIS by texting that she was afraid of being alone? Did she really believe that putting a little boy in a shirt that said THE FUTURE IS FEMALE would quash his dreams and desires? Did she know that it seemed like every time she said something this, it felt like she was saying she did not believe in my rights, that she had never taken a step back to consider my reality?

When we talked about politics and the future, it felt like we could not even agree on the existence of the same present. Lingering behind all of these conversations was my knowledge that we couldn't share a future, because each of us already lived in separate worlds. She was afraid of taking a shower because of a documentary on ISIS, but she'd never asked about my fear of racists, of going through passport control, of the current US president.

Worse, I was terrified she wouldn't understand me if I tried to explain.

And two months later, when I finally asked her to examine her white privilege, those fears were confirmed. "It feels like you don't even want to be friends with me," she said. "It's like you blame me for being white."

I didn't respond to her comment directly. Instead, I said, "I do this thing. I see you say some of the most problematic things I've ever heard from another person and I choose not to tell you how I feel."

Suddenly, I felt liberated. I was a feather, a particle of dust, an autumn leaf picked up by wind. It's this easy, I thought to myself. I can just tell her that this is not the beginning of the fight. We can finally talk about the fight that has been going on for years, raging in the hollow of my ribs and in the cavity of my chest. In that moment, I felt compelled to tell her that if she wanted to know how I truly felt, she needed to know all of it.

When Trump was elected, my friend texted me to see how I was doing, a sign that she had listened to our conversation. "How are you doing?" I asked her. I didn't have words to express how I felt just yet. She had a four-month-old baby at home, a fair-skinned and blond-haired girl. "I always wished I wouldn't have a blond-haired, blue-eyed baby," she had said to me once after the baby was born. "And then I did." My friend had always struggled under the weight of what she considered conventional expectations of beauty, but I couldn't take her fear that her daughter would grow up stereotyped as "too beautiful" all that seriously while I worried that I might be attacked for my skin color. I wondered if she'd say this in front of other nonwhite women, if she could realize how it would sound. I carried my anger underneath my heart like a small rock.

"You just brought a daughter into this world," I said over text, trying to see what Trump meant to her. "Is that not terrifying?" Trump had bragged about grabbing women's pussies, proud of his history of sexual assault, convinced it was an act worthy of other men's awe. I knew that I would sob myself to sleep at night thinking about the young girls we were bringing into the world. Our country had chosen this man. It felt like a death sentence.

"I wouldn't have been thrilled either way," she said, and I spent the rest of the day feeling as though someone had punched me in the stomach, all the air leaving me in a whoosh and then returning with eye-watering pain.

The next day, I emailed her, asking for an explanation. Her answer was simple: "I also worried about what Clinton would have meant for the future of our country." I tried to swallow that down, but I couldn't. I grew up in Karachi, Pakistan, I wanted to yell. My city was crowded with people who were internally displaced, with Afghan refugees begging for jobs because of Secretary Clinton's AfPak policy. I, too, had strong reservations about her. But I had easily put those concerns aside—to me, given Trump's xenophobia and racism, there was no choice, but to my friend the two outcomes existed on the same plane.

Does the context even matter? I ask myself as I watch our friendship falter and struggle. My friend does not yet have a son. But already she is worried about how feminist slogans like "The future is female" might affect his ability to believe that he, too, can have a future. Around us, there is a president who has been supported by white supremacists. He endorsed a Senate candidate who has been accused of pedophilia. The president himself has been accused of rape. What future is unimaginable to her unborn, not-yet-conceived son? How can this be the thing she is worrying about?

It was so simple, I had told her in high school. Feminism is simply believing that women and men are equal. I believed that. I still do. But that also means believing all humans are created equal. And I no longer know if she believes that. Part of that is because I see her refuse to examine the inequality that does exist, and her own role in continuing that.

It's a discussion I've had with countless friends over the past year, one in which we talk about a moment when whiteness becomes aggressive and hostile to our way of being. One moment, it's a normal conversation, and in the next, the person we're with has revealed the limits of their understanding.

I am constantly working to convince my friend that I am the same as she, so that I can show her how differently the world treats us. "White on the Inside," reads the piece of notebook paper that I have carried around in a manila folder to every single city I have ever lived in. I still laugh about the list, laugh over the idea that loving Kelly Clarkson and believing in the power of literature are things that make someone white—that could make me white.

I spent years of our friendship weaseling my way into her space so that my race didn't seem alien to her whiteness. So now can I blame her that her whiteness centers her politics, her worldview? Didn't I convince her I was human like her by acting like my own race was negligible? I wonder now if she would have had a broader worldview if I hadn't forced myself into a shape that she'd be comfortable with. I am her only nonwhite friend. Is it too late for her to reconcile these ideas? Is it too late to prove that we will never be treated equally, even though we are the same?

DEVIANT BODIES

Soofiya Andry

What Is a Deviant Body?

I have always lived in a deviant body. When I think of my body as deviant, I think of it in relation to the dichotomies of beautiful and ugly, of dangerous and safe, of good and bad. A deviant body exists to be scrutinized, an unwelcome reminder to society that some bodies fail. When I speak of a deviant body I do so in the context of my personal deviations—my brown skin, hairy face, and chubby stature are my points of reference.

Almost all bodies deviate in some way and are met with similar repercussions and oppressions. However, deviant bodies are the ones that carry their deviations visibly and excessively. The reality of existing in a visibly gender-nonconforming body is nuanced and difficult, but it is also simple: My body isn't beautiful, my body isn't good, and most important, my body isn't safe.

The Deviant Body and Feminism

I first found feminism because of my deviant body. During my late teens I found myself participating in feminist body-positive movements, one of which was a body-hair-positive campaign. Women and nonbinary people grew out their body hair for a month to raise money for a charity for people with polycystic ovary syndrome. I was the only person of color in that group, and my hairiness is tied to my South Asian heritage. Being surrounded by white people, mostly women, who could choose to grow out their fair hair and not feel the same repercussions from society as I would was an alienating experience I couldn't quite articulate at the time. On the whole, this campaign and those like it within the body-positive movement draw on a feminism that fails to see intersectional bodies.

The feminism I consider to have failed is a monolithic, one-size-fits-all feminism. An example would be how in the fight for equal pay the statistic often quoted refers to the difference between men and white women in the UK; the pay gap for women of color is far greater. As a 2017 article in the *Guardian* pointed out, "Pakistani and Bangladeshi women see the biggest overall gender pay gap, at 26%, to white British men." The reasons for this aren't singular; the type of feminism needed for white women to achieve equal pay is very different from the one needed by women of color. Roxane Gay captures failure of a singular feminism profoundly in her essay "Feminism (Plural)." She writes, "historically, [feminism has] been far more invested in improving the lives of heterosexual white women to the detriment of all others." The feminism I want, and the one my deviant body needs, is one of pluralities. To quote Gay again, "We don't have to believe in the same feminism. Feminism can be pluralistic and messy." What is needed for one deviant body may not be enough for another. This is vital for deviant bodies—our bodies aren't neat; they're complex. Our bodies exist in multitudes and our feminism should, too.

The feminism(s) I found in my early twenties had an awareness of these multitudes and intersections, mostly because they existed within communities that introduced me to ideas that went beyond binary genders. Slowly, I started building an understanding of how feminism and bodies relate and the intersections of us, aided by experiences with anti-racist politics as well. However, this is yet to be the case for mainstream feminism, where nuanced discussions in which varying lived experiences are accepted and nurtured can be hard to come across except for at the fringes.

For example, I am a second-generation immigrant, the firstborn child of a Pakistani Muslim who left her home more than two decades ago in favor of a country that has been often hostile and alienating. Our experiences of the world are seen through a lens of brownness and the South Asian diaspora. Any feminist thought I apply to my body and being will always have to take into account this experience of growing up and living as the child of immigrants.

I grew up surrounded by white bodies, none hairy or brown like mine; my childhood was set in 1990s South East England. I was a quiet child; I tried to do as I was told, kept my head down, and just about survived school. It was an alienating experience; I was different from my peers in both body and culture. Socially awkward, I struggled to understand the maps those around me used to navigate the world with such ease. I couldn't at the time understand how, when compared to my own body, my peers were tolerated and treated kinder by society. Meanwhile my body experienced racial abuse and bullying for being too brown, hairy, and unfeminine.

I spoke fluent English and broken Urdu spliced together. I spent all my time and energy trying to learn, make, fight, and exist. Slowly, each of us in the family carved out a life for ourselves, finding our own individual ways of surviving and healing the hostility of living and existing in spaces we didn't always feel like we belonged in.

In my midtwenties, I found a home in friends I love fiercely, who understand the struggles of living in deviant bodies. I found a chosen family who have my heart and love me in ways my blood family are still learning to do. I found feminists (like Roxane Gay and Amina Wadud) who shifted my view of the world and my personal politics. It's through the words and work of activists like Aisha Mirza and Alok Vaid-Menon that I began to better understand my deviant body. Above all, I found the space to talk and think. Zines and other publications allowed me to explore ideas of feminism and bodies, becoming almost a form of art therapy. It was through writing and creating that I finally found a means to articulate the sort of home and the type of feminism I was trying to find—a feminism that can accept all parts of me, all deviations, and embrace them deeply. Yet despite this, my feelings of isolation remain. Even though I've found a home for myself, it's very difficult to move through the world in a deviant body like mine.

Beautiful Bodies

When I speak about beauty as a dichotomy, I refer to a normative set of predetermined qualities that constitute acceptable ways of presentation, qualities that are praised and valued and that carry social currency. These qualities can include (but are not limited to): whiteness, smoothness (opposite of hairiness), slimness, and cisness. If your body doesn't reflect all of these qualities in their entirety, then it has deviated and failed.

My body is one such failure. My body isn't beautiful. Beauty is a country, a fascist state with violent borders in which I can, at best, only ever be a tourist. I visit that country for fleeting moments, during which it doesn't feel so malicious. It's a country in which I cannot and will not live. I look around the country of Beauty and I see homogeneity; nowhere do I see a reflection of my own hairy face. I see laws all bodies must abide by; they are narrow, suffocating, and inescapable.

The laws of Beauty are ones to which my body, fundamentally, can never adhere. I can't change the color of my skin, no matter how aggressively tubes of Fair and Lovely skin-lightening cream are marketed in my mother's homeland. I can pluck, rip, and wax, but my face will always be hairy and so will my arms, my legs, my torso. My body is chubby, its rolls and flesh not always fitting in clothes.

Policed Bodies

Its worth noting that my deviations, my hairiness in particular, are tied intrinsically to my South Asian heritage. They are read as ugly and deviant, in part, because they subvert Western and Eurocentric standards of beauty. Subversion is a threat to the state. It dares to imply that there is another way to exist. This subversion must be fixed; it needs to be policed. Beauty is policed by your friends, parents, acquaintances and partners, your communities, no matter how radical, by strangers on the street, and even by you yourself. It's easy to paint these enforcers as every white-hetero-cis-capitalist man in the world. That is reductive. As a person of color I can internalize racism, and I use this to police myself and others despite good intentions and knowing better. I also find this policing in feminist spaces. Slut shaming, trans-exclusionary feminism, sex-worker-exclusionary feminism, white feminism—all of these areas take ideas and thoughts and use them to police women and bodies they deem as deviating. It comes back to the common wisdom that patriarchy is so lazy that it gets women (and other marginalized genders) to do its work for it. The state is not maintained by the establishment of aesthetic alone; it is maintained by you, by me, by bodies I love, I hate, I know, and bodies I don't.

Policing Beauty happens in public and in private. Private policing is when your mother puts facial bleach on your mustache when you are eleven even though you are crying because it burns and itches. It's when your grandma points to your face, and with nothing but care in her voice and love in her intentions, she says, "This looks dirty, beti." It's when your two close friends, both white, smooth, and skinny, laugh about your sideburns in secondary school and you pretend not to hear because what can you say? These words from the ones you love leave your body filled with shame and your heart filled with hurt. These words are reminders that your deviation is everyone's responsibility (just as much as it is yours) to correct.

Public policing of Beauty isn't always obvious, but it is constant. Its threat haunts every plan, every outfit, every decision you make before stepping out in public. It's when strangers openly stare at you; it's when people on the train try to take photos of you; it's when groups of men snigger and point, calling you a "dirty, hairy Paki." It's when people say, loud enough for you to hear, "Is that a man or a woman?" This public dialogue on your deviant body is a reminder that you do not belong in Beauty. My deviations strip me of my humanity and are read as consent to make my body a public discourse. Public and private policing of bodies is a reaffirmation that everyone is allowed an opinion on a deviant body except, of course, the body itself. This is because a deviant body showing autonomy is one of the most frightening things of all.

Refusing to assimilate frightens the state, and when the state is scared it is often at its most abusive and dangerous. When the state feels a loss of power, it will retaliate to recover lost ground. When the state sees a body that cannot be tamed, a deviant, it fears that which it cannot understand or control. What if other bodies start to empathize? What if this spreads to other bodies? What if they see through our laws? What if they rise up? This disruption must be stopped before it starts. The state has everything to lose; the deviant body has everything to gain.

Good Bodies

A law-abiding body is a good body. A good body will listen and put itself through all the requirements in order to occupy Beauty and goodness. Societal pressure and norms on how we can touch our bodies, the things we can change, take off, add, remove, put in, and take out are all ordained by the state. To deviate from this is a moral wrong as well as a criminal one. A good body, law-abiding and obedient, is frequently rewarded with safety and protection.

A beautiful body is one that meets all the benchmarks set by the state. It has much stricter parameters of presentation compared with a body that is only good. A good body that aspires to be beautiful, even if it isn't yet, will be tolerated. A body that is trying is a body of no threat. A good body can be permitted to carry weight, unlike a beautiful body, but this must be in moderation, carried in seamless proportion and coupled with hyperfemininity. We see this reflected in the depiction of "curvy" women as "real" women. However, to go beyond the quota and fail to moderate is a deviation. I occupy a chubby body with small breasts, big hips, and thunder thighs. My body carries weight in ways that deviate from how people think women "should" carry weight. "The state isn't all that fascist—look, it will allow people to carry weight," people will say. But this illusion of tolerance exists only because it cannot expect pure beauty from every body. What if everyone was beautiful—who would be left for the state to oppress?

A bad body is also considered an unhealthy body or a differently abled body. The medical-industrial complex regularly seeks to profit from the assimilation of deviant bodies who struggle to conform to the idea of a good body. This is even more so with the beauty industry. For example, I have polycystic ovary syndrome, a condition far more prominent in those of South Asian heritage. Treatment of my hirsutism and chubbiness was costly, including spending hundreds of pounds on monthly hair removal treatments, multiplied over a lifetime. My desire to be hair-free is a result of Eurocentricity and standards of beauty that uphold whiteness, it was this which led me to stop removing my hair and is now a reflection of how I am slowly trying to decolonize my body.

Hairy is seen as dirty, much like the brownness with which it is commonly associated. A good body is a clean body, a body that is smooth, plucked, and free of hair. Again, a good body can be gifted with tolerance here; if you are a beautiful white girl, society will allow you to have tiny wisps of armpit or leg hair, and you will be heralded for breaking the norms, but as previously mentioned, moderation is key for a good body. Moderation avoids proximity and associations with people of color and transness. Excessive hairiness will be penalized; hair on your face is not for anyone who wishes to align themselves with femininity.

Safe Bodies

Safety for my gender-nonconforming body is being able to exist in public without the threat of violence. Time and time again I feel unsafe in public. Danger articulates itself in various forms: like when you're stopped and searched by the police because someone reported you on your regular commute. Your being brown, hairy, and in a hijab was too suspicious, too threatening, and cannot be trusted. It can be a group of loud white men laughing as you walk past. The danger of living in a deviant body is having to measure every threat: Are they going to stare and take photos, or are they going to physically hurt me? It's a balance, a compromise in hopes of lesser harassment: "I'll sit silently and let them laugh because if I say something, I could leave with a broken nose or knee-caps." This is something many women experience, but for gender-nonconforming bodies it's different because society—and even mainstream feminism—condones the danger in which deviant bodies exist. This is evident in the violence perpetrated by trans-exclusionary feminism, in which the most vulnerable women and marginalized people are left outside feminist discourse. Most recently, conversations surrounding trans people's use of bathrooms and changing rooms highlights how toxic this type of exclusionary feminism can be. Use of bathrooms and changing rooms is predominantly about safety, and which bodies are deserving of safety. In opposing trans people's right to use the bathroom of their choice, exclusionary feminism aims to take away safety in public spaces for gender-nonconforming bodies.

Public harassment is often followed by silence; people are less likely to defend or protect deviant bodies. This needs to change in feminism as well as in society. Safe bodies don't have to weigh up how much energy they have to fight the world that day before stepping outside, and they rarely need to ask themselves, "Can I run in this chub? I want to wear eyeliner but can I with my mustache? What if something happens? Will someone help?" The answer all too often is no.

Good bodies and beautiful bodies can be recipients of this pressure, and violence—one in five have been sexually assaulted—its epidemic. However, often gender-nonconforming bodies, are ones that can feel the full extent of violence in public, with over a third of trans people having experienced a hate crime in the past twelve months. Sexual violence and harassment are all too commonly used to police the good and beautiful bodies of those who occupy forms of femininity.

However, should the good and beautiful bodies experience harassment, the structures in place for support, being believed, and healing are usually more accessible to them. Accessibility comes through the social worth that certain bodies possess. Deviant bodies carry little, if any, social value; as a result, safety is harder and more costly for them to access. When someone is laughing on the train about my hairy face, nobody steps in. To be visibly nonconforming to Beauty and binary gender is to consent to violence. Deviation concedes my safety, in the world at large but also within feminism and feminist politics.

A question might be forming in your mind: Why, if there is so much danger and pain tied to being gender nonconforming, do I persist in my deviance? My answer is uncomplicated and resentful: Do you think I have a choice in the matter? My body is mine, it grows in its own, and despite its deviance, I love my body because its my own. To believe that my deviant body is a choice is a luxury afforded by those with beautiful, good, and safe bodies. Surely, if this body were a choice, would I not have chosen, at the very least, a body that is safe? Despite this, I know I am still entitled to safety, love, and equality.

Loved Bodies

A deviant body is rarely loved. I don't know how to hold love or accept love. Instead of accepting it as a gift, you are forced to question: What are their motives? What is their agenda? My deviant body knows its worth to the state, to society, and to other bodies. A deviant body can be fetishized or tokenized; it can be put on a pedestal as either a warning or a performative celebration of diversity. But it does not seem possible for it to be loved, be it romantically or platonically, and held by the world, at least under the current regime.

Love isn't something my body or I were built for. My mother loves me, my family and my friends love me, but loving a deviant body is a burden. To love that body opens you up to the same hostility through association. Not everyone can carry this burden; it is heavy and exhausting. I remember once being out for dinner with a friend, and she said, "That couple keeps staring at us. Maybe it's my purple hair—do we look weird?" Her good body, despite the purple hair, wasn't weird. It was my deviant body that prompted the staring, and by letting herself sit close, she felt the hostility through association. For a fleeting moment she carried that burden.

Neutrality is the closest and most comfortable thing I hope for. But what if I learned to hold love? What if deviant bodies could be loving and loved bodies? When I imagine a world like this, I know I am tired of burning down my house because other people don't like my garden. I am tired of carrying the shame others project onto my body. I want to feel at home in a world where all bodies are good bodies, where all bodies are safe bodies and all bodies are beautiful bodies. A world that loves deviant bodies, my body, and treats us with softness and tenderness. I want a world that will hold me when I am hurt, make me laugh until I cry. I want you to see beyond my hairy face, brown skin, and chubby rolls. I want you to share my joys, my hopes, my fears and dreams. I want to celebrate and reclaim the ugliness of my body; I want to reject the state of Beauty and for those who love me to do so, too, in solidarity.

The Feminist Body

Being visibly gender nonconforming is tiresome. I'm tired of fighting, tired of it being the first and foremost thing about me. It's tiring not knowing who I could be beyond my deviant body if it weren't constantly defining me, who I am beyond my marginalization. Mainstream feminism also makes me tired: seeing Theresa May in a THIS IS WHAT A FEMINIST LOOKS LIKE T-shirt, despite the fact she advocated for violent detention centers for women. These models of feminism are superficial, like the statement T-shirts they wear; they fail to see the broader picture, relying on existing patriarchal structures to find success for themselves individually and others like them. It's tiring seeing women who already have a certain amount of privilege purport that feminism has won, saying that the bulk of the work in equality and change has been done. It hasn't—it's barely started, and I am tired of the lack of intersectional thought, of their failure to see beyond their personal struggle.

When your entire being is built on the trauma of surviving in a world that dehumanizes you because of the way you look you are always tired. But what would happen if all the bodies—the good bodies, the beautiful bodies, the safe bodies, and the deviant bodies—decided that the state had had its day? What would happen if the deviant bodies had felt too much pain? What would happen if the good bodies started becoming bad bodies? What would happen if the beautiful bodies joined the ugly? What would happen if the safe bodies helped those in danger? What would happen if we demanded radical change of both mainstream feminism and the world?

The day we decide to uproot this toxicity is the day we stop trying to find solace in assimilation. We must build a feminism reliant on community rather than on hierarchy. I urge all feminists, put gender-nonconforming people at the heart of your work; with alliance and empathy we can truly move toward radical change. Let us speak; give us platforms; ask us to write, talk, and lecture, we can share, create, and thrive if given spaces to do so. And after that, protect us. There will always be repercussions for speaking out and demanding safety, this is where feminism can step in when it sees us being hurt. You can campaign for our safety in public, pay for taxis home, defend us and our humanity. The day the state begins to fall is the day you walk your friend home because they are too anxious to be alone in a hostile world. Help us feel at home in the world by first helping us feel at home within feminism(s). A feminism which strives to help gender-nonconforming people live a life without fear or threat of violence is one we need. With this inclusive, nuanced, and intersectional feminism we can, together, take steps to overthrow the state of Beauty. By liberating the deviant body, you liberate us all.

ACKNOWLEDGMENTS

Putting together this anthology would have been impossible without the community of people who love and support me every day:

To Julia Kardon, for being a superstar agent, a confidante, my biggest advocate, and my friend. Thank you to you and Max for showing me what real love is, for opening your heart and home to me. I would not be the woman I'm becoming without your unconditional love and mentorship.

To Ailah Ahmed, Sarah Savitt, Gretchen Schmid, Lindsey Schwoeri, and the wonderful teams at Penguin Books US and Virago UK for taking a chance on me. It has been my absolute dream to work with such an impeccable all-female team. Special thanks to Lindsey Schwoeri, who spearheaded many aspects of this project.

To Ore Agbaje-Williams and Eishar Kaur, for being the older sisters I never knew I needed. Thank you for being chosen family and for loving me so fiercely that I am forced to love myself, too.

To Catrin Cooper, for carrying me through the hardest parts of being estranged from my family so I didn't have to go it alone. You mean so much to me—thank you.

To Attyat Mayans, for your love and humor that sustains

me, even on my worst days. I am so lucky to have you by my side.

To Lilinaz Evans, for inspiring me every day to choose my own path. I hope our four years of friendship becomes forty, and then, even more.

To Izin Akhabau, you being in my life is a cause for celebration every day. I'm excited to see how far you soar.

To my babies, Jemima and Albachiara, your Auntie June loves you so much and is forever proud of you. To Aunt Connie and Aunt Josephine, thank you for loving me like your own.

To Arlene Arevalo, Ce'Ondra Ellison, Mumbi Kanyogo, Johnna Lambert, Parmida Mostafavi, and Tatayana Richardson, for friendship and joy. Here's to more years of friendship, more nights of eating barbeque wings at 2 a.m., more evenings spent dancing in our rooms, and more love, so much love.

To Nimco Ali, Laura Bates, Daisy Buchanan, Gemma Cairney, Kira Cochrane, Lynn Enright, Ifrah Hassan, Muna Hassan, Jude Kelly, Catherine Mayer, Hannah Azieb Pool, and Lisa Zimmermann, for your support of me and my activism over the years.

To the staff and professors at Duke, who have trusted my ability to execute this project and supported me and my goals: Jill Anderson, Valerie Ashby, Debbie LoBiondo, John Blackshear, Tsitsi Jaji, Tori Lodewick, Jarvis McInnis, and Karin Shapiro. A very special mention goes to Tiarra Wade, for always making me feel like I can succeed. You're the best and I am indebted to you.

Finally, to my little sisters, Joan and Erica, I love you both so much. I hope we'll be able to reunite soon.

Thank you to those listed, and to those not listed. I am immensely grateful to have all of you rooting for me. I am such a lucky, lucky girl.

NOTES

Introduction

x   **I came across a definition of feminism:** hooks, bell, *Feminist Theory: From Margin to Center* (Boston: South End Press, 1984).

xii   **In what is now a famous speech:** Truth, Sojourner, "Ain't I a Woman?" *National Anti-Slavery Standard*, May 2, 1863, reproduced at http://sojournertruthmemorial.org/sojourner-truth/her-words. Truth's speech was originally published by Marius Robinson in 1851 in the *Anti-Slavery Bugle*. The version cited here was published by Frances Dana Barker Gage. In this transcription, Gage gave Truth many of the speech characteristics of those enslaved in the South and included new material that Robinson had not reported in 1851. Gage's speech is now the historical standard, but there are several issues that have been raised about her version. This includes but is not limited to the fact that Truth's speech style was not like those enslaved in the South because she was born and raised in New York and had spoken Dutch exclusively until she was nine years old. Other inaccuracies include Gage's introduction of the idea that Truth could bear the lash as well as a man, and mention of her thirteen children being sold into slavery, when it is widely believed that Truth had only five children, with one sold away.

xiii   **I feel I have the right:** "Celebrating Dr. Martin Luther King Jr.: Black Women & the Suffrage Movement: 1848–1923," Wesleyan University, http://www.wesleyan.edu/mlk/posters/suffrage.html.

xiii   **There is a great stir:** Ibid.

xiv   **I will cut off this right arm of mine:** Ibid.

xiv   **Fast-forward to the 2016 presidential election:** Segal, Corinne, "Hundreds of 'I Voted' Stickers Left at Susan B. Anthony's Grave," PBS, November 8, 2016, https://www.pbs.org/newshour/politics/hundreds-voted-stickers-left-susan-b-anthonys-grave.

xiv   **For example, in 1913:** Yandoli, Krystie Lee, "People Are Upset About Meryl Streep's 'I'd Rather Be a Rebel Than a Slave' T-Shirt," *BuzzFeed*, October 5, 2015, https://www.buzzfeed.com/krystieyandoli/people-are-upset-about-meryl-streeps-id-rather-be-a-rebel-th.

xiv   **In her words:** Crenshaw, Kimberlé, "Why Intersectionality Can't Wait," *Washington Post*, September 24, 2015, https://www.washingtonpost.com/news/in-theory/wp/2015/09/24/why-intersectionality-cant-wait.

xv   **ableism, racism, and sexism, for example:** Beal, Frances, *Double Jeopardy: To Be Black and Female* (Ann Arbor, MI: Radical Education Project, 1971).

xv   **at the next national conference:** "1969: The Year of Gay Liberation: Radicalesbians," New York Public Library, http://web-static.nypl.org/exhibitions/1969/radicalesbians.html.

xvi   **Governments that consists of:** Greer, Germaine, *The Whole Woman* (London, UK: Black Swan, 2007).

xvi   **all transsexuals rape women's bodies:** Raymond, Janice G., *The Transsexual Empire: The Making of the She-male* (New York: Teachers College, 1994).

xvi   **According to the National Center for Transgender Equality:** "Issues: Anti-Violence," National Center for Transgender Equality, https://transequality.org/issues/anti-violence.

xvi   **A 2011 study from the Anti-Violence Project:** National Coalition of Anti-Violence Programs, *Hate Violence Against Lesbian, Gay, Bisexual, Transgender, Queer and HIV-affected Communities in the United States in 2010* (New York: New York City Anti-Violence Project, 2011).

xviii   **But come election day, 53 percent of white women:** Rogers, Katie. "White Women Helped Elect Donald Trump," *New York Times*, November 9, 2016, http://www.nytimes.com/2016/12/01/us/politics/white-women-helped-elect-donald-trump.html.

xix   **In the United States, Black women and girls:** "#SayHerName," The African American Policy Forum (AAPF), http://www.aapf.org/sayhername.

xix   **In 2015, Amnesty International published:** Murphy, Catherine, "Sex Workers' Rights Are Human Rights," Amnesty International, August 14, 2015, https://www.amnesty.org/en/latest/news/2015/08/sex-workers-rights-are-human-rights.

xix **white feminists from Hollywood:** Staff and agencies, "Actors Call on Amnesty to Reject Plans Backing Decriminalisation of Sex Trade," *Guardian*, July 27, 2015, https://www.theguardian .com/society/2015/jul/28/actors-streep-winslet-thompson -dunham-amnesty-decriminalisation-sex-trade.

xx **Then there's rural America:** McKay, Betsy, and Paul Overberg, "Rural America's Childbirth Crisis: The Fight to Save Whitney Brown," *Wall Street Journal*, August 11, 2017, https://www.wsj .com/articles/rural-americas-childbirth-crisis-the-fight-to-save -whitney-brown-1502462523.

xx **one in three Hispanic or Latina women:** "Prevalence and Occurrence," National Latin@ Network, https://www.nationallatinonet work.org/learn-more/facts-and-statistics/prevalence-and-occurrence.

xxi **Instead, I seek a feminism:** Lorde, Audre, *Sister Outsider: Essays and Speeches* (Berkeley, CA: Crossing Press, 2007).

xxiv **a womanist is:** noteasybeingred, "Alice Walker's Definition of a 'Womanist,'" Tumblr, October 6, 2009, http://noteasybeingred .tumblr.com/post/206038114/alice-walkers-definition-of-a -womanist-from-in.

No Wave Feminism

4 **The challenge of the twenty-first century:** Davis, Angela Y., *Abolition Democracy* (New York: Seven Stories Press, 2005), 26.

Unapologetic

23 **[Black women] stumbled blindly through their lives:** Walker, Alice. "In Search of Our Mothers' Gardens: The Creativity of Black Women in the South," *Ms.* magazine, 2002, http://www .msmagazine.com/spring2002/walker.asp.

Fat Demands

31 **In it, she instructs women:** Orbach, Susie, *Fat Is a Feminist Issue*, vols. I and II (London: Arrow Books, 1998).

32 **We can see this in the ongoing appropriation:** See Dionne, Evette, "The Fragility of Body Positivity: How a Radical Movement Lost Its Way," Bitch Media, https://www.bitchmedia.org /article/fragility-body-positivity, for an excellent in-depth exploration of this.

33   **fat's inception as a discrediting factor:** Erdman Farrell, Amy, *Fat Shame: Stigma and the Fat Body in American Culture* (New York: New York University Press, 2011).

34   **endless articles about just how fat:** Randall, Alice, "Black Women and Fat," *New York Times*, May 5, 2012, http://www.ny times.com/2012/05/06/opinion/sunday/why-black-women-are -fat.html.

34   **how we fail to recognize:** "Large Discrepancies Between Parental Perceptions of Child's Weight and Official Classifications," London School of Hygiene and Tropical Medicine, https://www .lshtm.ac.uk/newsevents/news/2015/parental_perceptions_child _weight.html.

34   **this fat is just another example:** Harris, Tamara Winfrey, *The Sisters Are Alright: Changing the Broken Narrative of Black Women in America* (Oakland, CA: Berrett-Koehler, 2015).

37   **obesity tax on foie gras:** Garwood, Emma, "An Interview with Amy Lame," *Outline*, February 3, 2018, http://www.outlineonline .co.uk/content/interview-with-amy-lame/comedy/109658/2499.

38–39 **With every failure:** Brown, Harriet, "The Weight of the Evidence," *Slate*, March 24, 2015, http://www.slate.com/articles/health_and _science/medical_examiner/2015/03/diets_do_not_work_the _thin_evidence_that_losing_weight_makes_you_healthier.html.

40   **building your activism around the individual:** Cooper, Charlotte, *The Fat Activist Vernacular* (UK: Charlotte Cooper, 2016).

42   **Fatphobia is rampant in veganism:** Shire, Emily, "PETA Is Now Fat-Shaming Women into Vegan Diets," *The Week*, December 3, 2013, http://theweek.com/articles/455240/peta-now-fatshaming -women-into-vegan-diets.

42   **discussions of fat within transfeminism:** Various, "The Many Faces of Eating Disorders," *Do What You Want: A Zine About Mental Wellbeing* (UK: Ruby Tandoh and Leah Pritchard, 2017).

Intersectionality and the Black Lives Matter Movement

66   **As columnist Jarvis DeBerry explained:** DeBerry, Jarvis. "For Rekia Boyd and All the Overlooked Black Women Victims of the Police, *Times-Picayune,* April 24, 2015, http://www.nola.com/ opinions/index.ssf/2015/04/rekia_boyd_police_killings.html.

69   **As McGuire told NPR in 2011:** "Hidden Pattern of Rape Helped Stir Civil Rights Movement," NPR's *Tell Me More*, February 28, 2011.

No Disabled Access

83   **the pay gap between disabled women:** "The Wage Gap: The Who, How, Why, and What to Do," National Women's Law Center, https://nwlc.org/resources/the-wage-gap-the-who-how-why -and-what-to-do.

83   **research by the Equality and Human Rights Commission in 2017:** "Shake Up of Working Culture and Practices Recommended to Reduce Pay Gaps," Equality and Human Rights Commission, August 15, 2017, https://www.equalityhumanrights.com/en/our -work/news/shake-working-culture-and-practices-recommended -reduce-pay-gaps.

85   **disabled women are twice as likely to experience domestic violence:** "The Survivor's Handbook: Support for Disabled Women," Women's Aid Federation of England. Accessed via https://www.womensaid. org.uk/the-survivors-handbook/the-survivors-handbook-disabled -women.

85   **in the United States, there is a 40 percent greater chance of a woman being abused if she is disabled:** "Abuse of Women With Disabilities: Facts and Resources," American Psychological Association, http://www.apa.org/topics/violence/women-disabilities.aspx.

A Hundred Small Rebellions

93   **the ethnic group hailing from:** Chanda, Rupa, and Sriparna Ghosh, *The Punjabi Disapora in the UK: An Overview of Characteristics and Contributions to India* (Fiesole, Italy: European University Institute, 2013).

93   **The first significant migration:** Pitkänen, Pirkko, and Ahmet Içduygu, *Migration and Transformation: Multi-Level Analysis of Migrant Transnationalism* (Heidelberg, Germany: Springer Science & Business Media, 2012).

95   **whiteness positions itself as the norm:** Eddo-Lodge, Reni, *Why I'm No Longer Talking to White People About Race* (London: Bloomsbury, 2017).

97   **I'm lucky that this overt misogyny:** "Honor based violence," The Halo Project, https://www.haloproject.org.uk/honour-based-violence -W21page-3.

100 **The Pink Ladoo project:** www.pinkladoo.org.

Ends, Means, and Subterfuge in Feminist Activism

105 **I can't stand the thought:** A note here to acknowledge that lack of access to abortion affects all people who can get pregnant, not just women. This essay does use gendered language at times, partly for ease of communication, partly to reflect the reality of the discourse in Ireland, and partly because the vast majority of people affected by this issue are women. Irish trans and nonbinary folks: I see you, I feel you, your stories are important.

106 **conservative Catholic lobby groups:** That's right—contraception was only legalized in Ireland in 1980, and you needed a prescription to buy condoms.

Representation as a Feminist Act

138 **bad hair more than anything else:** Rumbelow, Helen. "Originally My Headscarf Was Probably to Cover Up My Bad Hair More Than Anything Else," *Times* (London), August 9, 2016, https://www .thetimes.co.uk/article/nadiya-hussain-i-was-the-only-child-at -school-in-a-headscarf-my-mum-said-whats-wrong-with-her -xmzgl52g8.

138 **I heard it constantly, 'Oh, she's the Muslim:** "Nadiya Hussain Feard Being Labelled 'The Token Muslim' During Great British Bake off Apperance," *Radio Times,* July 11, 2017, http://www.radio times.com/news/2017-07-11/nadiya-hussain-feared-being-labelled -the-token-muslim-during-great-british-bake-off-appeerance.

139 **figures from *The Bookseller*:** Shaffi, Sarah, "Publishing Seeks to Address Industry's Lack of Diversity," *The Bookseller,* November 4, 2016, https://www.thebookseller.com/news/publishing-seeks-address -industry-s-lack-diversity-426031.

141 **This resulted in an article:** Gani, Aisha, "Here's What Muslim Women Authors Have to Say About Finding Their Voice," *Buzz-Feed*, January 28, 2017, https://www.buzzfeed.com/aishagani /what-muslim-women-authors-write-about.

143 **a quote by Nora Ephron:** "Nora Ephron's Commencement Address to Wellesley Class of 1996," *HuffPost,* June 26, 2012, http://www .huffingtonpost.com/2012/06/26/norah-ephrons-commence ment-96-address_n_1628832.html.

146 **The study found 19.8 percent:** House of Commons Women and Equalities Committee, *Employment Opportunities for Muslims in the UK* (London: House of Commons, 2016), https://publications .parliament.uk/pa/cm201617/cmselect/cmwomeq/89/89.pdf.

146   **Eight percent of Muslim women in the UK:** Social Mobility Commission, "Young Muslims in the UK Face Enormous Social Mobility Barriers," Gov.UK, https://www.gov.uk/government/news/young-muslims-in-the-uk-face-enormous-social-mobility-barriers.

146   **Their recent study (the Social Mobility Commission):** Asthana, Anushka, "Islamophobia Holding Back UK Muslims in Workplace, Study Finds," *Guardian*, September 7, 2017, https://www.theguardian.com/society/2017/sep/07/islamophobia-holding-back-uk-muslims-in-workplace-study-finds.

146   **in the United States, 29 percent of Muslims:** "U.S. Muslims Concerned About Their Place in Society, but Continue to Believe in the American Dream," Pew Research Center, http://www.pewforum.org/2017/07/26/demographic-portrait-of-muslim-americans/.

147   **As Audre Lorde, the civil rights activisit, said:** "(1981) Audre Lorde, 'The Uses of Anger: Women Responding to Racism,'" BlackPast.org, http://www.blackpast.org/1981-audre-lorde-uses-anger-women-responding-racism.

Body and Blood

167   **It's not a fear of men going to bed with men:** Eckman, Fern Marja. *The Furious Passage of James Baldwin* (New York: M. Evans, 1966).

169   **We must walk the streets everyday:** King, Martin Luther Jr. "Some Things We Must Do," Address Delivered at the Second Annual Institute on Nonviolence and Social Change at Holt Street Baptist Church, https://kinginstitute.stanford.edu/king-papers/documents/some-things-we-must-do-address-delivered-second-annual-institute-nonviolence.

Loving Two Things at Once: On Bisexuality, Feminism, and Catholicism

176   **In 2015, Pope Francis:** Pope Francis, "Apostolic Letter: *Misericordia et Miseria*," Libreria Editrice Vaticana, November 20, 2016, http://w2.vatican.va/content/francesco/en/apost_letters/documents/papa-francesco-lettera-ap_20161120_misericordia-et-misera.html.

Imperial Feminism

182   **as the Kenyan writer Binyavanga Wainaina reminds us:** Binyavanga Wainaina, "How to Write About Africa," *Granta*, January 19, 2006, https://granta.com/how-to-write-about-africa.

184 **another disturbing trend:** Rosaldo, Renato, *Culture and Truth* (Boston: Beacon Press, 1993), 69.

184 **a seminal essay by bell hooks:** hooks, bell, "Eating the Other: Desire and Resistance," in *Black Looks: Race and Representation* (Boston: South End Press, 1992), 21–39.

185 **the Braid Bar, a braid service:** Tweedy, Jo, "'We've Been Naive': The Braid Bar Says SORRY to Radio One DJ Clara Amfo After She Accused the Trendy Salon of Racism for Not Featuring Black Women," *Daily Mail*, March 7, 2017, http://www.dailymail.co.uk /femail/article-4286628/Braid-Bar-APOLOGISES-One-DJ-Clara -Amfo.html

186 **Appropriation: the act of taking:** Cambridge Dictionary, s.v. "cultural appropriation," https://dictionary.cambridge.org/us/dictionary /english/cultural-appropriation.

186 **The context is so significant a factor:** Jourdan Dunn, for example, one of the most recognizable fashion faces in the UK, revealed after she was canceled from a fashion show because she didn't fit the clothes, "I'm normally told I'm cancelled because I'm 'coloured' so being cancelled because of my boobs is a minor." Wiseman, Eva, "I Want to Talk About What Goes On," *Guardian*, September 20, 2013, https://www.theguardian.com/fashion/interactive/2013/sep /20/twiggy-cara-delevingne-25-years-supermodels.

186 **"Ethnicity," bell hooks reminds us, "becomes spice,:** hooks, bell, "Eating the Other: Desire and Resistance," in *Black Looks: Race and Representation* (Boston: South End Press, 1992).

187 **A small town in southern England:** Booth, Robert, "Lewes Bonfire Society Agrees to Stop Blacking Up in Annual Parade," *Guardian*, November 3, 2017, https://www.theguardian.com /world/2017/nov/03/lewes-bonfire-society-agrees-to-stop -blacking-up-in-annual-parade.

188 **the advertisement by the cosmetics company:** Rehman, Maliha, "Getting Rich from the Skin Lightening Trade," *Business of Fashion* (blog), September 27, 2017, https://www.businessoffashion.com /articles/global-currents/profiting-from-the-skin-lightening-trade.

188 **the commodification of anti-Blackness:** Hirsch, Afua, "Nivea's Latest 'White Is Right' Advert Is the Tip of a Reprehensible Iceberg," *Guardian*, October 22, 2017, https://www.theguardian.com /media/media-blog/2017/oct/22/niveas-latest-white-is-right -advert-is-the-tip-of-a-reprehensible-iceberg.

188 **When white feminists have sought:** Feris, Sachi, "Moana, Elsa, and Halloween," *Raising Race Conscious Children* (blog), Septem-

ber 5, 2017, http://www.raceconscious.org/2017/09/moana-elsa
-halloween.

The Machinery of Disbelief

192 **How could it not be:** Briddick, Catherine, "Sex Discrimination
and UK Immigration Law," University of Oxford Faculty of Law,
http://bordercriminologies.law.ox.ac.uk/sex-discrimination
-and-uk-immigration-law.

192 **increased levels of exploitation:** Ibid.

192 **Their visa is described as:** Roberts, Kate, "Looking Back: The
Fight to Protect Domestic Workers with the Modern Slavery Act,"
OpenDemocracy, https://www.opendemocracy.net/beyondslavery
/msaoh/kate-roberts/looking-back-fight-to-protect-domestic
-workers-with-modern-slavery-act.

194 **We need to crack down on abuse:** UK Border Agency, *Family
Migration: A Consultation*, July 2011, https://www.gov.uk/govern
ment/uploads/system/uploads/attachment_data/file/269011/fam
ily-consultation.pdf.

195 **Great scrutiny is generally focused:** Alexander, Claire, "Marriage,
Migration, Multiculturalism: Gendering 'The Bengal Diaspora,'"
Journal of Ethnic and Migration Studies 39, no. 3 (2013): 333–51,
http://www.academia.edu/11259715/Marriage_Migration_Multi
culturalism_Gendering_The_Bengal_Diaspora.

195 **The shaping of immigration law:** Politics 97, "Immigration Rules
Relaxed," BBC, 1997, http://www.bbc.co.uk/news/special/politics97
/news/06/0605/straw.shtml.

195 **the primary purpose rule:** Hussain, Asifa Maaria, *Revival: British
Immigration Policy Under the Conservative Government* (Farnham,
UK: Ashgate Publishing, 2001).

195 **men and women from white countries:** Wray, Helena, "Spousal
Migration, Gender and UK Immigration Law," University of Oxford Faculty of Law, http://bordercriminologies.law.ox.ac.uk
/spousal-migration-gender.

196 **Such invasiveness was based:** Travis, Alan, "Virginity Tests for
Immigrants 'Reflected Dark Age Prejudices' of 1970s Britain,"
Guardian, May 8, 2011, https://www.theguardian.com/uk/2011
/may/08/virginity-tests-immigrants-prejudices-britain.

196 **This probationary period was justified:** Bloch, Alice, and Sonia
McKay, *Living on the Margins: Undocumented Migrants in a Global
City* (Bristol, UK: Policy Press, 2016), 44.

197 **Thanks to years of campaigning:** Southall Black Sisters were formed in 1979 in the aftermath of the Southall riots. At the time, *Black* was often used to refer to all people of color in the UK; it was used as a marker of political allegiance and solidarity.

197 **Despite these small victories:** Gill, Aisha, and Kaveri Sharma, "Response and Responsibility: Domestic Violence and Marriage Migration in the UK," in *Women and Immigration Law: New Variations on Classical Feminist Themes*, ed. Thomas Spijkerboer and Sarah Van Walsum (New York: Routledge-Cavendish), 183–203.

197 **let alone specialist ones:** "Definitions," Institute of Race Relations, http://www.irr.org.uk/research/statistics/definitions.

197 **If nothing could be done:** Amnesty International and Southall Black Sisters, *No Recourse No Safety: The Government's Failure to Protect Women from Violence* (London and Southall, UK: Amnesty International UK and Southall Black Sisters, 2008).

198 **practical and emotional support:** Sharma, Sandhya, and Vicky Marsh, *Migrant Women's Rights to Safety Pilot Project 2016* (Manchester, UK: Safety4Sisters Northwest, 2016), 14.

199 **six hundred women a year:** Amnesty International and Southall Black Sisters, *No Recourse No Safety*.

200 **Abusers frequently used the women's:** Sharma and Marsh, *Migrant Women's Rights to Safety*, 4.

201 **I went to the Adult Education Centre:** Ibid.

201 **If I could change one thing:** Ibid., 20.

205 **the Home Office is making it as difficult:** Blinder, Scott, *Briefing: Non-European Migration to the UK: Family Unification & Dependents* (Oxford, UK: Migration Observatory, 2017), 6, http://www.migrationobservatory.ox.ac.uk/resources/briefings/non-european-migration-to-the-uk-family-unification-dependents.

206 **the application depends on:** Bhuyan, Rupaleen, Woochan Shim, and Kavya Velagapudi, "Domestic Violence Advocacy with Immigrants and Refugees," in *Domestic Violence: Intersectionality and Culturally Competent Practice*, ed. Lettie Lockhart and Fran Danis (New York: Columbia University Press, 2010), 161.

206 **various routes to permanent settlement:** Caplan-Bricker, Nora, "I Wish I'd Never Called the Police," *Slate*, March 19, 2017, http://www.slate.com/articles/news_and_politics/cover_story/2017/03/u_visas_gave_a_safe_path_to_citizenship_to_victims_of_abuse_under_trump.html.

207 **unsure whether to advise:** Ibid.

207   **perhaps too early to see:** Wang, Karin (1996), "Battered Asian American Women: Community Responses from the Battered Women's Movement and the Asian American Community," *Asian American Law Journal* 3 (1996): 151–84.

207   **Language barriers are a major obstacle:** Ibid., 163.

209   **If they did not comply:** Douglas, Debbie, Avvy Go, and Sarah Blackstock, "Canadian Immigration Changes Force Women to Stay with Sponsoring Spouse for Two Years," *Toronto Star*, December 5, 2012, https://www.thestar.com/opinion/editorialopin ion/2012/12/05/canadian_immigration_changes_force_women _to_stay_with_sponsoring_spouse_for_two_years.html.

210   **legal advocates stated that the Conservatives:** Ibid.

210   **one of several changes to immigration routes:** "Speaking Notes for The Honourable Jason Kenney, P.C., M.P. Minister of Citizenship, Immigration and Multiculturalism," address to the Empire Club, Royal York Hotel, Toronto, Ontario, May 25, 2012, https://www .canada.ca/en/immigration-refugees-citizenship/news/archives /speeches-2012/jason-kenney-minister-2012-05-25.html.

210   **what spurred him to make permanent residency:** Ibid.

210   **in the wake of the amendment:** Faruqui, Ferrukh, "Domestic Violence Cases Spike After Immigration Law Amendment," *Rabble*, October 16, 2014, http://rabble.ca/news/2014/10/domestic-violence -cases-spike-after-immigration-law-amendment.

211   **As a result of the requirement:** Government of Canada, "Notice— Government of Canada Eliminates Conditional Permanent Residence," Canada.ca, http://www.cic.gc.ca/english/department/media /notices/2017-04-28.asp.

211   **The Conservatives, led by Theresa May:** Smith, Katie, and Charlotte Miles, *Nowhere to Turn* (Bristol, UK: Women's Aid Federation of England, 2017), 44.

213   **the £200 per year immigration health surcharge:** In February 2018, the government announced that they would double the health surcharge to £400 a year, which means that for her second family visa application, Liz will be paying £1,000 in total for the health surcharge alone. (The family visa only allows non-EU family member immigrants to stay in the UK for two and a half years, so to qualify for a permanent residency visa, which requires you to have lived in the UK for a minimum of five years, non-EU family immigrants must apply for a second family visa once the first visa is close to expiration. All fees must also be paid a second time.) In

their 2017 election manifesto, however, the Conservatives promised to triple the health surcharge for non-EU immigrants, to £600 a year (£450 for students). Given that the 2018 fee increase is actually a watering-down of this Conservative manifesto promise, it is likely the Home Office will further increase the health surcharge and other immigration fees in the near future.

Deviant Bodies

226 **Pakistani and Bangladeshi women:** Brinkhurst-Cuff, Charlie, "Serena Williams Is Right About the Pay Gap for Black Women—but We Need Radical Change," *Guardian*, https://www.theguardian.com/world/shortcuts/2017/aug/01/serena-williams-pay-gap-black-women-radical-change.

233 **One in five have been sexually assaulted:** Travis, Alan, "One in Five Women Have Been Sexually Assaulted, Analysis Finds," *Guardian*, https://www.theguardian.com/uk-news/2018/feb/08/sexual-assault-women-crime-survey-england-wales-ons-police-figures.

233 **Over a third of trans people:** Butcher, Ryan, "More Than a Third of All Trans People Suffered Hate Crimes in 2017, Research Suggests," *The Independent*, https://www.independent.co.uk/news/uk/crime/trans-hate-crimes-stats-figures-2017-more-than-third-a8166826.html.

ABOUT THE CONTRIBUTORS

Soofiya Andry is a visual artist and designer. Soofiya's art practice and writings aim to articulate a commentary on gender nonconformity, bodies, and race as part of the South Asian diaspora. You can see more of their work here: *soofiya.com*.

Gabrielle Bellot is a staff writer for *Literary Hub*. Her work has appeared in *The New Yorker, The Paris Review Daily, The Atlantic, The New York Times, Tin House, Electric Literature, them, New York* magazine's "The Cut," *VICE, Guernica*, and many other places. She lives in Brooklyn.

Brit Bennett is the author of *The Mothers*. She earned her MFA in fiction at the University of Michigan, where she won a Hopwood Award as well as a Hurston/Wright Award for College Writers. She is a National Book Foundation "5 under 35" honoree, and her essays are featured in *The New Yorker, The New York Times Magazine, The Paris Review*, and *Jezebel*.

Caitlin Cruz is a Chicana reporter and writer focusing on reproductive rights and women's health. She is a contributing writer at *Pacific Standard* and has been published by *Jezebel, The Village Voice*, Digg, and *The Seattle Times*, among others. She lives in Texas.

Nicole Dennis-Benn is a Lambda Literary Award winner and a finalist for the 2016 John Leonard Prize National Book Critics Circle Award, the 2016 Center for Fiction First Novel Prize, Dublin Literary Award, and the 2017 Young Lions Fiction Award for her debut novel, *Here Comes the Sun*, a *New York Times* Notable Book of the year. Her work has appeared in the *New York Times, Elle, Electric Literature, Ebony*, and the *Feminist Wire*. She was born and raised in Kingston, Jamaica, and lives with her wife in Brooklyn, New York.

Evette Dionne is a Black Feminist culture writer, editor, and scholar. Presently, she's the editorial director at Bitch Media and regularly contributes stories about race, size, gender, and popular culture to *Teen Vogue*, the *Guardian*, *Cosmopolitan*, *The New York Times*, Refinery29, *Harper's Bazaar*, MIC, and other print and digital publications. Find her online at EvetteDionne.com.

Aisha Gani is an award-winning British journalist specializing on underrepresented communities and world news. Previously, she was a senior reporter for BuzzFeed News UK and has written on issues from fake news, Muslim women in politics, human rights abuses, and has reported on Europe's refugee crisis and on the Burkini ban from the South of France. She has well-read exclusive reports on the UK general elections, terror attacks, and the Grenfell Tower fire. She has made TV appearances including the newspaper review on the BBC News Channel and Sky News. She is passionate about human interest stories and telling her stories in accessible ways. Before this she was a reporter at the *Guardian* news desk in London.

Afua Hirsch is a writer and broadcaster, and the author of the UK bestselling book *Brit(ish): On Race, Identity and Belonging*. She writes widely about social justice, race and gender, as well as narratives of Africa, development, and law. She has worked as a barrister, as the social affairs editor for Sky News, and as West Africa correspondent for the *Guardian*, where she is a regular columnist. *Brit(ish)* is the recipient of a RSL Jerwood Prize for Non-Fiction.

Juliet Jacques is a writer and filmmaker. In addition to publishing two books, *Rayner Heppenstall: A Critical Study* (Dalkey Archive, 2007) and *Trans: A Memoir* (Verso, 2015), her fiction, essays, and journalism have appeared in *Granta*, the *Guardian*, *The London Review of Books*, *Sight & Sound*, *Frieze*, and many other publications. She lives in London.

Wei Ming Kam has written for the bestselling essay collection *The Good Immigrant*, the graphic novel anthology *We Shall Fight Until We Win*, Media Diversified, and Gal Dem. She works in publishing and is the cofounder of BAME In Publishing, a network for people of color who work in publishing in the UK, and Pride in Publishing, a network for queer people who work in publishing in the UK.

Mariya Karimjee is a freelance writer based in Brooklyn, New York. A graduate of Mount Holyoke College and Columbia University School of Journalism, Mariya was a Logan Nonfiction Fellow at the Carey Institution of Global Good and a writer-in-residence at Hedgebook, where she was the recipient of the Elizabeth George Award in 2015. Her work has been featured on *This American Life*, and in *BuzzFeed*, *Vulture*, and *LitHub*, among others, and her memoir is forthcoming from Spiegel & Grau.

Eishar Kaur is a twenty-five-year-old Londoner working in children's publishing by day, and writing by night. She can be found on Twitter @eisharkaur.

Emer O'Toole is Associate Professor of Irish Performance Studies at Concordia University, Montréal. She is author of the book *Girls Will Be Girls* (Orion: 2015) and coeditor of the collection *Ethical Exchanges in Translation, Adaptation and Dramaturgy* (Brill: 2017). Her work appears in academic journals including *Sexualities*; *Éire-Ireland*; *Literature, Interpretation, Theory*; and *Target*. She is also a regular contributor to the *Guardian* and *The Irish Times*.

Frances Ryan is a *Guardian* columnist and broadcaster. She appears on radio and television, from BBC Radio 4's Woman's Hour and The World Tonight, to BBC Sunday Politics and Sky News, as well as public speaking for campaign groups, universities, and other political events. She has a doctorate in political theory, with a focus on inequality in education. She will release her debut book on disability in Britain with Verso in 2019.

Zoé Samudzi is a writer, photographer, and sociologist of race, and a doctoral student at the University of California–San Francisco. She is the coauthor (along with William C. Anderson) of *As Black as Resistance*, and her work has been published on the Verso Books Blog, in *The New Inquiry*, *ROAR* Magazine, *Teen Vogue*, and many other spaces.

Charlotte Shane is the author of two memoirs: *Prostitute Laundry* and *N.B*, and the coauthor, with merritt k, of the chapbook *3 Conversations*. She is a cofounder of TigerBee Press and of Tits and Sass, a group blog by and for sex workers. She is currently at work on a book about heterosexuality, sex work, desire, and damage.

Selina Thompson is a performance artist and the artistic director of Selina Thompson Ltd, an interdisciplinary performance and visual art company based in Birmingham, UK. Her practice is primarily intimate, political, and participatory, with a strong strand of public engagement and investigation. She makes joyous, highly visual work that seeks to connect to those often marginalized by the arts, and tries to extend this in her writing, too.

SUGGESTIONS
FOR FURTHER READING

Women and Gender in Islam: Historical Roots of a Modern Debate by
　　Leila Ahmed
Before I Step Outside [You Love Me] by Travis Alabanza
Queer Ultra-violence: Abridged Bash Back Anthology edited by Fray
　　Baroque and Tegan Eanellli
Everyday Sexism: The Project that Inspired a Worldwide Movement
　　by Laura Bates
Fun Home: A Family Tragicomic by Alison Bechdel
*Sex Workers Unite: A History of the Movement from Stonewall to
　　SlutWalk* by Melinda Chateauvert
Are Prisons Obsolete? by Angela Y. Davis
Women, Race, & Class by Angela Y. Davis
Stone Butch Blues by Leslie Feinberg
Chicana Feminist Thought: The Basic Historical Writings by Alma
　　M. Garcia
Bad Feminist: Essays by Roxane Gay
Hunger: A Memoir of (My) Body by Roxane Gay
Ain't I a Woman: Black Women and Feminism by bell hooks
Trans: A Memoir by Juliet Jacques
Sister Outsider by Audre Lorde
Woman, Native, Other: Writing Postcoloniality and Feminism by
　　Trinh T. Minh-Ha

Aisha Mirza (various writings: see AishaMirza.net)

Redefining Realness: My Path to Womanhood, Identity, Love & So Much More by Janet Mock

This Bridge Called My Back: Writings by Radical Women of Color edited by Cherríe Moraga and Gloria Anzaldúa

Pushout: The Criminalization of Black Girls in Schools by Monique Morris

The Argonauts by Maggie Nelson

The Good Immigrant edited by Nikesh Shukla

Alok Vaid-Menon (various writings: see AlokVMenon.com)

The Rejected Body: Feminist Philosophical Reflections on Disability by Susan Wendell

Shrill: Notes from a Loud Woman by Lindy West

Oranges Are Not the Only Fruit by Jeanette Winterson